LET FREEDOM RING

SEAN HANNITY

LET FREEDOM RING

Winning the War of Liberty over Liberalism

ReganBooks
An Imprint of HarperCollins*Publishers*

HarperCollins books may be purchased for educational, business, or sales promotional use. For information please write: Special Markets Department, Harper-Collins Publishers Inc., 10 East 53rd Street, New York, NY 10022.

FIRST EDITION

Designed by Kris Tobiassen

Printed on acid-free paper

Library of Congress Cataloging-in-Publication Data has been applied for.

ISBN 0-06-054820-7

02 03 04 05 WBC/RRD 1 2 3 4 5 6 7 8 9 10

To my wife, Jill, the love of my life, and the greatest gift God ever gave me—our two children, Patrick and Kelly

CONTENTS

ACKNOWLEDGMENTS

With a schedule as crazy and intense as mine, I never could have completed a project like this without the wise counsel, incisive insights, and good humor of some tremendously close friends, kindred spirits, and confidants, all of whom gave beyond measure, put up with my whining, and made the whole thing more fun than I'd expected.

First and foremost, I want to thank David Limbaugh, a fantastically gifted lawyer, a great syndicated columnist, author, and one of my closest friends. His intellectual and conceptual contributions were absolutely invaluable, as was his editor's eye. As always, he was a great source of inspiration and support and this book wouldn't have happened without him.

Mark "The Great One" Levin is a great loyal friend, and one of the smartest lawyers in the business. This book is much better for his intellectual stimulation on a daily basis.

Joel C. Rosenberg became a good friend and a great asset during this project. He assisted in the research and development of this book from the beginning and I'm deeply grateful for his enthusiasm, support, and dedication to excellence.

Judith Regan, Cal Morgan, Monica Crowley, and the team at Regan Books were wonderful. They believed in this project from the start, and helped me navigate the white-water rapids of book publishing.

My family at Fox News also deserves thanks.

Roger Ailes gave me my big break and I'll forever be grateful to him. If he hadn't taken a chance on me back in September of 1996, I'd never have had the chance to experience the fun, challenge, and professional fulfillment in doing live, daily television. Whatever I do right on TV, I give credit to his influence on my career. Whatever I do wrong, I must blame on my own stubbornness. Roger had a great vision for what Fox News—and I—could be. Long ago, he predicted many of the good things that have happened to me, and not a week goes by that I'm not amazed that he was right and so many of his predictions are coming to fruition.

I'm also grateful for Chet Collier and Kevin McGee, both of whom have helped teach me the art of live television.

One of my closest friends—and the best executive producer in TV today—is Bill Shine. He told me back in October of 1996 that I'd be writing this book. I just laughed at him at the time. I'm not laughing now. Bill, this is for you.

The *Hannity & Colmes* team is the best in television, beginning with Alan himself. Meade Cooper is our senior producer, one of the nicest and hardest-working people I have ever met in my career. Chet Lishawa is our talented director. I would also like to thank our dedicated staff, including: Maureen Murphy, John "Fin-Man" Finley, Erin Rider, Tara Nicaj, Matt Linder, and Nicole Goodman. And I want to thank the behind-the-scenes folks at Fox, from the hair and makeup people to the camera crew—they make coming to work fun each and every day. I also want to say thanks to Rob Monaco and Peter Zorich, both former producers of *Hannity & Colmes,* who have contributed greatly to the show's success.

My ABC Radio family:

I want to say a special thanks to Phil Boyce. Not only has he become one of my closest friends, but Phil also believed in my radio career and supported me before anyone else in the big leagues did. It was his idea to take the show national, and he predicted the great success we would enjoy. Thanks, Phil.

Mitch Dolan of ABC is the greatest radio executive in America today, and a man who always keeps me humble. The greatest thing he taught me was *not* to focus on ratings and revenue, but to focus on "What Is Coming Out of the Speaker"—that everything else will take care of itself—and he was, and is, right.

I also want to thank Traug Keller of ABC Radio Networks. Traug makes radio battles so much fun you just can't wait to get to work every day. If you're ever in a radio war, you will *need* and *want* Traug on your side.

John McConnell—a conservative-in-waiting—constantly inspires me to go out and win. More important, John always finds a way to solve the day-to-day problems that we encounter, and he was always there supporting the show from the beginning. Thanks, John.

Thanks, too, to Tim McCarthy, the GM of our flagship station in New York City, 77 WABC, The Most Listened-to Talk Radio Station in America. Tim has also mastered the Art of Radio War—and has been a big supporter from day one.

The Sean Hannity Show radio staff is the best around:

James "Sweet Baby James" Grisham, my senior executive producer, is also one of my closest friends, and one of the hardest-working people I know. There is no doubt in my mind that the radio show would not be half as successful as it is without his dedication—and I am very grateful.

I also need to thank Flipper—Jill Vitale, my associate producer and call screener—who makes each day a new experience with her crazy liberal views. Greg Ahlfe, our creative and dedicated engineer and production manager. Bill Russell, my number one affiliate relations guru, is the best in radio today. I should also mention the fun I have working with two of the most talented radio people in NYC: Bruce Anderson and Heather O'Rourke.

I also want to thank Eric "Stanginator" Stanger, a great friend and the assistant PD at KABC in L.A. Eric produced the show for a number of years, and is destined to be a star in radio management for years to come. Eric and I perfected our own style of radio combat, and had a lot of fun learning the game.

A few other names:

Throughout my career, I've been very fortunate to develop lasting friendships with bosses and colleagues who helped me learn, grow and always keep moving forward.

Eric "Sluggo" Siedel—a "diamond in the rough"—gave me a chance in my first major market even when the research said to fire me. Thanks, Sluggo.

Nancy Zintak, my first producer in the big leagues—who has a personality bigger than life.

Mike Rose, who tried to get me to flirt with the dark side (liberalism)—I thankfully never listened.

Also a very close friend of mine by the name of Bob Just, a writer and talk show host himself. Bob has been a huge support in all aspects of my career, and has helped me to improve not only as a host but as a person as well—thanks, Bob.

The guys at WVNN who gave me my first real radio job—Dave Stone and Bill Dunnavant—both remain good friends and I'm forever in their debt. We're still in touch, and I greatly value their continued inspiration, advice, and counsel. There is no doubt the success I enjoy today is due to the fact that both of them took a chance on me when I was breaking into this business—both have also helped me develop my own unique style.

I'm also grateful to Duane Ward at *www.PremiereSpeakers.com,* who has done such a fantastic job of putting together my speaking tours and my book tour. He's a great guy, a true professional, and I'm really blessed with his help.

The most important acknowledgment I make is to my family—my wife, Jill, and my two children, Patrick and Kelly, to whom I dedicate this book. They are the ones who put up with the long work hours I needed to invest in this project. They are the ones who make it worth doing—and who make my life complete and happy on more levels than I can explain. I am blessed to have them in my life.

Also a special thanks to my extended family—my sister Therese Grisham, her husband James and baby Christopher, and my sister Mary-Jo Kuchta, her husband Dr. Steven Kuchta, and their three children Cassandra, Brandon, and Michael. They, along with my immediate family, are the most important people in my life, and the ones who bring me the most happiness. This project would never have been possible without their daily love and support.

And finally, I would like to thank two people who were instrumental in shaping my way of thinking and instilling great values in me: my parents, Hugh and Lillian Hannity. Though they have both passed on in the last five years, there is not a day that goes by that I am not thankful for the love they showed me, which has helped me grow into the person I am today. None of the good things that are happening in my life now would have been possible without the unconditional love they gave me on a daily basis.

[ONE]

CIVILIZATION
IN THE BALANCE

First things first: I'm a New Yorker.

It's not just home—it's who I am.

I was born and raised here. I grew up on Long Island, in Franklin Square, and went to Catholic schools for twelve years here. I am a New Yorker in every way. I was born combative. I love Sabrett hot-dogs. I have a thick accent, which I didn't realize until I began to travel a bit in my early twenties and started working in places like Rhode Island, California, Alabama, and Georgia. But I came back to the Big Apple because my roots are here. It's where I've chosen to settle down with my wife, Jill, raise my kids, and make my career.

I love New York. I love every cliché about this wild, wacky, wonderful city. And they're all true. Sure, it's loud. And brash. And bright. And gritty. Sure, everyone here thinks he lives at the center of the universe. So what? We do.

People don't dream all their lives of escaping the hellish countries they live in and pay their life savings to underworld types for the privilege of being locked up in a freezing, filthy, stinking container ship and hauled like cargo for weeks until they finally arrive in . . . Moscow . . . or Beijing . . . or Baghdad . . . or Kabul.

People risk their lives to come here—to New York. The greatest city in the world, where dreams become reality.

Why shouldn't they? It's a city of immigrants and indigents. Busboys and billionaires. Big dreamers and big idiots. Every race and every religion. Every idea and every "ism." They're all here. Competing for your time, attention, and bucks. And Sinatra was right: if you can make it here, you can make it anywhere. This is the place where all my dreams are coming true.

Welcome to New York, city of dreams.

As much as I love New York, though, on a deeper level I am also a proud American. I believe in the American dream, the American ideal, the unique American culture, and traditional American values. Indeed, my core political beliefs—my conservative ideals—are grounded in my respect for the traditions that make up America's foundation.

At the core of those traditions is the idea of freedom. Freedom was the idea that inspired our Founders, that moved them to break free of an oppressive regime and envision a better system of government. The framers of our Constitution were determined to establish a governmental structure that would ensure freedom. They understood that freedom was the exception rather than the rule in world history, and they were determined to right that wrong.

But the framers also recognized that democratic participation in government wouldn't be enough, for even a parliament could become corrupt in the absence of restraints on government. So in order to safeguard liberties, they knew they would have to impose limitations on government—limitations that would be etched in a permanent (though amendable) Constitution and would be bolstered by a complex scheme of checks and balances among the various levels and branches of government.

At heart, American conservatives like myself are believers in the Constitution. We believe that the principles embodied in the Constitution are enduring, and that to whatever extent we deviate from them we put our liberties at risk. Our views are consistent because we believe in absolute truths and in the essential soundness, even righteousness, of the Founders' vision of government.

In this book I'll talk about a wide array of issues—from the perennial questions of education, government spending, and abortion to the many urgent concerns that have been raised in this uncertain time, when we face a threat from an elusive and powerful new enemy. If you've watched me on *Hannity & Colmes,* or listened to *The Sean Hannity Show* on the radio, you already know you're in for some strong opinions. But if you read carefully, you'll notice how often my beliefs come back to that basic idea: that as Americans we have a basic right to enjoy freedom in our lives—including freedom from governmental interference. For the first time in generations, Americans are now forced to confront an immediate and genuine threat to our way of life. And for me this is the strongest reason that we must win the war on terror: to secure, in those unforgettable words, the blessings of liberty.

The conservative vision is that America return to its founding principles—because these principles are the pillars of freedom. Without them America will not continue to be great; with them there is no limit to our future.

Monday, September 10, 2001.

That's the day my radio show became nationally syndicated.

We talked about cutting taxes, reforming education, strengthening the military, and defending the Judeo-Christian values too often being driven out of our schools. It was a great first day—fun, fast-paced. I was doing what I love, debating the hot news and burning issues of the day. When it was over, I went to sleep happy.

John Gomez, a friend since third grade, called me at home a few minutes before nine on Tuesday morning, September 11. He told me a plane had just crashed into the side of one of the World Trade Center towers. He thought it might have been a small commuter plane. It wasn't quite clear. I couldn't believe it; at first I thought he was kidding. I turned on the Fox News Channel—just in time to see the second jumbo jet slam into the side of the second tower and erupt into a monstrous ball of fire and thick black smoke. How could this be happening? This was clearly no mistake, but most certainly a kamikaze. Without a doubt it was an act of terrorism—indeed, an act of war.

It was a moment of incomprehensible horror, for every American and for freedom-loving people around the globe. But as a New Yorker I was seeing more than just an attack against America. For me, it was personal. Some sick cell of psychotic suicide bombers had just attacked *my* world. *My* city, *my* friends. As I stared at the video replays—at the planes and the people and the terror and the devastation—I knew I was staring into the face of evil, glimpsing a vision born in the minds of savages. And I knew that, unlike that atrocity at Pearl Harbor sixty years before, the miracle of twenty-first–century communications would soon be bringing this same horrific vision to a billion people all over the world. The experience was as disorienting as it was surreal.

Then came word of smoke at the Pentagon—another plane, another attack.

A plane crash near Pittsburgh.

A car bomb in front of the State Department (a rumor that later proved false).

Air Force One's destination was unknown.

The White House was being evacuated.

Members of Congress were being rushed to a secure, undisclosed location.

Then the ghastly image of one tower collapsing.

Then the other.

People jumping from the towers, running for their lives.

A city of smoke, and a skyline scarred forever.

Hell was breaking loose—and it was just beginning.

I was due on the air in a few hours, but there was no way I was going to be able to get to the studios in Manhattan. New York was under siege, locked down by the military. F-16s were flying combat air patrols overhead. I'd have to do the show from a studio on Long Island. What would I say? What was happening? And what might happen next?

Welcome to New York, city of nightmares.

On September 11, 2001, the world changed—forever.

Yours did. Mine did, too.

When I think back, a year later, to those horrifying images . . . to those huge passenger jets, filled not only with thousands of pounds of jet fuel but with fathers and mothers and sons and daughters . . . to those Twin Towers—home of some fifty-five thousand workers every day—engulfed in flames and collapsing in mushroom clouds of smoke and dust and ash . . . to those human bodies raining from the sky . . . to the frantic, desperate, 24/7 search for the three thousand souls who perished . . . to all those policemen and firemen, New York's finest and bravest, weeping uncontrollably for their lost brothers . . . to all those children, sitting in classrooms all over New York, orphaned and frightened and alone . . . to brave, stoic, heartbroken Ted Olson, the U.S. solicitor general, at the memorial service for his wife, Barbara . . . when I see these images—even a full year later—I get angry.

I get angry because I'm convinced those attacks might have been prevented.

I get angry because I'm convinced the Clinton-Gore administration never truly focused on protecting the American people from terrorism in general and Osama bin Laden in particular.

I get angry because it is now clear that President Bill Clinton's sworn obligation to preserve, protect, and defend this nation took a backseat to his personal and political pursuits. Instead of leading an all-out war against those whose express goal was to murder innocent Americans, he wasted precious time and resources fighting with federal prosecutors, federal courts, and the Republican Congress—over sins and crimes he'd committed.

I get angry because for decades the Left in America has foolishly and relentlessly attacked and undermined the very policies and institutions that have made our country a beacon of liberty and prosperity. They have wasted decades bitterly attacking conservatives as "extreme" and "dangerous"—conservatives whose mission it has been to stand up for the rule of law, free enterprise, limited government, and a strong military.

And I am amazed that so many liberals still don't get it. They still don't seem to grasp the very real dangers we face—or what we need to do about them.

From the moment those two planes hit those two towers, it was crystal clear to me: America is at war.

Not an old, cold, Communist war, but a new, hot, holy war.

Not against an evil nation—a regime with a capital, an army, a navy, and an air force—but against an evil network that is wealthy, stealthy, and extremely deadly.

To win, we must fight with bullets, bombs, spy satellites, special ops, and the latest weapons in our high-tech, high-intelligence arsenal. But we must understand that this is also now a war of ideas: between good and evil; between right and wrong; between the Judeo-Christian values upon which this country was founded and the violent nihilism of radical Islam.

And make no mistake: it's winner take all.

The shadowy, clandestine forces arrayed against us will not slow their progress until they have decapitated our leaders, destroyed our freedoms, and ushered in a new age of slavery and darkness—unless we stop them with deadly force. Even now, as they have been for years, they are feverishly pursuing weapons of mass destruction. And when they have them, they will use them.

Our enemies have not been distracted or softened by the allure of modern liberalism, feel-good feminism, or radical environmentalism. They are not distracted from their murderous mission by absurd notions of political correctness. They are focused. They are fearless. They are disciplined. And they will pay any price to advance their jihad—until they win, or die. Period.

Therefore we now face two fundamental questions.

First, are we Americans truly prepared to fight this new war to wipe out terrorism and terrorist regimes and win it decisively—no matter what sacrifices it requires or how long it takes?

You might think the answer would be an obvious yes. But the fact is that just months after September 11, liberal politicians and opinion-makers were already seeking to tie President George Bush's hands by publicly announcing their opposition to a much-needed increase in defense spending and demanding "endgame" strategies for a war whose end could not now be known. And they did this while our courageous servicemen and women were defending our country on the battlefields and in the caves of Afghanistan and elsewhere.

Unfortunately, this is nothing new. During the Reagan administration, the Left opposed the modernization of our aging bomber fleet, a six-hundred-ship navy, the modernization of nuclear missiles in Europe, the Strategic Defense Initiative, and our efforts to uproot communism in this hemisphere—including the liberation of Grenada and support for the freedom fighters in Nicaragua. They mocked Reagan for denouncing the Soviet Union as the Evil Empire, rather than condemning the Soviet Union for *being* an evil empire.

The Left may be sincere, but they're sincerely wrong. And they must be challenged and defeated if we are to win this war on terror and preserve our way of life for this and future generations.

Second, are we once again prepared to teach our children the fundamental principles and values that made this country great—the values that made this country worth fighting for, living for, and dying for?

Far too many liberals see no connection between values, education, the moral health of our nation, and America's security and prosperity. And that's precisely the problem. For the past half-century, liberals have been engaged in a dangerous and destructive effort to morally disarm our children. Here, too, they must be confronted and defeated if America is to lead and succeed in the twenty-first century.

Whether the issues are social, cultural, economic, or international, every significant policy debate and every election of consequence from this point forward will be weighed against the events of September 11, 2001.

Let me put it bluntly: for those who have so long and fiercely opposed giving our military and intelligence forces the tools they need to defend our nation and defeat our enemies, it is now time to answer in the court of public opinion. Why should their message prevail any longer? Why should we entrust our country's future to those whose track record is so miserable?

So, too, it's time for those who disparage and dismiss the importance of faith, family, and the flag in our lives to be held to account. Liberals preach that there is nothing wrong with American education that more money and social engineering, fewer standards, and less competition can't solve. They teach our children multiculturalism rather than American culture, revisionist history rather than American history, the thinly disguised religion of secular humanism and extreme environmentalism rather than capitalism. They train our young to criticize America, not celebrate it. They welcome condoms into the classroom but ban God and the Ten Commandments. They encourage tolerance for the teachings of the Koran but not for the teachings of Jesus Christ. They oppose the Pledge of Allegiance, tell us that "God is dead," that "Christianity is for losers," and that evangelical and Catholic conservatives are more dangerous than radical Islamic militants. They tell us that fuel-burning SUVs are bad for America, but flag-burning SOBs aren't.

But they are wrong. And it is time to ask: Why, particularly in time of war, should we entrust the education of our children to people who loathe and ravage so many of our core values and traditions?

In 1992 Al Gore—then a senator from Tennessee hoping one day to become president of the United States—published a rather bizarre political manifesto. Its title? Not *Civilization in the Balance,* significantly, but *Earth in the Balance.*

Gore didn't concern himself with the threats to our national security—and to the freedom of all mankind—posed even then by global terrorism and the spread of weapons of mass destruction. Instead he fretted about global warming and the spread of the internal combustion engine. He didn't express concern about the growing concentrations of radical Islamic cells in the United States or around the world. Instead he agonized about the "growing concentration of carbon dioxide (CO_2) now circling the earth."

What's wrong with this picture?

"Consider that the United States spends tens of billions of dollars on frenzied programs to upgrade and improve the technology of bombers and fighter planes to counter an increasingly remote threat to our national security, but we are content to see hundreds of millions of automobiles using an old technological approach not radically different from the one first used decades ago in the Model A Ford," wrote Gore. "We now know that their cumulative impact on the global environment is posing a mortal threat to the security of every nation that is more deadly than that of any military enemy we are ever again likely to confront."

Let's parse that paragraph for a moment, shall we?

At the time Gore wrote his book, the Gulf War against Saddam Hussein had just ended. So had the fifty-year Cold War. The lessons of what Ronald Reagan called "peace through strength" were crystal clear. Yet despite the fact that Gore wished one day to become commander in chief of the world's greatest military, he wrote a book in which he disparaged America's *"frenzied"* effort to *"upgrade and improve"* our military.

Why? Because Gore perceived the rise of foreign military threats and terrorist networks to be *"an increasingly remote threat to our national security."*

Why? Because he believed that the bigger threat—*"the mortal threat"*—to our way of life came not from foreign fanatics opposing freedom around the world but from American families and workers exercising their freedoms here at home by driving their own cars and trucks and SUVs.

Moreover, Gore believed that this threat—this domestic threat— was *"more deadly than that of any military enemy we are ever again likely to confront."* Really?

How could anyone really believe this? Or admit it publicly? Yet this was (and presumably remains) Al Gore's worldview. Today, in his hapless effort to reestablish himself in the public eye, Gore has even stooped to critiquing the Bush administration's war efforts. Which is why Al Gore was overwhelmingly chosen as the Democratic Party's presidential nominee and liberalism's standard-bearer in the year 2000.

Does this suggest that Al Gore is somehow un-American? Of course not. It does, however, suggest that his views don't square with those that have contributed to America's singular tradition of freedom. It suggests that he is unqualified to be an effective commander in chief.

It explains why he and the administration in which he served for eight years (and whose record he still enthusiastically endorses) so radically downsized the military and did so little to protect the American people from the likes of Osama bin Laden. And its suggests that we are genuinely indebted to those patriots in Florida—and the other states and territories—who went to the polls and voted for George W. Bush.

Protecting our air, land, and water from pollution is certainly important. But isn't electing leaders committed to a "frenzied"—that is, *urgent*—effort to rebuild our military and protect our homeland security far more important?

Which brings me to a point sure to be controversial. But it happens to be true.

The views of the American Left—and the policies that flow from them—aren't just wrongheaded; they're reckless.

Let me be clear: Liberal ideas are *not* responsible for the terrorist attacks of September 11, 2001. They are, however, responsible for making America more vulnerable, for creating confusion in our society and among our children about what is right and wrong, and thus for placing our freedom and security at risk.

If the Left succeeds in gaining and retaining more power, the well-being of future generations will be at greater peril. I fear they will inherit a nation that is less free and less secure than the nation we inherited from the last generation.

It is therefore our job to stop them. Not just debate them, but defeat them.

Please understand that I'm not saying that liberals like Bill Clinton and Al Gore and Tom Daschle and Dick Gephardt and many of the elitists in academia and the media are evil. I'm saying they have a disturbing habit of winking at evil—of ignoring it, or turning a blind eye to it. And in so doing, they put us all in jeopardy.

I'll make this case in detail on a range of issues throughout this book. But for now, let me give you a sense of what I'm talking about.

HOW CLINTON AND GORE
TURNED A BLIND EYE TO TERRORISM

In the weeks and months following September 11, Americans began asking hard questions. *Wasn't there any way these attacks could have been prevented? Why didn't the CIA know what was coming? How could we spend billions of dollars on intelligence and have such a massive failure?*

After all, the rising threat of global terrorism—particularly the threat of Osama bin Laden and his al Qaeda terrorist network—had been clear to U.S. policy-makers for years, from the 1988 bombing of Pan Am 103 over Lockerbie, Scotland, to the 1993 World Trade Center bombing, to the 1998 bombings of two American embassies in East Africa, to the suicide attack on the USS *Cole* in the fall of 2000.

From the beginning, President Bush expressed the outrage of the American people. He immediately took charge; there was no mistaking who was commander in chief. He made it clear that his first priority would be to hunt down the evildoers and bring them to justice. He and his team also made it clear that determining the causes of America's security failures and finding and remedying its weak points would be central to their mission. Other Republicans concurred.

"I absolutely believe that we have to go back and see what happened," said Senator John McCain, the Arizona Republican, on NBC's *Meet the Press* just one month after the attacks. He stressed the importance of determining what went wrong "so that we will not make the mistakes again that we made before and can reorganize our intelligence services."

Curiously, however, liberal Democrats—many of whom historically criticized, attacked, and sought to defund the CIA—at first showed little interest in an investigation of the roots of this massive intelligence failure. (It was only after they smelled political advantage that they began to jump on the bandwagon.)

"We don't need a witch hunt now, or certainly not next year in an election year," Representative Jane Harman, a California Democrat on the House Intelligence Committee, told the *New York Times.*

A witch hunt? That's pretty strong language. What might Representative Harman fear that the American people might learn— especially "in an election year"?

Maybe this: that the Clinton-Gore administration—starting with the president and vice president themselves—had turned a blind eye to the growing threat posed to Americans by global terrorist networks. And it cost us. Big time.

On December 30, 2001, *New York Times* reporters Judith Miller, Jeff Gerth, and Don Van Natta, Jr., wrote a 7,237-word story titled "Planning for Terror But Failing to Act." The story detailed how the Clinton-Gore administration did little or nothing to crack down on terrorism in the wake of the 1993 bombing of the World Trade Center.

The *Times* story revealed that "in 1996, a State Department dossier spelled out Mr. bin Laden's operation and his anti-American intentions. But Clinton chose not to act." The *Times* reported that "in 2000, after an Algerian was caught coming into the country with explosives, a secret White House review recommended a crackdown on 'potential sleeper cells in the United States.' That review warned that 'the threat of attack remains high' and laid out a plan for fighting terrorism. But most of that plan remained undone."

The *Times* even quoted former Clinton senior adviser George Stephanopolous admitting that the Clinton-Gore administration never gave much attention to protecting the American people from bin Laden and his ilk, despite the growing number of deaths of innocent Americans at the hands of al Qaeda operatives.

"It wasn't the kind of thing where you walked into a staff meeting and people asked, what are we doing today in the war against terrorism?" said Stephanopolous.

To which I ask: Why not?

Why were issues like gays in the military and global warming and promoting race-based set-asides more important to the Clinton-Gore administration than waging a war against terrorism?

As time passes, other Clinton-Gore advisers and supporters are going on the record to describe just how uninterested the president and vice president really were in defending American citizens from the terrorist threat.

Dick Morris, for example. Smart, clever, and now a Fox News consultant, Morris has known Bill and Hillary Clinton for more than two decades. He worked with them during their political days in Arkansas. More recently, he was the chief political strategist for the Clinton-Gore reelection campaign in 1996. That put him at the epicenter of the Clintons' political lives. It now makes him a window into the soul of the Clintons for conservatives like me who otherwise wouldn't have gotten within a hundred miles of that White House inner sanctum.

In interviews over the past year on *Hannity & Colmes* and elsewhere, Morris has shed light on some very disturbing aspects of the Clinton-Gore approach to terrorism. It hasn't been pretty. But it has been instructive.

Morris points out that President Clinton—known for his unctuous phrase "I feel your pain"—never visited the site of the 1993 World Trade Center attack, in which six people died and more than one thousand were injured. Clinton didn't even meet privately with the director of the Central Intelligence Agency for *two years* following that attack.

The lack of focus by President Clinton and Vice President Gore on the 1993 bombing caused the investigation to move forward so slowly that the White House had no idea of Osama bin Laden's complicity in the attack until 1996, three years after it happened.

Even after a bomb exploded at the 1996 Atlanta Olympic Games, and nineteen American soldiers died in the bombing of a U.S. military barracks in Saudi Arabia, Morris says that President Clinton "seemed curiously uninvolved in the battle against terror."

This curious inattention wasn't just the result of negligence—which would have been bad enough. Sandy Berger, then President Clinton's deputy national security adviser, "seemed to work overtime at opposing tough measures against terror," says Morris. According to Morris, Berger advised Clinton to veto a bill designed to cripple Iranian funding of terrorism by mandating American retaliation against companies that aided its oil industry. Berger said Clinton should only sign the bill if a provision were added to it authorizing the president to waive the retaliatory sanctions. And Morris observes that, when the bill eventually passed with the waiver provision, Berger blocked the imposition of sanctions almost every time.

In addition, Morris notes, Stephanopolous and Deputy Chief of Staff Harold Ickes lobbied Clinton against approving a measure that would have forced aliens' driver's licenses to expire with their visas—which would have meant that routine traffic stops could trigger deportation proceedings. The bill would have resulted in the interfacing of state motor vehicle records with FBI and INS data concerning illegal aliens, visa expirations, and terrorist watch lists. But Ickes and Stephanopolous opposed it because it could be viewed as racial profiling, thereby alienating Clinton's political base. If the bill had passed, Morris concludes hauntingly, hijacker Mohammed Atta might have been deported when he was cited for driving without a license several months before September 11.

To make matters worse, neither President Clinton nor Vice President Gore did much to fight for stronger airline security, despite the rising terrorist threat. Clinton essentially ignored recommendations to require X-ray screening for baggage, to restore air marshals to commercial flights, and to federalize air security checkpoints. Similarly, Gore did nothing to implement these suggestions when his Commission on Air Safety issued its recommendations in 1997. Only after September 11, observed Morris, were any of these initiatives instituted.

Clinton was apparently so afraid of being accused of racially profiling Islamic charities that he even refused to create a list of extremist and terrorist organizations along with their members and donors in order to alert the public to the possibility of donations that might further terrorism.

What conclusion does the man who was once President Clinton's chief political strategist draw after observing these facts?

"Everything was more important [to Clinton] than fighting terrorism," says Morris. "Political correctness, civil liberties concerns, fear of offending the administration's supporters, Janet Reno's objections, considerations of cost, worries about racial profiling and, in the second term, surviving impeachment, all came before fighting terrorism."

HOW CLINTON AND GORE
LET OSAMA BIN LADEN SLIP AWAY

Clinton Kool-Aid drinkers will defend the Clinton-Gore administration regardless of such serious evidence and seek to paint as obsessive those of us who try to assign it blame. It's the Clinton-honed tried-and-true tactic of deflecting criticism by attacking your accusers.

Liberals argue that the administration had many issues to deal with, not just terrorism, and that some things were bound to fall through the cracks—particularly with the rabid Republicans trying to impeach the poor man. That's the pathetic case left-wing filmmaker Michael Moore, author of *Stupid White Men*—a vicious screed against conservatives like President Bush, among others—tried to make to me one night on *Hannity & Colmes*.

"Frankly, I don't think we're handling this war on terrorism in the correct way," Moore objected. "What did we have two hundred FBI agents doing three or four years investigating the president's zipper? Seriously, think about this."

"Not his zipper," I shot back. "His lying under oath, just to remind you—his lying. He put his hand on a Bible, Michael."

"Let's see," Moore snapped back. "His lying under oath? Or would I rather have had the two hundred FBI agents finding the terrorists who were planning to kill three thousand people?"

Clever, Michael, oh so clever. Just one problem. It turns out that we didn't need two hundred FBI agents tracking down the terrorist mastermind. Sudan actually offered Osama bin Laden to the Clinton-Gore administration on a silver platter back in 1996. Before he bombed our embassies in Kenya and Tanzania. Before he attacked the USS *Cole*. Before thousands of Americans died on September 11, 2001. But the Clinton-Gore administration repeatedly turned down Sudan's offer and in so doing let Osama bin Laden slip away to unleash an epoch of evil against us.

In fact, in February of 2002, my cohost, Alan Colmes, and I had the opportunity to talk with the man who tried to broker the deal between the Sudanese and the Clinton-Gore White House to deliver bin Laden into U.S. custody—the deal the administration turned down. His name is Mansoor Ijaz, and his story is remarkable.

Ijaz is an American citizen, a Muslim, a Democrat, and a financial contributor to the Democratic Party and the Clinton-Gore campaigns. The chairman of a New York–based investment company, Ijaz counts among his partners former CIA director James Woolsey and retired U.S. Air Force Lt. Gen. James Abrahamson, the former director of President Reagan's Strategic Defense Initiative. Ijaz is now a Fox News Channel foreign affairs analyst. But during the 1990s he was a middleman deep inside the Middle East.

"In February of 1996," Ijaz told me, "the Sudanese had come to the conclusion that their Islamic experiment had gone bad, essentially, that the fanatics had gotten out of control. Bin Laden was part of that problem. They offered Saudi Arabia an extradition treaty—extradition of bin Laden. The Saudis turned them down. They came to the United States and said, 'Do you guys want him?' And [the Clinton-Gore administration] said: 'No, we don't have a case. We can't do it now.'"

"Clinton turned it down?" I pressed, unsure I'd heard Ijaz correctly.

"They turned it down," he confirmed, adding that the United States "made a huge mistake" in not nabbing bin Laden when we could. After all, he noted, "Sudan was the place in which all this Islamic extremism was born."

Between 1996 and 2000, Ijaz opened unofficial back channels between Sudan and the Clinton-Gore administration. He met with Clinton National Security Adviser Sandy Berger and explained that Sudanese President Omar Hassan al-Bashir wanted terrorism sanctions against Sudan lifted. He was therefore offering to arrest and extradite Osama bin Laden to the United States and provide detailed information about global terrorist networks run by Islamic Jihad, Hezbollah, and Hamas, including information about the two hijackers who would eventually pilot the planes that slammed into the World Trade Center. But to Ijaz's astonishment, the Clinton-Gore administration wasn't interested.

In fact, Sudan kept offering important information on bin Laden and top al Qaeda operatives. But the Clinton-Gore administration kept turning it down—first in February 1996, then in August, then in April 1997, then in February 1998, and finally in July 2000, a little over one year before the attacks.

Ijaz also tried to get the interest of liberal Democrats in Congress. On April 5, 1997, he forwarded a letter from the Sudanese president to Indiana Rep. Lee Hamilton, then the ranking Democrat on the House Foreign Affairs Committee, offering to let the FBI's counterterrorism team go to Sudan to review their information. But Hamilton never responded to Ijaz. On June 10, 1997, Ijaz testified before the House Judiciary Subcommittee on Crime, describing ways to work with Sudan to hunt down terrorists and make them pay. A full four years before the tragic events of September 11, Ijaz argued that "the real danger for the West lies in revivalist Islamic movements disintegrating into unguided, genuinely radical states, pushing terrorist networks underground where they can only be seen at a sidewalk café, with a bomb strapped to the body of a fanatic. He was right. But no one listened.

In the days after Ijaz first revealed the substance of these foiled negotiations, former Clinton-Gore officials, including former national security adviser Sandy Berger and former UN ambassador Bill Richardson, came forth to dispute them. But their contentions—that there was no proof of the story, that Saudi Arabia may have been intended to act as a go-between—rang hollow. The more plausible story is the more regrettable one: that the administration chose not to pursue the opportunity because they still treated bin Laden as a criminal threat, not a terrorist enemy, and feared they would not have the legal grounds to hold him pending a trial.

What conclusion does Mansoor Ijaz draw on the basis of such facts?

"The silence of the Clinton Administration in responding to these offers was deafening," wrote Ijaz in an op-ed piece in the *Los Angeles Times*. "As an American Muslim and a political supporter of Clinton, I feel now, as I argued with Clinton and Berger then, that their counter-terrorism policies fueled the rise of bin Laden from an ordinary man to a Hydra-like monster."

It's truly astonishing. Bill Clinton, Al Gore, and their liberal allies on Capitol Hill were offered Osama bin Laden by the Sudanese government, and they turned the offer down. They could have taken him into custody and begun unraveling his terrorist network almost six years ago. But they didn't. And now more than three thousand innocent Americans have paid with their blood.

HOW CIVILIZATION IS AT RISK

Why is the Left so contemptuous of our military and intelligence services, yet so ignorant of those who would do us harm?

This is a critical question we'll explore in the pages ahead. For now I want you to begin to see the pattern, and understand what is at risk if misguided liberal ideas continue to distract our nation and drain our resolve. Next time it might not be hijacked planes and traces of anthrax powder. It could be a suitcase bomb with radioactive material. It could be a tactical or intercontinental ballistic missile armed with biological, chemical, or nuclear warheads. It could be attacks of apocalyptic proportions; attacks aimed at obliterating our civilization as we know it—unless we act decisively.

"The militant Islamic terror that we're facing sees the United States as the main enemy," former Israeli prime minister Benjamin Netanyahu told me on *Hannity & Colmes* just weeks after the September 11 attacks. "In their desire to reverse the course of Western history over the last thousand years, they view the U.S. as being the West. . . . So they're going to attack America again and again. And the great danger that we face—and I say this every time I'm here, and I'll say it again tonight—if they acquire nuclear weapons, if any part of this terror network acquires nuclear weapons, they will use it."

Netanyahu knows what he's talking about. He's fought terrorism on the front lines as a commando, and lost his brother in the daring rescue of Israeli hostages in Entebbe in 1976. He's written perhaps the definitive book on the subject, *Fighting Terrorism: How Democracies Can Defeat Domestic and International Terrorists.* And on September 20, 2001, Netanyahu was invited to testify before the Government

Reform Committee of the United States Congress on the dangers facing us all.

"What is at stake today is nothing less than the survival of our civilization," Netanyahu stated bluntly. "There may be some who would have thought a week ago that to talk in these apocalyptic terms about the battle against international terrorism was to engage in reckless exaggeration. No longer. Each one of us today understands that we are all targets, that our cities are vulnerable, and that our values are hated with an unmatched fanaticism that seeks to destroy our societies and our way of life."

Other nations may decide not to join us in our war on terrorism, Netanyahu warned, but we must not be deterred. Even if at first we must go it alone, eventually our moral position will win the day and the world's other democracies will be compelled to join us. The very freedom the terrorists are trying to extinguish will ultimately impel us to victory over them and deliver us security in the future. But having the military power to crush the terrorists, he warned, will not be sufficient. We will also need to muster the will.

Words of wisdom in an age of liberal confusion.

Liberals told us that global warming and gays in the military were top priorities, well above securing our nation. September 11 and subsequent revelations have proven them wrong. We must wake up and put to use the lessons we've learned. For the sake of our children and grandchildren, we must devote ourselves to putting conservative ideas back to work to defend our nation, strengthen our economy, and preserve our values.

TWO

THE LEFT VS. THE CIA

Two men.

Same first name—John.

Same homeland—the United States of America.

But between them stood a great chasm.

Johnny "Mike" Spann served his country in the marines and the CIA.

Johnny Walker Lindh betrayed his country as a soldier for a militant Islamic terrorist cell.

A hero, Spann died defending our freedoms.

A traitor, Lindh fought to extinguish those freedoms—and though our government has decided not to seek the death penalty in prosecuting him, for his crimes against his country he deserves execution.

On November 25, 2001, America suffered her first battlefield casualty in the first war of the twenty-first century. His name was Johnny Spann; he was known as Mike. CIA Director George Tenet called Spann "a precious life given in a noble cause." And he was absolutely right.

At thirty-two years old, Spann was a husband and the father of an infant son and two young daughters. He was a brother of two sisters and the son of Johnny and Gail Spann of Winfield, Alabama. A Christian and a conservative, he grew up in the Bible Belt, loving his family, his football team, and his American flag and heritage. His senior quote in his high school year book was taken from Proverbs 13:20: "He that walketh with wise men shall be wise; but a companion of fools shall be destroyed." Studying criminal justice and law enforcement, Spann graduated from Auburn University in 1992, joined the marines, and served eight years. In 1999 he joined the CIA and quickly became a field officer in the service of the Directorate of Operations. When the war began and President Bush ordered U.S. forces into battle, Spann eagerly answered the call and was sent to the front lines. He believed he had been born for that moment, and he was ready.

And it was there—in the early days of our military and covert operations deep inside Afghanistan—that John Spann came face-to-face with John Lindh.

With a scraggly beard and wild, uncut hair, Lindh looked like a madman. Named after John Lennon, John Lindh was born and raised in Marin County, a wealthy, liberal suburb of San Francisco. He grew up in a veritable ideological Disneyland of moral relativism, political correctness, and not-too-subtle anti-American multiculturalism, the kind that preaches that America is a racist, sexist, bigoted, imperialist, homophobic, and thus fundamentally evil and oppressive nation. He grew up feeding his mind on *The Autobiography of Malcolm X*, not Moses or Peter or Paul. He grew up in a world where devout Christians are regarded as part of the despised "radical religious right" and considered a serious threat to American pluralism and tolerance. Radical Muslims, by contrast, are often considered victims of Western cultural and political oppression.

In time, Lindh converted from anything-goes liberal agnosticism to hard-core Middle Eastern radical Islam. He moved to Yemen, then

Pakistan, then Afghanistan. He began memorizing the Koran. He began training with Osama bin Laden's military forces. He began serving with al Qaeda forces against his own country, and continued doing so even after learning that al Qaeda terrorists had just killed more than three thousand Americans in New York, Washington, and Pennsylvania.

In a makeshift prison at Mazar-e-Sharif, Afghanistan, Spann came to interrogate Lindh. (No evidence has yet surfaced that the twenty-one-year-old Lindh ever suggested to any American official, including Spann, that he had been kidnapped or caught up in something beyond his control, despite his lawyers' claims to the contrary.) Lindh was soon part of a bloody, chaotic prison riot in which al Qaeda forces tried to murder their way out of custody. And in the terrible ensuing events, Spann was blown up with a hand grenade, defending his colleagues and his country.

From the beginning, John Walker Lindh's parents have persistently insisted that their son did nothing wrong.

"John loves America," Frank Lindh told reporters the day his son pled not guilty to a ten-count indictment in U.S. federal court, including the charge of conspiracy to kill Americans. "We love America. John did not do anything against America."

Spann's family couldn't disagree more.

"Mike was a hero, not because of the way he died but because of the way he lived," says Gail Spann, the slain CIA agent's mother. "I would also like to say that John Walker is a traitor because of the way he lived."

Even a year after September 11, it is amazing to me to consider that a young American man could actually do what John Walker Lindh did—join a radical Islamic terrorist group and take up arms against his fellow countrymen. But even more amazing to me is the incredible bravery and sacrifice of young people like Mike Spann— who eagerly go to war against these murderous lunatics, joining our armed forces and the CIA and taking up arms in the defense of liberty and their fellow countrymen. Even though it may cost them everything they have to give.

Such commitment, in the face of such grave danger, requires a measure of love and devotion to country that only the finest among us can truly muster. And when we see people make these kinds of commitments—and pay the ultimate price, with the currency of their own blood—it is our duty to them, their families, those who have gone before them, and those who will follow, to honor them. Thank them. And lift them up as models for us and our children to follow. For such men and women represent the best America has to offer. And we dare not forget them.

One reason I have such deep respect for President Bush is that he has set about to ensure that our young men and women will not serve or sacrifice in vain. He has called them to a just and noble cause. he has rallied the nation behind them, and he has pledged to give them every tool necessary to finish the job.

Do you remember during President Bush's first State of the Union address, when he turned to look up at the young woman sitting beside the first Lady? There was Shannon Spann, the sweet, strong, and classy widow of Mike Spann. I will never forget that image, or the surge of emotions it triggered in me.

"Last month," said Bush, his own heart clearly full of emotion, "at the grave of her husband, Michael, a CIA officer and marine who died in Mazur-e-Sharif, Shannon Spann said these words of farewell: 'Semper Fi, my love.' Shannon is with us tonight." The House chamber erupted with applause. Everyone in the chamber gave a warm and deeply deserved standing ovation to a woman who, along with her young children, truly gave her country her full measure of devotion.

"Shannon," the president continued, "I assure you and all who have lost a loved one that our cause is just, and our country will never forget the debt we owe Michael and all who gave their lives for freedom."

I found myself thinking of the words of Jesus: "Greater love has no man than this, that he lay down his life for his friends."

A few weeks later, Alan and I had the honor of welcoming Shannon Spann on our program. Because it is vitally important that we not permit this cause to be dehumanized, we must always be aware that there are real people behind the arresting headlines in this war on terror—real people who risk their real lives so that the rest of us may enjoy real freedom.

I began by asking her how she was holding up.

"Well, we're doing really very well," she said stoically. "It depends what day you catch me, really. One day is different from the next. But we're moving along."

I asked her about reports that many of her friends and neighbors had no idea that her husband worked for the CIA and were totally surprised to find out about his profession—and tragic death—on the news.

"Well, the colleagues that we work with at CIA are certainly a unique group of individuals, dedicated to working toward America's freedom in a quiet sort of way. And so, when your neighbors and friends aren't aware, I guess that's when you're doing your job just right."

We talked about their eight-month-old son and young daughters and how hard it must be on all of them.

"I was thinking about this just before we came on," Shannon told me. "It sure is [difficult]. I mean, I look at my little son and just the smile on his face, just what a bright little life he has. And just knowing that he isn't even aware just exactly what he's missing, it's a heartbreaker. It really is."

Did she believe Lindh should be found guilty of treason?

"I certainly should have liked to see treason charges laid against him, sure. I mean, I think he has, very purposefully, aligned himself with . . . al Qaeda and has dedicated himself to their stated goals over the past three years. And they certainly are not shy about the fact that they are dedicating themselves as organizations to the destruction of the West and to the killing of Americans."

Did she believe Lindh should be executed?

"I do, sure. I mean, good grief, Sean, he's a terrorist, you know?"

I asked Shannon if she remembered the last time she spoke with her husband.

"It was Thanksgiving Day," she said. "He was able to phone every once in a while from the field."

She concluded the interview by appealing to the American people to understand "that it's real lives" at stake in this war, not just numbers and news reports. "You know, we have colleagues and friends, and your next-door neighbor, and your friends' sons, and your own sons and daughters are putting themselves in harm's way every day to protect our freedoms. And we need to not forget that . . . it's real people."

Indeed it is.

HOW RONALD REAGAN DEFENDED THE CIA

The stark contrast between Lindh and Spann is only the latest evidence of the tension between the CIA and the Left, a conflict that has been ongoing for decades. Such attacks especially infuriated Ronald Reagan, who recognized that at the same time the Left was emasculating our intelligence services, the Soviet Union was strengthening theirs.

In a radio commentary broadcast in August of 1975, Reagan cited newly released government information that "the number of Communist government officials in the United States has tripled since 1960, and is still increasing," and that nearly two thousand of them "have been identified as members of intelligence or security agencies."

Reagan questioned why liberals in government and the media seemed determined to undermine the very institutions designed to protect the American people. "What disturbs me most about the witch-hunting mood [against our intelligence services] that came into being almost overnight and the investigations that resulted, including most especially the congressional hearings now going on, is the inestimable harm that has been done to this nation's entire intelligence-gathering ability," Reagan told his audience on nearly three hundred radio stations across the country. "There is no doubt that information sources worldwide have been frightened into silence, and certainly our own personnel must be retreating into a 'don't stick your neck out' posture."

In a June 15, 1977, radio commentary, Reagan criticized a report by the Senate Select Committee on Intelligence—chaired by left-wing senator Frank Church, an Idaho Democrat—that "makes one wonder if they know who really is the enemy."

Thirty-eight of the report's forty pages, Reagan pointed out, were consumed with determining whether the CIA was operating lawfully, not whether they were operating effectively against the Soviets, the Chinese, the Cubans, the Arab world, and other threats. Reagan also noted that criticisms of the CIA by Senator Daniel Patrick Moynihan, a New York Democrat, "made it sound as if the chief threat to our liberties was our own intelligence apparatus rather than the enemies that apparatus was supposed to protect us from."

"Isn't it time for someone to ask if we aren't threatened more by the people the FBI and the CIA are watching than we are by the FBI and the CIA?" he asked.

For such wisdom Reagan was castigated by the Left as an extremist and a warmonger. But, of course, he was right.

THE VAST LEFT-WING CONSPIRACY

Which brings me to the vast left-wing conspiracy against the CIA.

For decades, liberals and conservatives have been deeply divided over the importance of and the need for the CIA. Conservatives have long fought to strengthen and expand our intelligence services. Liberals have long sought to attack and undermine America's intelligence community.

"Is it time to get rid of the CIA?" asked a post-9/11 story by Ted Gup in the left-wing magazine *Mother Jones.*

In the face of the death of heroes like Mike Spann, how do liberals have the gall to ask such questions? Get rid of our most important intelligence organization? During wartime? Is that what liberals really want in their heart of hearts? Few would admit it on the record. But the *Mother Jones* article does provide a fascinating, if deeply disturbing, insight into the Left's mindset:

> Today, the CIA is hamstrung by its own sullied past. At home, critics suspect it of having had a hand in the assassination of John F. Kennedy, of introducing crack cocaine into South Central Los Angeles, and of a host of other conspiracies that remain utterly unproved. Overseas, its past shadows it from country to country and continent to continent, clouding America's moral standing and its ability to gather the kind of intelligence that the nation will need in the years ahead.
>
> Americans have long viewed the CIA as a rogue agency, its errant missions the work of covert cowboys. The truth—that everything it did, good and bad, originated in the Oval Office with either a presidential directive or a wink and a nod—is less comforting. It means that we as a nation bear a measure of responsibility for its actions, and its failures. Whether the CIA is still capable of effectively serving the nation is a question that can no longer be ignored.

So not only is the CIA a rogue agency—I guess we're a rogue nation!

Mother Jones also condemned the CIA for having too few spies—

or was that too *many* spies? "Human intelligence—the network of spies on the ground—was allowed to degrade steadily," an article argued in its January/February 2002 issue. "To the fore came satellite imagery and the National Security Agency's capacity to intercept communications. High-tech spying had proved effective against foreign states during the Cold War. Against terrorism, its value was dubious at best."

But in a previous issue of *Mother Jones*, in January/February 1995, writer Robert Dreyfuss seemed to be saying that conservatives were unwise in wanting to build up the CIA's human intelligence capabilities.

"Though the CIA is being downsized and there are calls to abolish it, there are also calls from CIA insiders, some congressional Republicans, and a few outside conservatives to expand the CIA's use of spies—known in the trade as human intelligence (humint)—at the expense of techint, or intelligence gathered by satellites, listening devices, or other technical means," wrote Dreyfuss. "Robert Steele, a former CIA officer who has put forward a number of otherwise thoughtful ideas about reforming the CIA, recently called for a doubling of the agency's clandestine espionage and for placing all of the new spies under 'nonofficial cover.'" Dreyfuss went on to point out that Congress may have been more receptive to expanding the CIA given a greater number of Republicans and the commitment of soon to be House Speaker Newt Gingrich to the idea.

So which is it? Are there too few Mike Spanns or too many? Are we conservatives off base for wanting to make the CIA too big or too small? Or is that really the point? Rather, isn't this just the Left demonstrating its visceral (and incoherent) contempt for the CIA— and ultimately seeking to diminish its effectiveness and public support?

The Nation, another leading left-wing magazine, has also long been a foe of the CIA. But a 1998 feature story titled "Bioterrorism: America's Newest War Game" really takes the cake. Writing just three years before September 11, author Peter Pringle mocked former CIA director John Deutch and his colleagues for warning that "an act of catastrophic terrorism" could "have the effect of Pearl Harbor" and "divide America into a 'before and after.'"

The Nation article conceded that terrorism's toll in the 1990s was rising. "In 1983, 271 Americans were killed by terrorist attacks, most of them in the bombing of the Marine barracks in Lebanon. Then came bombs at the World Trade Center in 1993 (six dead, 1,000 injured), the Oklahoma City federal building in 1995 (168 dead, 500 injured) and the Khobar Towers Air Force housing complex in Saudi Arabia (nineteen dead, 500 injured)." But then Pringle sniped, "In the rush to play a new war game there is always a tendency to hype the threat," specifically ridiculing the potential threat of an anthrax attack in Washington. It also quoted a professor who argued that "despite the lurid rhetoric, a massive terrorist attack with nuclear, chemical, or biological weapons is hardly inevitable. It is not even likely. . . . Terrorists wish to convince us that they are capable of striking from anywhere at any time, but there is really no chaos. In fact, terrorism involves predictable behavior, and the vast majority of terrorist organizations can be identified well in advance."

The article concluded by criticizing Republicans for adding $9 billion to the military budget, "including several additional millions for antiterrorism projects" and suggested the GOP might try to politicize the issue in the future.

Then came September 11 and the subsequent anthrax attacks. Did *The Nation*'s staff possess the intellectual integrity to admit or reassess its monumentally flawed judgment? Did it refrain from mocking further the CIA's prescient concerns about terrorism? Did it come to value a strong, vibrant, aggressive CIA to make sure such attacks could never happen again? Hardly.

In an October 1, 2001 essay, David Corn, Washington editor of *The Nation* and a Fox News contributor, attacked Republicans, conservatives, and "the national security cadre" for raising questions "of how best to bolster the military and intelligence establishment." He criticized former secretary of state James Baker "for "blaming the Church Committee, the Senate panel that investigated CIA misdeeds in the 1970s, for what happened: 'We went on a real witch hunt with our CIA . . . the Church Committee. We unilaterally disarmed in terms of intelligence.' " Corn also couldn't resist taking a shot at former House Speaker Newt Gingrich, who "assailed rules on intelligence gathering that limit CIA interaction with known terrorists, and he asserted that the intelligence budget (about $30 billion) was 'too small.' "

Is it really all that surprising that a leading leftist like Corn would vilify the CIA and those who have tried to strengthen it? Of course not. Corn has never been a fan of the CIA. In 1994 he wrote a book entitled *Blond Ghost: Ted Shackley and the CIA's Crusades,* which the *New York Times* described as "a scorchingly critical account" of the career of a major agency figure.

What *was* surprising and disappointing—to me, at least—was that Corn's ideological disdain for the CIA runs so deep that even the murder of three thousand Americans didn't persuade him of our need for a strong intelligence agency. But frankly I shouldn't be surprised. This is part of the liberals' pattern of hamstringing various reform measures (such as efforts to bolster the CIA or to reduce marginal tax rates to stimulate the economy), then blaming the other side for the inevitable consequences (security failures and recession, respectively).

JOHN KERRY'S CRUSADE AGAINST THE CIA

It's not just liberals in the press who despise the CIA and question its necessity, though. It's liberal politicians as well.

Take Senator John Kerry, for example, the Massachusetts Democrat who wants to be president. Kerry—a decorated Vietnam vet who was also once a leader of Vietnam Veterans Against the War—deserves great credit for his military service to our country, particularly in a war with which he did not agree. But one thing that bothers me about Kerry and causes me to question his wisdom and judgment is the ferocity of his attacks against the CIA since the 1980s.

Kerry has tried repeatedly to link the Agency to illegal drug-running, and accused it of having "abandoned the responsibility our government has for protecting our citizens from all threats to their security and well-being." It was Kerry and his advisers who, in 1989, released a 1,166-page report purporting to detail the supposed evils of the Reagan-Bush CIA. At the time, the report got little mainstream media coverage because few took it seriously.

In 1996, however, Gary Webb, an investigative reporter with the *San Jose Mercury News,* picked up on the Kerry report. He wrote an explosive series of articles titled "Dark Alliance," in which he tried to link the CIA to the introduction of crack cocaine in America. The story was quickly picked up by black radio stations, Internet sites, and black political leaders, among others. It created a firestorm of outrage against the CIA, fueling notions that the Agency was trying to encourage racial genocide in black, inner-city communities. There was just one problem: the story was false.

The CIA vigorously denied the explosive (and preposterous) allegations. The Agency's inspector general then put together a seventeen-member investigative team, pored over 250,000 pages of documents, conducted more than 365 interviews, most of them under oath, and issued a report on January 29, 1998. Bottom line: the *Mercury News* story was utterly groundless. And the CIA wasn't alone in reaching that conclusion. Between 1996 and 1998, major news outlets such as the *Los Angeles Times,* the *New York Times,* the *Washington Post,* and the PBS *NewsHour* ran stories exposing Webb's dubious reporting and making it clear that the allegations against the CIA were simply not true. Eventually, even the *Mercury News* itself backed off the story and admitted its errors (though Webb continues to deny the charges).

But none of this stopped congressional liberals like Congresswoman Maxine Waters, a California Democrat, in their anti-CIA cause. Waters bitterly attacks the CIA as a bunch of illegal drug traffickers, irrespective of the facts.

"I applaud Senator Kerry," said Waters. "Senator Kerry has worked for fifteen years to bring the truth to light, having chaired the Senate investigation that first uncovered the sordid details of Contra drug trafficking in the 1980s. . . . The Contras were a creation of the Reagan-Bush administration and run by Reagan's CIA and Oliver North. . . . I cannot understand why a CIA report, which details the illegal efforts of Reagan-Bush administration officials to protect the involvement of top level Contras in drug trafficking, should continue to be protected."

"The list of misdeeds by our intelligence agencies is long, and much of it still remains shrouded in secrecy," raged Waters.

Sadly, Waters was not the only one. Congresswoman Cynthia McKinney, a Georgia Democrat, also piled on, coining the phrase "Central Intoxication Agency" to describe the nation's premier intelligence organization.

On May 1, 1997, Kerry took to the Senate floor to question the CIA's budget, its usefulness, and even its status as an "essential" priority of the federal government.

"Why is it that our vast intelligence apparatus, built to sustain America in the long twilight struggle of the Cold War, continues to grow at an exponential rate?" Kerry demanded of his Senate colleagues. "Now that that struggle is over, why is it that our vast intelligence apparatus grows even as government resources for new and essential priorities fall far short of what is necessary? Why is it that our vast intelligence apparatus continues to roll on even as every other government bureaucracy is subject to increasing scrutiny and, indeed, to reinvention?"

MOYNIHAN'S CRUSADE

Among the most shortsighted and committed critics of the CIA was former senator Daniel Patrick Moynihan, the senior Democrat of New York. This may surprise some, given Moynihan's foreign policy experience and the media's fawning praise for his vaunted wisdom. Yet it was Moynihan who proposed and doggedly pursued the CIA's demise after the end of the Cold War.

In February 1992, the *New York Times* reported Moynihan as asking, "Without the Soviet threat, why not just abolish the CIA and let the State Department take over? For 40 years the threat of nuclear war drove the CIA, along with the other agencies and departments that make up the $30 billion-a-year constellation that is often called 'the intelligence community.'"

On January 4, 1995, Moynihan actually introduced Senate Bill 126—The Abolition of the Central Intelligence Agency Act—in which he sought to assign overall intelligence authority to the secretary of state. Under Section 202 of the bill, entitled "Findings," Moynihan included the following language: "The Congress finds that (1) the creation of the Central Intelligence Agency as a separate entity during the Cold War undermined the role of the Department of State as the primary agency of the United States Government in formulating and conducting foreign policy and providing information to the President concerning the state of world affairs; and (2) it is desirable for the Secretary of State to serve as the official primarily responsible for coordinating and managing the gathering of intelligence."

Moynihan's proposal was defective on many levels. Having served for years as a diplomat, including as UN ambassador, he above all should have known that combining diplomacy and spying into a single department would not only have created an internal tension between the two distinct operational activities but would cause foreign governments to wonder whether every American diplomat on their soil was in fact an intelligence operative. In some countries, this kind of confusion would have endangered the very safety of American diplomatic personnel.

Furthermore, had Moynihan's bill become law, interference by State Department foreign service personnel with the dirty but crucial business of intelligence activities would have become more prevalent, thereby making intelligence gathering less effective.

As for Moynihan's congressional "findings," suffice it to say that his bill never became law.

What, then, are we to make of congressional liberals' relentless broadsides against the CIA? Do they believe America will be safer, stronger, or more secure without it? Even they aren't that delusional, are they? Do they believe their irresponsible attacks will somehow gain them political points with the American people? Or are they just mired in their postmodern worldview, unable to grasp that the world will always be a dangerous place? Even before we won the Cold War, liberals were soft on national security and defense. But since then— and even since the start of the War on Terror—Moynihan has not been alone in his naive assumption that we have no urgent need for the CIA's intelligence services.

HOW CLINTON AND GORE UNDERMINED THE CIA

It would be bad enough if only liberal writers and members of Congress impugned the CIA. But it's worse than that.

The Clinton-Gore administration, which was constitutionally obligated to look after our national security, actively undermined our intelligence-gathering capabilities and demoralized our intelligence community.

Case in point: After listening to Representative Robert Torricelli, a New Jersey Democrat (and now a U.S. senator) rant and rave about how evil the CIA was for using creeps and crooks and scum as informants, the Clinton-Gore administration instituted a series of so-called reforms that tied the hands of U.S. intelligence agencies engaged in keeping and recruiting foreign spies, despite the crucial importance of these human assets to effective intelligence gathering.

The crippling effect of these reforms was corroborated by *The Hill*, the Washington, D.C., newspaper covering Congress and the White House, based on October 2001 interviews with members of the House Intelligence Committee. "In the wake of disclosures by Torricelli that a Guatemalan colonel linked to the murder of an American was on the CIA payroll, the agency fired one-third of its informants—roughly 1,000 'assets'—and instituted new rules on the recruitment of sources." The conclusion: "The Central Intelligence Agency's ability to gather intelligence in the Middle East has been injured by reforms triggered in 1995 by then-Representative Robert Torricelli."

Robert Baer, a former CIA operative in the Middle East, confirms the essence of the story. "In the mid-1990s," he asserts, "the CIA underwent what we called an 'agent scrub.' That meant that we let go of approximately sixty percent of our human sources, perhaps more, which seriously damaged the CIA."

Does the CIA need to be accountable to Congress and the people? Of course. Regardless of whether Torricelli's accusations were true, there is no question that the CIA shouldn't be paying foreigners who kill Americans. But Torricelli's hyperventilating about this case led to a series of policy changes that went way too far. Torricelli (and his fellow alarmist colleagues) created a public perception that the CIA was doing something wicked by working with informants involved in the dirty business of international espionage—the very people with the inside information we need and don't have. The Clinton-Gore administration was more than happy to accommodate the CIA's worst critics. The result: the United States has even fewer human intelligence resources in the Middle East than we had at the start of the 1990s. Here was this same liberal mindset injecting itself back into the policy mix: just as they naively assumed the world was no longer dangerous, liberals were demanding that our intelligence agents deal only with the pure and the clean. Sounds good in theory, but as anyone in the intelligence business will tell you, if you want to learn about the bad guys, you can't rely on choirboys.

Representative Porter Goss, a Florida Republican on the House Intelligence Committee who once worked for the CIA, told *The Hill* that the so-called agent scrub had a "dampening effect" on the CIA's ability "to gather intelligence in Afghanistan, Iran and other nations that sponsor terrorism."

It is a charge echoed by Representative Larry Combest, a Texas Republican also on the House Intelligence Committee. "I was very much opposed to what Mr. Torricelli did," Combest told *The Hill*. "Intelligence gathering is a nitty-gritty, dirty business, and you have to work with the kind of people you might not have over for dinner."

The bottom line? Torricelli's actions, combined with the approach of the Clinton-Gore White House, severely undermined the CIA in the 1990s.

Robert Baer, who worked for the CIA for two decades, says that when he was in charge of Central Asia operations for the CIA in the 1990s, he had no human sources. Not a single one. In his bestselling book, *See No Evil: The True Story of a Ground Soldier in the CIA's War on Terrorism,* Baer reported:

★ The CIA's London office "couldn't claim a single Arabic speaker."

★ British authorities prevented the CIA from recruiting sources in their country—even Islamic fundamentalists.

★ The CIA was shrinking throughout Europe by the mid-1990s and lacked the manpower to place sufficient numbers of officers in Middle Eastern communities. Those who were available for such placement were undertrained and unmotivated.

★ The same was true in the Middle East, where rarely were more than one or two officers assigned to any country.

★ "In 1995," Baer wrote, "the CIA made an analyst with no experience overseas, the director of operations. His successor was a retiree, who was followed by an officer with a similar dearth of 'spying experience,' having risen to his position through his political skills. The agency, for all practical purposes, had taken itself out of the spying business." It is not surprising, then, that we had no sources in the mosques of Hamburg to alert us that Mohammad Atta was recruiting fellow hijackers for the September 11 attacks.

Whose fault is all this? Baer pulls no punches. He says the Reagan and first Bush administrations made mistakes. But he is toughest on the Clinton-Gore administration.

"Whether it was Osama bin Laden, Yasir Arafat, Iranian terrorism, Saddam Hussein, or any of the other evils that so threaten the world, the Clinton administration seemed determined to sweep them all under the carpet," wrote Baer, adding that "the mantra at 1600 Pennsylvania Avenue seemed to be: Get through the term. Keep the bad news from the newspapers. Dump the naysayers. Gather money for the next election—gobs of it—and let some other administration down the line deal with it. Worst of all, my CIA had decided to go along for the ride. Now that such horrendous neglect has come home to roost in such misery-provoking ways, I take no pleasure whatsoever in having been right."

OLLIE, ME, AND THE WAR OF IDEAS

Soon after the September 11 attacks, an email began circulating on the Internet. Actually, there were several emails, all variations on the same theme. And they spread like wildfire through all fifty states and at least thirteen countries.

Here's the version I received.

Subject: Oliver North—remember him?

I was at a UNC lecture the other day where they played a video of Oliver North during the Iran-Contra deals during the Reagan Administration. I was only 14 back then but was surprised by this particular clip.

There was Ollie in front of God and Country getting the third degree. But what he said stunned me. He was being grilled by some senator I didn't recognize who asked him, "Did you not recently spend close to $60,000 for a home security system?"

Oliver replied, "Yes I did, Sir."

The senator continued, trying to get a laugh out of the audience, "Isn't this just a little excessive?"

"No sir," continued Oliver.

"No? And why not?"

"Because the life of my family and I were threatened."

"Threatened? By who."

"By a terrorist, sir."

"Terrorist? What terrorist could possibly scare you that much?"

"His name is Osama bin Laden."

At this point the senator tried to repeat the name, but couldn't pronounce it. A couple of people laughed at the attempt. Then the senator continued.

"Why are you so afraid of this man?"

"Because, sir, he is the most evil person alive that I know of."

"And what do you recommend we do about him?"

"If it were me I would recommend an assassin team be formed to eliminate him and his men from the face of the earth."

The senator disagreed with this approach and that was all they showed of the clip. It's scary when you think 15 years ago the government was aware of bin Laden and his potential threat to the security of the world. I guess like all great tyrants they start small but if left untended spread like the virus they truly are.

Turns out the interchange wasn't true. Not entirely, at least. But it felt true. That's why so many people read it and forwarded it to their friends.

Ollie quickly put out a statement correcting the story: It wasn't a senator but the committee counsel, John Nields, who did the questioning. The security system installed in Ollie's home cost $16,000, not $60,000. The terrorist who threatened to kill Ollie in 1986 wasn't Osama bin Laden. It was another major international terrorist, the Libyan mastermind Abu Nidal.

"I never said I was afraid of anybody," Ollie points out. "I did say that I would be glad to meet Abu Nidal on equal terms anywhere in the world, but that I was unwilling to have him or his operatives meet my wife and children on his terms. I did say that the terrorists intercepted by the FBI on the way to my house in February 1987 to kill my wife, children, and me were Libyans, dispatched from the People's Committee for Libyan Students in McLean, Virginia. And I did say that the federal government had moved my family out of our home to a military base [Camp Lejeune, North Carolina] until they could dispatch more than thirty agents to protect my family from those terrorists (because a liberal federal judge had allowed the Libyan assassins to post bond and they fled)."

In the end, the government spent more than $2 million protecting the North family, and the terrorists sent to kill them were never reapprehended.

When I read this email message, I have to admit it brought back a flood of memories. For it was precisely this controversy—the intense, dramatic televised showdown between Marine Lt. Col. Oliver L. North and the liberal, Democrat-controlled U.S. Congress over how to wage and win the war against terrorism—that pushed me off the sidelines and into the war of ideas.

It was the summer of 1987. I was living in California, trying to make some money to get myself back into college because after two and a half years I had run out of money. I was painting, doing construction, and remodeling homes. But suddenly I became engrossed in the televised Iran-Contra hearings. I was appalled at the unbelievably vicious liberal attacks on honorable and patriotic men like Lt. Col. Ollie North, Admiral John Poindexter, and the entire Reagan administration, including Reagan himself. Let's not forget what was driving these men: not the quest for power or money but the noble pursuit of the cause of freedom for the oppressed in our own hemisphere. (The Monroe Doctrine meant something to President Reagan.) They were trying to drive the Sandanista Communists from power in Nicaragua. But as soon became painfully evident, the Left's goal was to destroy the Reagan administration and drive the president from office.

The liberals were dead wrong in their condemnation of U.S. policy. Ollie North and Ronald Reagan were right. Evil people and regimes threatened Americans then as they do now, and the Reagan administration was determined to do something about it, whether that led to the Middle East, North Africa, or Central America. Did they make some mistakes? Maybe. But we were engaged in a Cold War against an evil empire and a hot war against terrorism all over the world. Ollie North—decorated for courage and bravery in Vietnam with the Silver Star, the Bronze Star, two Purple Hearts, and three Navy Commendation medals—helped plan the Reagan administration's liberation of Grenada. He helped plan the raid against Libya, in response to repeated rounds of Libyan terrorism. He helped the president wage a relentless campaign for freedom and democracy in Central America. And for his efforts, Ollie and his family were not heralded as American heroes. They were targeted—first by Libyan terrorists, and then by liberal Democrats.

These hearings had a profound impact on my life. I found myself getting furious at the sight of congressmen and senators excoriating a dedicated patriot like Ollie. I was so riveted by the Iran-Contra hearings that I wouldn't go to work. I'd stay home and watch the hearings all day. I even taped them so I could watch them over again. I still have my copies. The more I watched and listened, the angrier I got. And in my search to express my views—to hear a different viewpoint on the subject from what was available on TV—I began calling in to radio talk shows to defend Ollie and beat up on the sanctimonious congressman and senators. Their attacks on the CIA and covert operations and the Reagan administration's policy of "peace through strength," I argued, would end up damaging our national security and making all Americans more vulnerable to attack. As it turns out, Ollie was way ahead of the curve on the question of terrorism and the dangers of foreign aggression. Had we listened to him then, I am convinced America would be less vulnerable to attack today.

And somewhere along the way, I found my calling in life.

THREE

COAST TO COAST, BORDER TO BORDER

Let me say this before I go any further: My quarrel with liberals and liberalism is not personal. Just because I think liberals are wrong on the issues doesn't mean I don't like them. The vast majority of liberals are good, sincere, well-meaning people. They love their kids. They love their neighbors. I am sure most love their country. They're sickened by terrorism. And they certainly don't set out to make our country or our kids more vulnerable to people or policies or ideologies that would do any of us harm. It's just that now, in a post 9/11 world, the stakes are too high, and the case needs to be made that liberal policies will put our freedoms at risk.

I certainly don't have any personal beef with my Fox News partner-in-crime, Alan Colmes. He is a great guy and a great American. Sure, we disagree. But we try hard not to be disagreeable. Yes, some nights he wants to smack me. Some nights I want to smack him. After all, I'm right. He's wrong. But at least we have fun duking it out with each other.

Rank-and-file liberals with big dreams and big mouths don't bother me. Why should they? I am confident in my views. God bless them. Let freedom ring. As we say at the end of our TV show every night, "We have our opinions. You have yours. Debating is what makes America strong." More power to ya!

This is America, after all; whatever you think, you're free to say it out loud—as long as you're prepared to defend it. And if you get lucky, as Alan and I have, someday you might even get paid for it.

But the question remains: Why is it that so many leading liberals seem to think that the real threat to America isn't Communism, or Islamic radicalism, or terrorism—but conservatism?

Over and over again in the past decade, rather than deal with the real and rising threat of terrorism and a lethal Islamic jihad, liberals have acted as though American conservatives were members of the Taliban or al Qaeda.

Bob Herbert of the *New York Times* wrote that "The Republican jihad against the poor, the young and helpless rolls on."

Washington Post columnist Mary McGrory declared that "Human sacrifice is much in vogue right now. The Republican right thinks that people who get on its nerves, especially women, should be sent to the stake."

Allen Ginsberg, the leftist poet of the 1960s, chided, "I have no doubt that if Rush Limbaugh or Pat Robertson or Ollie North ever got real power, there would be concentration camps and mass death."

What are these people thinking? Can't they disagree with conservatism without being so mean-spirited about conservatives? Apparently not, which is ironic when you consider that these same liberals often accuse conservatives of having a monopoly on meanness. Throughout the 1990s—especially after the conservative revolution of 1994 that put the GOP in charge of the House and Senate—such venomous attacks were par for the course. And it wasn't just leftist pundits making these reckless accusations but also liberal politicians—those with official power—from whom we should expect a higher standard of responsibility and comportment. But they were deter-mined to use extremist rhetoric to paint Republicans as vicious soldiers engaged in a war against everything sacred in America.

President Clinton vilified the conservative Congress. "What they want to do," he said, "is make war on the kids of this country." Vice President Gore charged that "the Republican leadership in this Congress is conducting a jihad on the environment in the most right-wing agenda we have seen in America this century." Bill Clinton's White House chief of staff Leon Panetta told the *Washington Post* that he feared Republicans were poised to launch a "philosophical jihad." And Representative Martin Frost, a Texas Democrat and one-time chief fund-raiser for the House Democrats, took the image one step further, charging in a campaign letter that Newt Gingrich "is one of the most dangerous figures to emerge in American politics during our lifetime. He calls himself a revolutionary but he promotes the policies of a ter-rorist." (Apparently embarrassed, Frost later retracted his remarks.)

Few issues seem to evoke more hysteria from the Left than when conservatives argue that cracking down on illegal immigration, reforming our deeply flawed immigration and Naturalization Service, and protecting America's coastlines and borders are essential to defending our national security. As early as 1983, President Ronald Reagan was pointing out that "this country has lost control of its bor-ders" and that "no country can sustain that kind of position." The product of a rich and wonderful heritage of Irish immigrants, Reagan was strongly pro-immigration—pro-*legal* immigration. He celebrated the strength of an America created by men and women in pursuit of freedom coming from all over the globe to work hard and play by the rules. But Reagan believed that such new Americans must be encour-aged to assimilate and become part of the unique American culture; that they should not just live in America in segregated, balkanized enclaves but actually become Americans. At the same time, he believed that no country could tolerate or long survive criminals and terrorists sneaking across its borders and burrowing into its society with impunity.

The Left didn't like such notions of border security then, and they haven't warmed to them since. They spuriously contend that opposing illegal immigration means opposing all immigration. Worse, some of them apparently believe that conservatives are racists for insisting on defending the nation's borders against illegal intrusions.

Before going into more detail on this, let me share a bit more of my own heritage, which has obviously contributed to the way I see these issues.

A SON OF THE IRISH

I have a sign hanging in my office: IRISH CATHOLICS NEED NOT APPLY.

It's a daily reminder to me that racism is real. Religious bigotry is real. Anti-immigrant sentiment is real. Real and ugly. My Irish Catholic family experienced such ugliness, and it's not something I take lightly.

I am a second-generation American and proud of it. My grandparents were all born and raised in Ireland. They came here in the early part of the twentieth century. They came by boat, entered at Ellis Island, and settled in New York. And along with many other immigrants, they carved out a life for themselves against the odds through their industriousness in this land of opportunity.

My maternal grandfather, a man by the name of Cornelius Flynn, settled in the Bronx. He had a tremendous work ethic. He also had the gift of gab. He was smart, funny, and opinionated—not a bad legacy to leave behind. During the dark days of the Depression, he didn't let the fact that he was a poor Irish Catholic immigrant keep him down. He never regarded his race, religion, or ethnicity as a burden. He considered (and proudly claimed) them as assets. My grandfather went out every day and made friends with people wherever he could. In the process he managed to find jobs all over the city. Then, once he'd been working in a job for a while and had earned his employer's trust, he'd ask if one of his family members could take over the job for him. At first his employers would be surprised, but sure enough most of them said yes. Then off he'd go to find a new job. In his kindness and his shrewdness, my grandfather fought back against racism, helping one Irish Catholic after another find work to feed his family.

Along the way, my grandfather taught his family the values he held dear. He made sure his kids went to the best possible schools. He believed that an immigrant kid with an education could go places in America, and he was right. My mom, Lillian Flynn, went to school in the Bronx back when public schools in New York were good, and she graduated as valedictorian of her class. She learned to work hard, save her pennies, and plan for the future. In turn, she passed those values on to my three sisters and me.

My paternal grandfather, a man by the name of Hugh Hannity, was a good man who did his best in tough times. He settled in the Bedford-Stuyvesant section of Brooklyn, a rougher neighborhood than the Bronx. More racism. More violence. His wife—my grand-mother—died from complications related to childbirth soon after my father was born in 1925. My dad, also named Hugh Hannity, grew up without much money, without a mother, and his father wasn't around much either, since he had to work so hard to make ends meet. My father got shuttled around among relatives a lot. His wasn't an easy life.

Then came December 7, 1941, and the attack on Pearl Harbor. The worst sneak attack on American soil in history, until 9/11 hap-pened sixty years later. As soon as he could, my father—like all his friends—signed up with the navy. He served four years, mostly in the Pacific. He didn't talk about it much when I was growing up. He didn't brag about it. But I've got to tell you, I'm proud of my father and grateful for him. He was the son of immigrants, working shoulder to shoulder with thousands of others just like him who put their lives on the line for their new country. No, it was not a perfect country, but it was surely a free one.

I came to understand why we call such men part of "the greatest generation." I want my kids to understand it someday as well. So many of these men were new to these shores. Yet they instinctively understood the value of freedom, hard work, and sacrifice. They understood that despite America's flaws, she was a force for good in the world, a beacon of freedom and an island of hope in an ocean of tyranny. They understood deep in their souls that if America went down in flames, the liberties of men and women all over the globe would eventually be lost as well. For America was not just another place to hang their hats. These men hadn't simply come to America. They had become Americans, part of a dream worth living for and dying for.

After the war, my father came home and lived that dream. He got a job in the restaurant business. He met and married my mother and moved to Long Island. It was a big deal when they saved enough to put a down payment on a Levitt-style Cape Cod house in Franklin Square, with an asking price of about $13,000. It was a tract house, the kind builders were putting up by the thousands in the postwar baby boom years. It was small, and sat on a 50- by 100-foot lot with one bathroom for four kids. But it was ours. It was home.

Just like their parents, my parents put a huge emphasis on education. They sent us to Catholic schools when I was growing up—Sacred Heart Seminary in Hempstead for middle school and St. Pius X Seminary for high school. They really had to struggle financially to do this, and they sacrificed a lot. Why? In part because both were great schools academically. In part because they were schools that would reinforce the faith, the heritage, and the values they were trying to instill in my sisters and me at home. Even when putting their roots down as full-fledged Americans, my parents never shied away from their Irish

Catholic roots. They celebrated them. And we went to mass every Sunday.

I was fortunate. I never personally experienced any anti-Irish or anti-Catholic bigotry, the way some people have, the way my parents or grandparents did growing up, though they rarely if ever spoke of it. My parents' primary concern was for us to know who we were, where we came from, and to be proud of it while learning how to pursue the American dream for ourselves. They wanted us to succeed beyond their wildest dreams. They wanted us to appreciate the freedoms they'd fought and worked so hard for us to enjoy. And they wanted us to take advantage of those freedoms and to do our best to succeed.

No one has to tell me that life isn't easy for people coming to America to make new lives for themselves. I get it, because my family lived it. And I believe in my heart and soul that our laws have to protect those who work hard and play by the rules. It doesn't matter who they are, where they are from, or what they look like. It's only fair that we do not discriminate.

But you know what? When I look at that sign hanging in my office—"Irish Catholics Need Not Apply"—I don't get discouraged about that darker time in our country's history. Instead, I'm reminded of how far America has come. As I said, we're not a perfect country. We have flaws and warts and sins. But unlike most countries, we've always been big enough to atone for those sins and make constructive changes. That's one of the many great things about this country: we've had the humility to make adjustments when we didn't like what we saw or did. And we continue to move forward, overcoming challenges and making progress. In less than a century, America transformed itself from a place where Irish Catholics and blacks and Jews and dozens of other minorities could barely find work to a society where millions of kids like Sean Hannity could succeed beyond what his parents and grandparents ever could have imagined.

Which brings me back to liberals and the troublesome issue of illegal immigration.

THE VITRIOL OF LIBERAL IMMIGRATION RHETORIC

Just as the Left has demonized Republicans on a host of other issues, they have been particularly vicious toward the Right with respect to their stand on immigration. Instead of constructively contributing to the debate, liberals have used the issue as a racially charged political football.

In 1995 a Stanford University professor named Dale Maharidge wrote a blistering article in *Mother Jones*. He described Pete Wilson, then California's Republican governor, as a "symbol of American racism" for wanting to stop the flood of illegal immigrants pouring into California. He warned of "Wilson's skillful manipulation of white fear" and quoted the Reverend Jesse Jackson describing Wilson as the "new George Wallace," fueling deep racial divisions. Maharidge charged that "Wilson has been chiseling in the dark mine of fear that was El Dorado for Richard Nixon and Ronald Reagan, both of whom had political roots in California. Theirs was a racial message tailor-made for the suburbs." He wrote that "Republicans across the nation have copied Nixon and Reagan's use of the racial wedge issue," particularly on the topic of illegal immigration.

Professor Maharidge's conclusion? "Like the ghoul from the Friday the 13th movies, [Governor] Wilson is the Jason of politics: The prognosis is often six feet under but he routinely claws his way out of the soil" and does so by standing "at the forefront of the old, European America" and "rejecting the new, multiracial America."

Maharidge's vicious comments stemmed in part from his political opposition to Wilson's support of Proposition 187, which would have cut off health and social services, including access to public education, to illegal aliens and their children. In the politically charged atmosphere surrounding the issue of immigration, you can't have an honest difference of opinion without running the risk that some hard-line left-wing critic like Maharidge will play the race card. And Maharidge's venom was hardly an isolated case.

Writer Bill Berkowitz wrote a piece for *The Nation* in which he charged that "Conservatives are fond of fashioning a connection between immigration and terrorism." Then he tried to smear Pat Buchanan, Texas Republican Representative Ron Paul, and conservatives in general as part of "white supremacist organizations" and an "anti-immigrant" movement that included six hundred "active hate groups," some of which subscribed to a "racially charged conspiracy theory."

Newsweek's Eleanor Clift attacked her fellow McLaughlin Group pundit Pat Buchanan, calling him "David Duke with a word processor and without the sheet, although sometimes he comes close to putting on the sheet. His views on immigration—he talks about it as suicide of a nation—where he talks about the hordes of immigrants coming to dilute our Western civilization, to me is thinly veiled racism."

Anthony Lewis, the recently retired *New York Times* columnist, accused conservatives running the GOP Congress of passing "draconian" immigration laws, fueled by "anti-immigrant zealotry."

Cecilia Munoz, deputy vice president of the National Council of La Raza, told the *New York Times* that "the immigration debate has reached a point where Republicans are apparently prepared to attack newborns."

And just as with other issues I highlighted at the beginning of this chapter, liberal pundits and policy wonks weren't the only ones slinging mud. They were joined by their soul mates in elective office.

During the 1996 campaign, President Clinton clearly insinuated that racism had motivated recent church burnings and the move to curb illegal immigration. "We really fall into a dangerous trap when we start blaming our problems on other people just because they're different from us," Clinton told a crowd in San Diego. "I say that because even though I'm a long way from there, my heart has been in my native South for the last several weeks as we have dealt with this incredible rash of church burnings."

Vice President Gore took the same tack when courting Latino voters in the 2000 presidential race, by pointing to Republican support of three California ballot propositions. Gore urged Latino voters to take their resentment out against Republicans at the polls for favoring measures on illegal immigration, affirmative action, and bilingual education. "If a candidate wants to divide the nation instead of unifying it, if a candidate wants to appeal to fear instead of hope, they're going to pay at the ballot box," Gore told the Latino Vote '99 conference.

House Minority Leader Dick Gephardt similarly showed no hesitation about invoking the race issue during the 2000 campaign. "The Republican leadership in Congress," he said, "has spent the last six years blocking bills, stopping progress, strengthening the anti-immigrant forces in the culture, and in the country." Terry McAuliffe, chairman of the Democratic National Committee, echoed this contemptible mantra, railing against "the anti-immigration forces in the Republican Party." And Representative Luis Gutierrez, an Illinois Democrat, blasted "the anti-immigrant proposals put forward by the Republican party in recent years."

The rhetoric never stops, and sometimes its tone gets absolutely out of hand. Senator Ted Kennedy, the party's elder statesman, agrees: "The majority Republican Party," he charges, is "basically anti-civil rights, anti-immigrant, anti-women, anti-worker." And Representative Charlie Rangel, a New York Democrat, has gone so far as to say that "a wave of scapegoating is sweeping the country" and that "just like under Hitler, people say they don't mean to blame any particular individuals or groups, but in the U.S. those groups always turn out to be minorities and immigrants."

Further examples are legion, but this should be enough to demonstrate that it is the Democrats, not the Republicans, who have been divisive about race, by repeatedly leveling false and incendiary allegations against Republicans purely for political gain. It is time for the adults in their party to rise up and rein in the reckless and destructive rhetoric; there is simply no excuse for reasonable people to descend so far into calumny.

THE DANGER OF LIBERAL IMMIGRATION POLICY

The Left's anticonservative rhetoric is damaging, but even worse are the politically opportunistic and dangerous immigration policies (or nonpolicies) they advocate.

Guess how many illegal aliens are in the United States at this very moment? Take a wild guess. A million? Two million? Five million?

Try more than eight million. According to the U.S. Census Bureau, in the year 2000 there were 8.7 million "unauthorized" immigrants living in the United States. That's some two and a half times the amount when Clinton and Gore were elected (3.4 million).

Disturbingly, the Census Bureau estimated that in the year 2000 there were 114,818 people from the Middle East living illegally in the United States. That included some 30,823 illegal aliens from Iran—named by President Bush as part of the "axis of evil" after 9/11—and 59,623 illegal aliens from Islamic countries such as Afghanistan—then the home base of Osama bin Laden, al Qaeda, and the Taliban. The majority of these illegal aliens were males.

On top of all this, an estimated two million foreign citizens come into the United States each year and illegally overstay their visas. All in all—thanks in large part to the Clinton-Gore administration—we have a huge illegal immigration problem.

The Clinton-Gore administration's dismal performance on immigration policy is best illustrated by our consideration of a number of disturbing questions:

★ How could Clinton-Gore have tolerated such a dramatic increase in the number of illegal aliens living in the United States?

★ Did Bill Clinton or Al Gore ever bother to distinguish between legal and illegal immigration—or were their only concerns in this area to discredit Republicans and pander to the various immigrant constituencies?

★ How could the Clinton-Gore Census Bureau and INS determine how many illegal aliens there were and what regions they were from but take little or no action to investigate, arrest, or deport them?

★ How could the Clinton-Gore administration have ignored the link between border security, illegal immigration, and terrorism even after learning that Mohammed Salameh—a Palestinian terrorist convicted of participating in the bombing of the World Trade Center in 1993—came into the United States in 1988 with a visitor's visa claiming to be a student but then overstayed his visa and never returned home?

★ How could the Clinton-Gore administration have ignored the link between border security, illegal immigration, and terrorism even after learning that Mir Aimal Kansi—a Pakistani terrorist convicted of killing three people during a horrific shooting outside the CIA headquarters in Langley,

Virginia, in 1993—came into the United States in 1990, overstayed his welcome, obtained a driver's license, bought an AK-47, and then tried to escape back to Pakistan?

★ How could the Clinton-Gore administration have ignored the issue of border security even after Gazi Ibrahim Abu Mezer (also spelled "Maizar")—a Palestinian terrorist convicted of trying to blow up the New York City subway system to kill scores of Americans, particularly Jews, in 1997—was found to be an illegal alien who had been repeatedly apprehended by U.S. Border Patrol agents as he tried to sneak in from Canada? Officials believed that Mezer worked closely with another Palestinian who was also convicted of breaking U.S. immigration laws.

This last case is particularly troubling because it was actually the subject of a special investigation by the Clinton Justice Department. In March of 1998, Michael Bromwich—the Justice Department's inspector general—issued a report entitled "Bombs in Brooklyn: How the Two Illegal Aliens Arrested for Plotting to Bomb the New York Subway Entered and Remained in the United States." Bromwich testified about it before Congress in April of 1999.

Bromwich's report is chilling. He found that though the U.S.-Canadian border extends for almost four thousand miles, the Clinton-Gore administration assigned only three hundred border patrol agents to keep criminals and terrorists from crossing it, and there was often "no coverage of the border from midnight until the morning." He found that "the vast majority of illegal aliens apprehended entering the United States from Canada . . . are voluntarily returned to Canada," yet "record checks are rarely done on these illegal aliens to see if they may be suspected terrorists." The terrorist Gazi Ibrahim Abu Mezer was actually apprehended three times by the border patrol but was released on bond by a judge. Then Mezer had the gall to apply for political asylum in the United States. And why not? After all, Bromwich found that "no terrorism checks are performed either by INS or by the Department of State" on "more than 90 percent of the 150,000 asylum applications filed annually."

This is a system that absolutely must be fixed before terrorists use such loopholes to strike us again. Illegal aliens must be incarcerated, not allowed to roam freely in the United States. If they're known terrorists, criminals, or drug cartel leaders, they must be arrested, prosecuted, and imprisoned upon conviction. Even if they are otherwise law-abiding citizens from countries that are merely poorer than the United States, they nevertheless must be deported.

Are there occasions for granting an illegal alien political asylum in the United States? Of course. If an otherwise law-abiding family flees in fear of their very lives from the religious or political persecution of their mother country—traveling on a rickety boat or inner tube through shark-infested waters to escape Cuba for South Florida, for example—shouldn't they be given a thorough background check and full protection here in the safest and freest nation on earth? Absolutely. That is part and parcel of America's history and moral heritage. And it happens to be the law of the land. But for the law to have any effect, it must be followed. Just as it was unconscionable for the Clinton-Gore administration to look the other way when our immigration laws were being flagrantly violated, it was indefensible for it to be selective about when it would afford genuinely endangered immigrants the protection of our laws.

These seemingly conflicting immigration policies of the Clinton-Gore administration—incredibly open to some, inexplicably closed to others—cannot logically be reconciled analytically unless you remember the consideration underlying most of Clinton's policies: pure politics.

He obviously deemed it politically advantageous for the nation in general to inhale as many immigrants as possible but not to accept Elian Gonzalas specifically. Nothing else makes sense.

LIBERALS AND THE INS

Which brings me to the U.S. Immigration and Naturalization Service.

For years the INS has been in desperate need of radical reform, or even outright abolition. Perhaps, as some have suggested, that agency could have been replaced with two separate agencies—one that fights illegal immigration and another that welcomes and processes legal immigration. Conservatives were urging such a restructuring throughout the 1990s. But the Clinton-Gore administration wanted nothing to do with it.

In January 1996, for example, conservative immigration expert Linda Chavez—president of the Center for Equal Opportunity in Washington—published a study by legal scholar Daniel Sutherland titled "Abolish the INS: How Federal Bureaucracy Dooms Immigration Reform." Sutherland noted that the INS's problems had been worsening for years. The Reagan and Bush administrations deserved their share of responsibility, he conceded. But the magnitude of the problems came to a head under the Clinton-Gore watch.

"In 1994," noted Sutherland, "an investigative series in the *New York Times* concluded that the INS is 'perhaps the most troubled major agency in the federal government,' and 'broadly dysfunctional.' In March 1995, Congressman Harold Rogers, a Republican from Kentucky, charged that the INS is 'the most inept, badly managed federal agency that we have.' Rogers concluded that the INS 'needs [deep reform] more than any agency I've ever seen.'"

What were some of the agency's worst problems? For one thing, it practically refused to deport people. "Several million immigrants currently living in this country should be deported (having entered the

United States illegally or violated the terms of their visas)," noted Sutherland. "Of these, an estimated 200,000 have been convicted of criminal acts while in this country. Yet the INS deports only about 40,000 people every year." Sutherland also pointed out that the asylum process desperately needed to be changed, the computer systems were out of date, agents rarely coordinated their actions with each other or other federal agencies, and that few inside the agency even fully understood the mission of the INS.

When Sutherland updated his research for the Center for Equal Opportunity in 2000, he found that little had changed. The General Accounting Office (GAO), for example, criticized the INS deportation program repeatedly, "finding in reports released in 1995, 1997, 1998, and 1999 that the program needs vast improvements." Sutherland identified two problems. First, because its agents seldom visit local jails, the INS fails to recognize many criminal aliens eligible for deportation. Second, on those rare occasions when the agents do visit jails, they make little effort to identify immigrants. In looking at one sample of some twenty thousand aliens, the GAO found that the INS only identified 64 percent of them. That means that more than seven thousand felons were released back into society. Sutherland noted that while most immigrants are legal, there could be as many as eighty-five thousand immigrants in state prisons and thirty thousand in the federal penal system.

"The bottom line is," concluded Sutherland, "the INS has been successful in deporting hundreds of people who everyone agrees should not be deported, but unsuccessful in targeting truly dangerous criminals."

Such stories of endemic INS failures abound.

The *Washington Post* noted in 1998 that the Clinton-Gore administration "pushed the INS to speed up the citizenship process before the last presidential election, only to prompt a congressional investigation into why at least 6,000 immigrants with criminal backgrounds were granted U.S. citizenship."

The inspector general of the U.S. Department of Transportation found that "more than eighty percent of the security screeners at Dulles International Airport"—the airport from which American Airlines Flight 77 took off before terrorists hijacked it and crashed into the Pentagon—"are not U.S. citizens." Federal law requires such screeners to be citizens or, at the very least, legal residents, but the Clinton-Gore administration never made it happen. Nor did it make sure the INS was diligent about immigration and criminal background checks on airport security screeners or the companies that hire them, even though airport security companies that supposedly protect U.S. airports have repeatedly been fined for failing to do such background checks.

I could go on, but here's the point: It is abundantly clear that the Clinton-Gore administration understood the real and increasing risks of not cracking down on illegal immigration. It knew how incompetent the INS was. Yet the administration did little, if anything, to make Americans safer from Middle Eastern terrorists who were using huge loopholes to gain access to our country.

But Americans, while an extraordinarily generous people, clearly understand the importance of an immigration system based on the rule of law. Consider a Harris Interactive poll of 1,017 Americans taken in August of 2001, just a month before the terrorist attacks.

★ 54 percent of Americans said they believed illegal immigration into the United States was "a serious problem" and that "the government was not doing an adequate job of stopping it." Only 27 percent believed at the time that the government was doing an adequate job.

★ Fully two-thirds of all Americans believed that granting amnesty (legal status) to illegal immigrants would "encourage more people to come here illegally, and therefore we should not do it." Only one in four Americans believed amnesty was a good idea.

After the September 11 attacks, Americans agreed that an even tougher crackdown on illegal immigration was needed, according to a Fox News/Opinion Dynamic poll taken in November of 2001:

★ "By 85 percent to 11 percent, Americans support imposing stricter control on foreign student visas."

★ "By 90 percent to 7 percent, Americans want these tougher limits on immigration from countries 'thought to be connected to terrorists.'"

★ "By 65 percent to 29 percent, they favor 'temporarily sealing U.S. borders and stopping all immigration in the United States during the war on terrorism.'"

Why, then, didn't the Clinton-Gore administration take such measures when they had the chance, before America was attacked? Because while the vast majority of the American people have held such commonsense views, the liberal elite in and around the White House and the Democratic National Committee did not. And more importantly, as I said, politics trumped policies: immigrants, by and large, vote Democrat.

Oh, sure, after Republicans took control of Congress, the Clinton-Gore administration made some halfhearted moves, using some conservative-sounding rhetoric to try to give the impression that they wanted to fix some immigration problems. And yes, like good liberals, the administration threw money at the problem. The INS budget grew from $1.1 billion to more than $4 billion during the Clinton-Gore years, and the bureaucracy nearly tripled, to more than thirty thousand people. But the simple fact remains: they failed to enforce existing immigration laws, and they failed to make bold reforms to the INS bureaucracy. And just look at the results.

The terrorists who hijacked American jetliners on September 11 were all from foreign countries. Some originally had legal visas, but they had expired, and the INS never followed up or deported them.

Others had legal visas but shouldn't have had them. They were on terrorist watch lists, but no one at the INS ever bothered to check those lists. Nor did the INS inform the U.S. embassies and consulates—or INS and customs officials at major American airports—that these men should have been denied entry into our country in the first place.

And then, of course, there is the astonishing story that even six months after the terrorists Mohammed Atta of Egypt and Marwan Al-Shehhi of the United Arab Emirates flew separate planes into the Twin Towers, the INS mailed the approval of their student visa applications to the very flight school where the men learned the skills to complete their ghastly last mission.

There are many hardworking, dedicated, and brave INS, border patrol, customs, and other law enforcement officials. They deserve high praise—and support. My problem isn't with the men and women who are trying to defend our country but with the politically driven policies imposed on our immigration system that make defending our country that much more difficult.

Are all illegal immigrants dangerous? Of course not. Are all immigrants who overstay their visas terrorists? No. But do we have any idea which are and which aren't? Apparently not. We must do a much better job of protecting our coastlines and borders. We need to screen all visa applications more effectively—particularly those from countries known or suspected to be harboring terrorists. We need to cross-check all visa applications against the FBI's terrorist watch list. We need to take special care with those who are granted temporary entry to our country. We need our colleges and universities to help us track foreign students and make sure they're really showing up in class. We need to deport illegal aliens, particularly those who commit additional crimes while on our soil. And that's just for starters. This is not racist. It's common sense. The kind of common sense that seemingly escapes far too many on the Left—including, unfortunately, Al Gore.

During the 1990s, Al Gore took personal responsibility for reforming the INS, making the agency a part of his National Partnership for Reinventing Government (formerly the National Performance Review) (NPR). In fact, even after the disasters of September 11, the INS continued to boast that it had won more than one thousand awards for excellence from Gore's NPR Office.

"INS is proud of its many successful reinvention efforts," declared the agency's web site in a posting last modified on December 19, 2001.

The INS reinvented—deserving one thousand awards?

Amazing.

WHAT LIBERALS (AND SOME OTHERS) WANT NOW

In fairness, some liberals are beginning to change their minds.

In the aftermath of the 9/11 attacks, some liberals are seriously rethinking their positions on illegal immigration and reforming the INS. Lo and behold, some are coming around to conservative positions.

That's good. But it's not enough.

Far too many still want to reward illegal immigration, not crack down on it.

Example: Giving Legal Driver's Licenses to Illegal Aliens

Some on the Left are actually agitating for illegal aliens to be allowed to obtain legal driver's licenses. Al Gore's home state of Tennessee made it legal in May of 2001, and incredibly, Republican Governor

Don Sundquist actually signed the bill—which, incidentally, demonstrates that not all liberals are Democrats, and not all liberal acts are committed by Democrats alone. Utah and North Carolina also have such laws on the books. California and Texas appear to be next. This is dumb and dangerous for a host of reasons, not the least of which is that a legal driver's license provides the false appearance of legal residence. And it has become a common form of identification, which can be used to buy a weapon or get on an airplane.

"The skyjackers had obtained U.S. identification that was used for boarding flights in the form of Florida, Virginia and New Jersey driver's licenses/ID cards," notes an "Issue Brief" by the Federation for American Immigration Reform. "One of the terrorists, Mohamed Atta, was detained in Florida for driving without a license, but subsequently obtained one. Thirteen of the terrorists had Florida driver's licenses or ID cards, seven had Virginia driver's licenses and two had New Jersey driver's licenses."

Example: Making Taxpayers Pay for Illegal Aliens to Go to College

Talk about reckless: In October of 2001, the California legislature passed—and Governor Gray Davis signed—a bill rewarding illegal aliens. California's new law actually allows illegal immigrants to pay the same subsidized in-state college tuition as full-fledged legal citizens of the Golden State. "At Cal State campuses, for example, undergraduate fees are $1,839 a year for residents and $7,380 for nonresidents," reported the *Los Angeles Times,* a savings for illegal immigrants of $5,541 a year. In other words, law-abiding California taxpayers will now subsidize people breaking the laws of our country, to the tune of thousands upon thousands of dollars each year for each student. This is utter foolishness, particularly during this time of war. It puts the welcome mat out for far more illegal immigration, even with eight million illegal immigrants already in the country.

Example: Giving Illegal Immigrants Amnesty

In 1986 Congress passed a bill called the Immigration Reform and Control Act. President Reagan signed it. But it turned out to be a big mistake. It allowed almost three million illegal aliens already in the United States to dodge detection by the INS for at least four years to stay without fear of being caught and prosecuted.

Yet we don't seem to learn from our mistakes. In February of 2000, the bosses who run America's labor unions called for blanket amnesty for all illegal aliens living in the United States, in an apparent bid to bolster the voting rolls of the Democratic Party. The Clinton-Gore administration embraced the idea, seeking to give a "get out of jail free card" to millions of illegal immigrants.

"Our response is: Let's not call it an amnesty at all," Maria Eschaveste, then White House deputy chief of staff, told a reporter. "Let people benefit from the amnesty that was passed by a bipartisan Congress in 1986."

Fortunately, congressional Republicans shut down the move, but not before Clinton actually threatened to veto a budget bill to fund the federal criminal justice system unless he got his way. "I have no choice but to veto this bill [because it] fails to redress several injustices in our immigration system as called for by the Latino and Immigrant Fairness Act," Clinton wrote in a letter to congressional leaders.

"To just give blanket amnesty to millions of illegal aliens and undermine the legal system, we think is not wise," Senator Trent Lott, the Mississippi Republican and then Senate majority leader, told reporters.

"In other words," said Senator Phil Gramm, the Texas Republican, "the president is threatening that he will veto a bill that funds DEA—the Drug Enforcement Administration—the FBI, the federal prison system, our system of criminal and civil justice. He will veto that bill unless we in Congress grant amnesty to people who have broken the law by coming to the United States illegally."

"I draw the line on illegal immigration," said Gramm. "I draw the line when it comes to breaking the laws of this country."

In the summer of 2001, however, President George W. Bush and some of his Republican colleagues on Capitol Hill shocked a lot of people—including me—when they began making noises about passing an amnesty bill of their own. I said it on radio and TV at the time, and I'll say it again here: amnesty for illegal aliens is a misguided and perilous notion, and it's no less so when Republicans are behind it.

Our side already tried amnesty back in 1986. It didn't work. Since then, millions more illegal immigrants have come to our country. We ought not repeat our mistake—especially not now.

We must learn from history.

Hopefully, President Bush and his advisers will reverse course and find a wise balance between sound policy and smart politics. After all, I love the fact that Bush is reaching out to immigrants in general and Hispanics in particular. I feel passionately that the GOP needs to do much more to get our message out to all Americans, and to counter liberal race-baiting in the process. But in the process of reaching out, we must remain true to our core principle that free people in a free society must honor the rule of law.

When an otherwise hardworking and decent person tries illegally to enter our country, a political party must have the courage to say that such conduct is wrong and won't be rewarded. For when people break the law with impunity, the freedoms of everyone are in jeopardy.

I don't harbor resentment or bitterness about the tough challenges my family faced almost a century ago. I'm grateful that America welcomed legal immigrants—however imperfectly—back when my grandparents were arriving. And I'm grateful that America keeps welcoming legal immigrants today as well. I support *legal* immigration. But we need to ensure that our laws are applied consistently, fairly, and impartially.

Of course we need to be passionate about stamping out racism, religious bigotry, and anti-immigrant sentiment wherever they rear their ugly heads. But we need to be careful not to ascribe such sins to those who simply make a distinction between legal and illegal immigration and who want to keep our country safe and secure from all enemies, foreign and domestic. This issue is far too important to be politicized; it must be approached in a way that best promotes our national security while preserving our civil liberties.

FOUR

DASCHLE, DEMOCRATS, AND DEFENSE

Americans deserve the most powerful military in the world.

Early in our nation's history, when our enemies faced us with muskets, we responded with superior tactics. When Europe ruled the seas, America responded by building a navy second to none. When air power was turned into a potent military weapon, America responded by building the most devastating warplanes and finding the best pilots in the world.

When the Soviet Union acquired nuclear technology, America developed and deployed the world's most accurate strategic arsenal. And as the nature of warfare evolves in the twenty-first century, America must always strive to make sure the brave men and women who serve in our armed forces—and the weapons and technology that they have at their disposal—are the very best America can offer. In the age of weapons of mass destruction, there can be no second place.

Freedom comes at a price. Sometimes that price is high in terms of time, talent, treasure, and human life. But it is a cost we must pay in the defense of liberty.

On September 11, we were reminded as at few other times in our history that we must always be vigilant. There are people who hate us with every fiber of their being. They despise our values, freedoms, wealth, and power. These people would annihilate us in an instant if they were capable. That's why they spend every waking hour trying to acquire that capability—through their own development, black-market purchase, or theft of weapons.

There was a time when Democratic leaders like Franklin Delano Roosevelt, Harry Truman, and John F. Kennedy understood the nature of evil. Whatever problems there may have been with their liberal domestic agenda, when it came to our country's national security, they helped unify America during some of its most challenging days. They led us to victory in World War II, even dropping two atomic bombs on a fierce enemy; they built NATO; and they stared down the imperial Soviet Union over its blockade of Berlin and nuclear missiles on Cuba.

Those were days when the Democratic Party was led by individuals who understood that there were sinister forces in the world and recognized the need to arm against and defeat them.

But along about the mid-1960s, the antiwar movement burst onto the public scene. A new generation of liberals, far more radical than their New Deal–era predecessors, not only opposed the Vietnam War but sought the evisceration of certain core American institutions, including the military, law enforcement, and capitalism. By the early 1970s this movement had virtually hijacked the Democratic Party, with the nomination of then senator George McGovern, a Democrat of South Dakota, for president.

Ironically, though McGovern lost in an electoral landslide, the movement that secured his nomination continued to gain, rather than lose, strength in the party. Despite further setbacks, it pressed forward with relentless persistence until it eventually became the Democratic Party establishment. This should serve as an object lesson for anyone who believes liberalism can be permanently defeated. Many modern Democratic Party leaders don't seem to grasp how truly dangerous the world is today. They consistently deny the gravity of the threats arrayed against us, which predisposes them against taking the requisite steps to defend America and our allies and leads them to draw the wrong conclusions about our security needs. They consistently seek to reduce the size of our military forces and oppose our urgent need to constantly upgrade and modernize our forces and weapons systems. They regard those of us who support increasing defense spending and placing a high priority on the development of new defense technologies as warmongers. During the half-century showdown with Communism, conservatives understood the Soviet Union and its continuing threat against freedom in much the same terms as brave Democrats like FDR, Truman, and JFK. But more recent liberals like McGovern, Ted Kennedy, Jimmy Carter, and Walter Mondale viewed things differently.

Conservatives took Communists at their word when they promised to take over the world. Modern liberals derisively dismissed the threat, despite mountains of evidence as to the Communists' expansionist designs.

Conservatives believed in the concept embodied in Ronald Reagan's phrase "peace through strength"—expanding and modernizing our conventional and nuclear arsenals (and being reluctantly prepared to use them) to prove to the Soviets that they could not defeat, blackmail, or intimidate us. Modern liberals fought for unilateral disarmament, including withdrawing our forces from Europe and Southeast Asia, turning our backs on freedom fighters in Africa and South America who were facing Soviet-backed regimes and insurgents, and drawing down our numerical and technological advantage in nuclear warheads. Conservatives knew that in a showdown with Communism, allowing our military to become rundown and weak and turning our back on others who shared our commitment to freedom was an invitation to Soviet aggression.

Modern liberals, led today by Senator Tom Daschle, a South

Dakota Democrat, are building on an ideological foundation that was laid forty years ago by the radical Left of the 1960s and 1970s. This movement utterly refused to acknowledge the Soviet threat and harbored an intense hostility toward the American military. They truly believed that conservatives represented a graver threat to freedom than did Communists. They refused to distrust the Communists, despite their record of deceitfulness, tyranny, and terror. They proposed "the gradual diminishment of the NATO forces." And they called for "the gradual transfer of sovereignties"—like control of the U.S. military and legal institutions—from the American people to "international rule-making and enforcement machinery beginning under the United Nations." Moreover, the New Left wanted to divert military spending to domestic spending, such as government-run health care for every American citizen.

People argued at the time that such radicals—and those sympathetic to them—were "just kids." But now those kids have grown up. Many have risen to high places in the Democratic Party. Many hold or seek to hold political office all over the country. Many work in the news media or the entertainment industry. They run television networks, national newsmagazines, Internet empires, and Hollywood movie studios. They have come to wield real power, and their ideas have taken root. They have succeeded in turning their radical theories into real policies, and consequently have weakened our national security and made us all more vulnerable—not to mention advancing the welfare state.

JFK'S YOUNGER BROTHER TEDDY

Somewhere, somehow—don't ask me how—Ted Kennedy lost his older brother John's courageous anti-Communism and fearless commitment to freedom. And I say this with sadness, because growing up I was a huge fan of the Kennedys. I was a fan because my parents were huge fans of Jack Kennedy's—and not simply because he was Irish Catholic, though that certainly played a part. My family loved Jack Kennedy because he loved freedom, and because he stood up to the Soviets. After all, it was JFK who said, in his brilliant 1961 inaugural address, "Let every nation know, whether it wishes us well or ill, that we shall pay any price, bear any burden, meet any hardship, support any friend, oppose any foe, to assure the survival and the success of liberty."

Pay any price. Would JFK have supported deep defense cuts? Of course not. In fact, he did not.

Bear any burden, meet any hardship. Would JFK have constantly complained that building a missile defense might be too difficult? No way. Indeed, it was Kennedy who responded to the Soviet space challenge by committing America to landing a man on the Moon before the end of the decade.

Support any friend. Would JFK have attacked Ronald Reagan for supporting the freedom-fighting Contras in Nicaragua against the Marxist Sandanistas? Not likely. He was keenly aware of the need to keep Soviet influence out of our hemisphere. The Cuban experience reinforced the wisdom of the Monroe Doctrine.

Oppose any foe. Would JFK have shrunk from the threat of Soviet nuclear expansion and called for a "nuclear freeze"? Not a chance. He was, after all, willing to risk nuclear war with the Soviets over their attempt to deploy nuclear missiles in Cuba.

The fact is, John F. Kennedy passionately wanted to "assure the survival and the success of liberty." He wasn't perfect, but he was no New Left liberal either. What, then, happened to his brother Ted?

On October 31, 1983, Senator Ted Kennedy called for a vote on an immediate U.S. nuclear freeze. Despite the fact that the Soviets had spent $140 billion more than the United States to modernize its nuclear forces since the signing of the SALT I arms reduction treaty in 1972, Ted Kennedy and many in his party insisted that America go in the opposite direction. They wanted us to shut down development and production of the MX Trident missile systems, the B-1 bomber, the Stealth bomber, air-launched cruise missiles, ground-launched cruise missiles, and a host of other weapons systems critically needed to reacquire American military superiority over the Soviets, which was lost under Carter. If truth be known, Kennedy and his colleagues and the Left today, including Clinton, didn't and don't believe that an America with superior military power is advisable or conducive to world peace.

One nuclear freeze measure had already passed the Democrat-controlled House of Representatives on May 4, 1983, by a vote of 278 to 149. Among those voting in favor of the freeze? None other than two future leaders of the Democratic Party: then representative Al Gore of Tennessee and Representative Dick Gephardt of Missouri. Fortunately, the Republican-controlled Senate was able to put a stop to such a reckless course. But not before 73 percent of all Senate Democrats—including current senators like Joe Biden of Delaware, Chris Dodd of Connecticut, and Fritz Hollings of South Carolina—voted in favor of the freeze. Governor Michael Dukakis, who became the Democratic Party's presidential nominee in 1988, was another big nuclear freeze proponent.

Locking into place American military inferiority in the face of Soviet expansionism was as foolish and dangerous an idea as a person could propose during the Cold War. Thank God President Ronald Reagan and Vice President George H. W. Bush were there to stop them. In fact, Bush framed the issue quite well during his October 13, 1988, presidential debate with Dukakis.

"I think the foremost responsibility of a president really gets down to the national security of this country," Bush told the country. "The governor . . . talked about a nuclear freeze back at the time when I was in Europe trying to convince European public opinion that we ought to go forward with the deployment of the INF weapons. And thank God, the freeze people were not heard. They were wrong. And the result is, we deployed, and the Soviets kept deploying, and then we negotiated from strength. And now we have the first arms control agreement in the nuclear age to ban weapons. You just don't make unilateral cuts in the naive hope that the Soviets are going to behave themselves. World peace is important, and we have enhanced the peace. And I'm proud to have been a part of an administration that has done exactly that. Peace through strength works."

How right Bush was. Peace through strength works. That's why the American hostages were released from Iran, the Contras were able to bring peace, freedom, and democracy to Nicaragua, the Berlin Wall fell, the Warsaw Pact collapsed, the Soviet Union collapsed, and global Communism ended up on the ash heap of history, just as President Reagan said it would.

Now just imagine if Jimmy Carter had been reelected in 1980, or Walter Mondale had been elected in 1984, or Michael Dukakis in 1988. Imagine if rather than standing up to the Soviets, the Iranians, the Libyans, and the Marxists of Central and South America, the United States had continued to back down and abandon its moral standing in the great war of ideas between Communism and freedom.

Would America and the West have won the Cold War? Would hundreds of millions of people living under the dark, cold, terrifying shadow of tyranny now be living under the bright, warm, invigorating sunshine of freedom? No. By God's grace, we elected the right leaders and in turn got the results for which we all so eagerly longed.

A LIBERAL WHO (ADMITTEDLY)
LOATHED THE MILITARY

On December 3, 1969, a bright, articulate young man named Bill Clinton wrote a letter to Eugene J. Holmes, a retired U.S. Army ROTC colonel.

Clinton began by thanking Colonel Holmes "for saving me from the draft."

He then went on to disparage the American government, the American military, and those who were fighting and dying in Vietnam. He concluded by saying that he hoped his letter would help Colonel Holmes "understand more clearly how so many fine people have come to find themselves still loving their country but loathing the military."

It was highly controversial stuff when the letter surfaced during the 1992 Democratic primary in New Hampshire. But amid the political firefight, the true importance of Clinton's letter was overlooked.

What should have truly disturbed us was not that Clinton disagreed with America's involvement in the Vietnam War but that he showed such disdain for the very brave young people who serve in our military and safeguard our freedoms. Clinton was tipping his hand. As president, he would be no friend of the military. Instead he would actively undermine the institutions charged with protecting our national security.

Loathing the military is a strong phrase—with unmistakable meaning. And based on his actions, there is no question that Clinton continued loathing the military to the time he became commander in chief and throughout his tenure. Why else would he have made gays in the military one of his top priorities? Why else would he have stretched U.S. military forces dangerously thin by simultaneously downsizing them and sending them all over the globe on UN peace-keeping missions?

Just look at the facts.

"The defense buildup in the 1980s increased active U.S. Army divisions from 16 to 18, and Reserve divisions from 8 to 10 by FY 1986," according to a study published in 2000 by The Heritage Foundation, a public policy research group based in Washington. Clinton slashed these forces more than 40 percent, leaving only 10 active army divisions and 5 reserve divisions.

During the Reagan era there were 26 tactical wings and 13 reserve wings. But Clinton cut them almost in half, leaving 13 active and 7 reserve wings. In addition, Clinton significantly reduced our mission-capable air force fighter aircraft and the marines, both active and reserves. During the Reagan years, our navy ships totaled 569, with 15 aircraft carrier battle groups. Clinton reduced the numbers to 315 ships and 11 aircraft carrier battle groups.

As if that weren't enough, "the military is suffering its worst personnel crisis since the draft ended in 1973," the Heritage study found. "The U.S. Navy missed its recruiting goal by nearly 7,000 sailors in 1998, forcing many ships to deploy understaffed. In response the Navy's leadership decided in 1999 to accept a higher percentage of recruits without high school diplomas. That same year, both the U.S. Army and U.S. Air Force missed their recruiting goals. As noted above, only the Marine Corps, by far the smallest of the four services, has avoided a major personnel crisis."

Did Clinton gut the military because there was no evidence that countries like Iraq, Iran, North Korea, and an increasingly aggressive Communist China would represent serious future threats to America and our friends and allies? No. Rather, it was because he loathed the military, he had little concern about the rising global terrorist threat, and he had difficulty foreseeing a moment in which he or one of his successors would be required to lead America in a full-scale war against an able, agile, and well-armed enemy. Perhaps more important, he wanted to use the money stripped from defense—the so-called peace dividend—to fund more domestic spending. The New Left found an adherent and voice in Bill Clinton, and the consequences were devastating to, among other things, our national security. And Clinton laid the groundwork for further mischief from his party colleagues.

THE INDEFENSIBLE TOM DASCHLE

Which brings us to Tom Daschle, the Senate majority leader and the effective leader of the Democratic Party. In his position Daschle wields considerable power and has been a thorn in President Bush's side on a wide range of domestic and foreign policy issues.

Tom Daschle masquerades as a nice guy—passing himself off as a mild-mannered moderate fighting for the average American. But don't let appearances fool you. Daschle is a New Left Democrat. And he has spent his long congressional career proving it.

Unlike Clinton, Daschle served in the U.S. Air Force from 1969 to 1972 as an intelligence officer assigned to the Strategic Air Command. He was elected to the U.S. House of Representatives in 1977 by the slimmest of margins. Ten years later he ran successfully for the Senate. When Senate Majority Leader George Mitchell, a liberal and partisan Democrat from Maine, retired in 1994, Daschle was elected his successor by merely one vote. Of course, Republicans gained control of the Senate in 1995, which meant Daschle would serve as Senate minority leader until 2001, when Vermont Senator Jim Jeffords abruptly quit the Republican Party and declared himself an Independent, but allied himself with the Democrats.

Through this regrettable turn of events, Tom Daschle became the world's most powerful liberal—the Senate majority leader.

Many believe Daschle is positioning himself for his ultimate goal: becoming president. Recently he's traveled to Iowa and other early caucus and primary states, speaking to the party faithful. He's raised truckloads of money for himself and other Democrats—while, by the way, railing against such "corrupting" campaign contributions. He's given major policy speeches. He's challenged President Bush almost daily. In short, he's been emerging from the shadows of obscurity into the bright lights of prime-time politics.

"So what?" you ask. Well, if you don't know much about Tom Daschle, I suggest it's time to find out who he is, what he believes, and why he couldn't be more ill suited to hold the power he has and the power he seeks. I've been watching him for years, and my conclusion is basically this: Daschle is arguably the most ideologically intransigent New Left liberal ever to serve in the Senate leadership.

Consider the following.

September 19, 1979. The Democrats controlled the White House, the House, and the Senate. Jimmy Carter was president. Islamic fundamentalist radicals in Iran were less than two months away from seizing the U.S. embassy in Teheran. The Soviet Union was just a few months away from invading Afghanistan. The U.S. military was run-down and demoralized after Vietnam. Congress voted on an amendment that would increase defense spending by $3 billion to upgrade our defense systems, but Tom Daschle, a freshman congressman, voted against it. In fact, so did most of his fellow Democrats, including Representative Dick Gephardt, a Missouri Democrat who, of course, is now the most powerful Democrat in the House (and another presidential hopeful). The promilitary amendment went down in flames, 221 to 191.

May 4, 1983. The U.S. House of Representatives passed a nuclear freeze bill by a vote of 278 to 149. Joining his liberal buddies Al Gore and Dick Gephardt in favor of the freeze was none other than Tom Daschle.

August 4, 1990. Two days after Iraq invaded Kuwait, Saddam Hussein was clearly one of the most dangerous men in the world. He was poised to seize control of some 60 percent of the world's oil supplies, had developed ballistic missiles capable of hitting Israel, Saudi Arabia, and other Arab neighbors, and was developing chemical, biological, and possibly nuclear weapons to be delivered by his ballistic missiles. Keep in mind that Hussein had already used chemical weapons against his own people.

The world was quickly plunging into a grave crisis. U.S. forces were preparing to move into the region to protect Saudi Arabia and liberate Kuwait. There could be no doubt that Saddam Hussein was a dangerous menace who was close to developing the capacity to strike directly at the United States with weapons of mass destruction.

Nuclear weapons in the hands of a ruthless dictator were no longer merely idle speculation but an inevitable reality. America had precious little time to prepare a defense.

Remarkably, liberals in Congress were not moved by this latest threat. In fact, they introduced an amendment to the defense budget that would slash ballistic missile defense research and development funding by $400 million. Fortunately, the amendment, sponsored by Senator John Kerry, was defeated, 54 to 43. Yet seven out of ten Democrats voted for Kerry's amendment, including Senators Ted Kennedy, Joe Lieberman, Bill Bradley, and—sure enough—freshman senator Tom Daschle. By contrast, almost nine out of ten Republican senators voted to protect missile defense spending, along with a handful of Democrats.

October 15, 1990. By this time, Saddam Hussein's forces had overrun Kuwait. Hussein announced that Kuwait had now been annexed as part of Iraq. President Bush drew a line in the sand, and a massive U.S. military buildup in the Persian Gulf was under way. Brave American soldiers were heading into harm's way. It was time for Congress to vote on the $268 billion defense budget that would, among other things, pay our troops, provide $1 billion more to expand sea lift capabilities, invest in more M-1 Abrams tanks, keep tank-making plants open, buy B-2 bombers, upgrade our submarine forces, and invest $3.57 billion in missile defense. Finally, the eve-of-war defense bill passed—but Daschle voted against it.

January 12, 1991. Decision Day. U.S. and allied forces were amassed in the Persian Gulf. Bush was ready to give the green light. But liberals in Congress again fought Bush tooth and nail. Hussein knew Congress was divided. Some Bush advisers didn't want a vote of Congress authorizing the use of force in the Gulf, for fear that Congress might defeat the joint resolution, tying the president's hands. But President Bush wanted America to go into battle united, so he called for a vote.

The House debate was intense and divisive. In the end, all but 3 of the 167 House Republicans voted yes to the use of force. But the vast majority of House Democrats voted no—voted against fighting to set the people of Kuwait free. A stunning 179 Democrats—including their leader, Dick Gephardt—voted no, while only 86 voted yes.

The Senate debate was even more intense, and the vote was even closer. In the end, the use-of-force resolution passed, but narrowly— 52 to 47. A full 95 percent of Senate Republicans voted yes to set Kuwait free. Even Senators Al Gore and Joe Lieberman voted yes. But an incredible 82 percent of Senate Democrats voted no—*82 percent*— including Tom Daschle and a number of other liberal presidential hopefuls, past and future, such as Senators Ted Kennedy, John Kerry, Bill Bradley, and Paul Wellstone.

Over the years the American people have come to expect a left-wing icon like Ted Kennedy to be out there on the floor of the U.S. Senate blaming America first and undermining U.S. national security and vital national interests. And in the lead-up to Operation Desert Storm, he was in his usual form. "I urge the Senate to reject the Orwellian argument that the only real hope for peace is for Congress to threaten war," Kennedy bellowed. "That is brinkmanship of the worst sort, and the U.S. Senate should not be an accomplice in it."

Accomplice? To a war begun by Saddam Hussein?

Kennedy actually maintained that Bush began the war. I kid you not. "President Bush lit the fuse for war on November 8, and the fuse has been burning steadily for the past two months," the senator said. "In three more days, the fuse will reach the powder. The Middle East may explode in war, unless the Senate puts out the fuse."

And there was more.

"In expressing his determination to roll back Iraq's aggression,"

Kennedy continued, "President Bush has frequently compared Saddam to Hitler. But that comparison is a gross exaggeration that has far more differences than similarities. Baghdad is not Munich. Iraq is not Germany. Kuwait is not Czechoslovakia. Saddam Hussein is not Adolf Hitler."

What can you say to such lunacy but thank God Ted Kennedy wasn't president of the United States. But you see, that was modern liberalism in action. In the liberal worldview, Saddam Hussein didn't start the war; George H. W. Bush did. Iraq wasn't to blame; Republicans were. There was no urgency to defeat an evil regime building weapons of mass destruction and to set an enslaved people free; the real urgency was to stop conservatives.

That's the way liberals think. And that's why their thinking can be dangerous. Because it's not just liberal dinosaurs like Ted Kennedy who believe such things. The real movers and shakers of the Democratic Party—people like Tom Daschle—also tend to believe them. It is Tom Daschle who now leads the Ted Kennedy party. It is Tom Daschle who wants to be president and commander in chief. Yet it's Tom Daschle who voted not just against the Gulf War but also against the defense budget that funded the brave American soldiers who put their lives on the line to fight it.

"I cannot look my seventeen-year-old son or nineteen-year-old daughter in the eye and say, 'Moving Saddam Hussein out of Kuwait, obtaining the necessary oil from the Persian Gulf, protecting our allies, or saving jobs is worth your life,'" Daschle declared on the floor of the U.S. Senate on January 10, 1991, in a speech broadcast around the nation and around the world. "I cannot say that. If at this time I cannot say it to them, how in good conscience can I say it to a mother or father? How can I say it to a sister or a brother?"

To me, it defies all understanding that a person in such a position of responsibility could oppose going to war against the likes of Saddam Hussein.

April 25, 1991. Despite all the fearmongering by the Left, America and our impressive international coalition won the war. We drove Hussein out of Kuwait. We decimated his military machine. Unfortunately, however, we left Iraq before destroying Hussein and his regime. No sooner had we left Iraq than Senator Bill Bradley, a Democrat from New Jersey, proposed slashing the defense budget by some $30 billion over five years. Fortunately, Bradley's amendment was shot down 73 to 22. But 21 Senate Democrats actually supported Bradley—including Daschle.

The Clinton-Gore Years. When Bill Clinton and Al Gore came to office the Cold War and the Gulf War were over, but there were still serious threats to U.S. national security. In 1996, although the Joint Chiefs of Staff unanimously requested a procurement budget of $60 billion to bolster a rapidly declining defense structure, the Clinton-Gore defense budget slashed that request by more than one-third, to $38.9 billion. To understand the significance of that cut, let's compare the 1996 Clinton-Gore defense budget with the Reagan-Bush defense budget ten years earlier.

COMPARISON OF DEFENSE BUDGETS

	Reagan-Bush 1986	Clinton-Gore 1996
New tanks requested in president's budget	840	0
New tactical aircraft requested in president's budget	399	34
New naval ships requested in president's budget	40	6

Not surprisingly, Daschle voted for the Clinton-Gore budget in 1996. In fact, the senator was even more extreme than Clinton and Gore. He voted for additional measures both large and small to cut military spending and further weaken our national defenses.

May 15, 1996. The Senate considered an amendment to cut the defense budget by $8.3 billion in the next fiscal year. Fortunately, the amendment was rejected—42 to 57—with 89 percent of Republicans voting against it and 78 percent of Democrats voting for it, including Daschle.

June 25, 1998. The Senate considered an amendment to cut the defense budget by $329 million. Again the amendment was rejected—by 38 to 55—with 90 percent of Republicans voting against it; 80 percent of Democrats voted for the cut, including Daschle.

June 13, 2000. It was just a little more than a year before terrorists would strike the Twin Towers and the Pentagon. The 2000 presidential campaign was white-hot. George W. Bush was beating up on the shamefully anemic national security record of the Clinton-Gore administration. Bush would soon name former defense secretary Dick Cheney as his running mate, signaling, among other things, that he was serious and ready to deal with tough foreign and national security policy issues. Gore, meanwhile, was trying to sound and act tough. He would soon name Senator Joe Lieberman as his running mate, one of the better Senate Democrats when it came to defense and security issues.

At that point the Senate considered an amendment to slash the defense budget by $1 billion. Yet again the amendment was rejected—15 to 83—with 100 percent of Republicans voting against it. What was interesting this time was that 66 percent of Senate Democrats voted against the cut, no doubt worried about looking weak on defense during an election year. But still 15 Democrats voted for it—and predictably, Daschle was among them.

Daschle is no left-wing campus hippie flake. He's the majority leader of the U.S. Senate and a possible candidate for the presidency. In his position as majority leader he sets the agenda, sets the tone, and speaks for the party. Yet the national security policies that he champions are right out of the New Left movement, and they are reckless, especially during this time of war. When it comes to America's national defense, Tom Daschle's ideas and actions—indeed, those of the entire Democratic Party—are indefensible and irresponsible.

A WORD TO THOSE WHO WEAR THE UNIFORM

In the next chapter, I'll survey the threats we still face around the world, those that put our very civilization at risk and for which we need a strong CIA, strong coastline and border security, and a strong military.

But I want to conclude this chapter by simply thanking God that our military remains the best in the world and by thanking the brave men and women who serve in our armed forces and put their lives on the line each and every day. To all who wear the uniform of our country—in the army, navy, air force, marines and coast guard—let me just say:

Thank you for all that you do, for putting yourself in harm's way so that your fellow countrymen can remain free and safe.

And to those on Capitol Hill or at home, I say:

It is time to do what the liberal Democrats have been so reluctant to do. It is time to defend our defenders. It is time to invest more in the defense of our nation, after nearly a decade of maltreatment. It is time to pay our soldiers, sailors, and air men and women far more in order to keep top-notch people in our military. It is time to offer recruiting packages that attract more bright, daring, courageous young people to join the armed forces and make the military and intelligence services their lifelong careers. It is time to rapidly rebuild our stockpiles of conventional weapons, ammunition, and spare parts. It is time to modernize our nuclear forces, to make certain that we're ready to confront the challenges of the evolving threats of the twenty-first century. It is time to get behind a missile defense system that will protect us from the nuclear advances and threats of our enemies. And it is time to invest in the development of other cutting-edge military technologies that have proven so important in our war against the forces of evil in our time. In short, it is time to enthusiastically embrace the people and policies that are committed to ensuring the survival of our civilization against those who are dedicated to destroying it.

[FIVE]

THREATCON DELTA

December 29, 1999.

It was almost two years before our new national nightmare began. The program was *Hannity & Colmes*. The topic was terrorism, the millennium celebrations, and the fact that Seattle had just canceled its Y2K party after the arrest of Arab terrorists allegedly trying to slip over the border from Canada and blow up the city's famous Space Needle. The guests on the program were Steven Emerson, one of America's leading experts on terrorism and Islamic radicalism, and Kirby Wilbur, a friend and fellow conservative talk-show host on Seattle's KVI, one of America's great talk radio stations.

"Unfortunately, we live in a dangerous world, in a dangerous time, and terrorism is one of those dangers," I told Alan and our guests.

The threat of terrorism has been a theme of mine ever since I began my career as a talk-show host, because as a conservative I don't turn a blind eye to the existence of evil in the world. I'm not a moral relativist. I don't believe in a politically correct foreign policy. I believe that while there may be plenty of gray in the world, there is also black and white—good guys and bad guys—and I don't have trouble distinguishing between the two. By 1999 there were serious threats on the horizon in terms of Islamic terrorism. They weren't hard to see. In fact, the Clinton State Department's own web site carried the following information:

> Middle Eastern terrorist groups and their state sponsors continued to plan, train for, and carry out acts of terrorism in 1999 at a level comparable to that of the previous year. Casualties remained relatively low, partly as result of counterterrorist measures by various governments, improved international cooperation, and the absence of major incidents that might have caused high numbers of fatalities. Nonetheless, certain terrorist groups remained active and continued to try to mount lethal attacks. These included Usama Bin Ladin's multinational al-Qaida organization as well as The Islamic Resistance Movement (HAMAS) and Palestinian Islamic Jihad (PIJ), both of which receive support from Iran.

Yet at the same time that his own State Department was identifying serious terrorist threats from bin Laden (among others), President Clinton was actually pardoning terrorists who had killed innocent Americans, including New York City cops. It was absolutely unbelievable. Remember when President Clinton pardoned terrorists who were members of the radical Puerto Rican faction called the FALN, responsible for one hundred bombings on American soil? We even have videotape of some of these guys making bombs; I aired it one night on *Hannity & Colmes.*

I also interviewed some of the victims who survived such horrors. I saw their anguish. I saw their astonishment that an American president would sell them out, presumably to court the Hispanic vote in New York City on behalf of his wife, Hillary, who was running for the Senate at the time. What kind of message did that send to the world? What might Osama bin Laden and his thugs have concluded when they saw Clinton pardon convicted terrorists? The administration's approach to terrorism was a disgrace—"a joke," as I said during that late December 1999 *Hannity & Colmes*.

"It is," Emerson agreed. "Clinton's antiterrorism policy is a joke, and that's part of the problem."

Conservative presidents like Ronald Reagan and George Bush 41 confronted Libya, Nicaragua, Panama, and Iraq firmly, decisively, victoriously, and in a way that enhanced America's international credibility and prestige. Liberal presidents like Jimmy Carter and Bill Clinton, on the other hand, handled these countries—not to mention others like Iran and Somalia—fecklessly and incompetently.

Osama bin Laden is "probably living in fear," Alan Colmes insisted on this night in December of 1999. "He knows he's a target. He knows he's vulnerable. But—"

"Not with this president, Alan," KVI's Kirby Wilbur interjected. "He has nothing to be afraid of."

"I beg your pardon?" Alan responded, genuinely perplexed.

"He has nothing to be afraid of with this president," Wilbur repeated. "We're not going to go after him."

"Look," Alan shot back, "you'd love to use this as an opportunity to knock Bill Clinton. We had lots of incidents of terrorism during the Reagan administration. The marine barracks in Lebanon and a number of other incidents . . . so let's not suggest [that] simply because Bill Clinton is president, we're therefore more vulnerable."

Emerson said the Clinton team was certainly doing a better job than the Europeans in trying to contain bin Laden, but it wasn't nearly enough. "I do believe we need much more aggressive policies," Emerson said prophetically.

"What else should we be doing?" Alan asked, almost incredulous. "What else—how much can you do? I mean, there's only so much you can do. You can't guarantee that there'll never be terrorist activity. And if we were to be more proactive and go after other leaders, we'd be more vulnerable here in America, wouldn't we?"

Alan may be right that you can't guarantee that there'll never be terrorist activity, but I would argue that we should *not* be giving pardons to convicted terrorists—or rejecting Sudan's repeated offers to deliver Osama bin Laden. Rather, how about getting a few more Arab-language interpreters working for the CIA? How about paying informants inside radical Islamic communities? How about untying the CIA's hands from the ropes of political correctness? How about sending a covert hit team over to the Middle East to take out bin Laden? All of these would have been good steps for the Clinton-Gore administration to take. By not aggressively and proactively defending Americans from the wide range of threats posed by global terrorism— and specifically by not effectively going after Osama bin Laden— America had made itself a target, just as Emerson tried to explain at the time.

"Well, I'm not so sure that we'd be more vulnerable if we went after Osama bin Laden," Emerson said. "I mean, there is the executive order prohibiting assassination, which is why we're not going after him. And that was a debate that, you know, maybe needs to be resurrected in Congress."

Emerson was referring to Presidential Executive Order 12333, which has been in place since the mid-1970s to prevent the United States from assassinating foreign heads of state, including ruthless leaders like Saddam Hussein, Muammar Qaddafi, and the Ayatollah Khomeini. But the executive order does not prohibit killing in self-defense, and it does not apply to killing a foreign combatant like bin Laden, who heads a terrorist network rather than a state. In any event, the president is free to rescind an executive order at any time with nothing more than his signature on another executive order.

There's something odd about the argument that the killing of a mass murderer is morally indefensible, yet the commitment of tens of thousands of troops to defeat his network or regime is legitimate. As I said in 1999, "I don't have a problem with rescinding that [order]. . . .

I'm a believer in covert operations. Especially when we can prove that these people were involved in terrorism on our soil."

The topic came up again in February of 2001, a mere seven months before New York and Washington were attacked by bin Laden and his terrorists. Representative Bob Barr, a Georgia Republican, had introduced the Terrorist Elimination Act of 2001 to repeal Executive Order 12333 and allow the U.S. government to take out terrorists when advisable. We debated it on *Hannity & Colmes*. I strongly supported Barr's legislation. But sure enough, the Democrats wanted nothing to do with it.

"We can protect ourselves from terrorist threats like Osama bin Laden," observed my guest, David Horowitz, the left-wing 1960s radical turned conservative writer and activist. "It would be nice if the CIA were able to assassinate him."

Amen, I thought. But Alan couldn't have disagreed more.

"It would be a bad policy for a number of reasons," he responded. Alan argued that such a move would be an invitation to target our leaders as well; I responded that they already are.

Alan wasn't alone in his view. Susan Estrich—once a top adviser to Democratic presidential candidate Michael Dukakis—was also on our show that night, and strenuously objected to assassinating terrorists like bin Laden.

Why?

"I'm a liberal," she said. "I'm a nice liberal."

True enough—I like Susan, as I like Alan. But I couldn't disagree more with her nice liberal ideas. FDR was a "nice liberal." But he also understood the imperative of victory. During World War II, in the spring of 1943 when Admiral Chester Nimitz learned that Admiral Isoruku Yamamoto—who was undoubtedly Imperial Japan's most brilliant and indispensable military strategist—would be flying from Rabaul to Bougainville in the South Pacific, he ordered U.S. fighters to shoot down his plane. They did, and Yamamoto was killed. As the brains behind Japan's navy operations, Yamamoto was a natural target, and his elimination was an important step in defeating Japan's war effort and ensuring American victory.

LIBERALS STILL DON'T GET IT

After 9/11, you'd think the Left would see the threats that face us and put aside petty political partisanship. While some have certainly become more conservative on national security issues—at least for the time being—many have not.

That's what worries me. And it should worry you, too.

America is at war. We may be at war for a long time. Today, whether our government officially classifies it this way each day or not, we live at Threat Condition Delta, which dictates the highest possible state of readiness. All Americans now understand that we have many enemies that could do us harm. We face threats from land, sea, and air. We face threats at home and abroad. We needn't be paranoid. But we must be vigilant and we must be prepared. And we must understand and accept one basic premise: the best defense is a good offense.

I'll sketch out some of these threats in a moment.

But first, a modest proposal: We ought to build a Museum of Modern Left-Wing Lunacy—a place like the Smithsonian or the Guggenheim where, instead of coming to see great art or artifacts, people can come to see great examples of contemporary liberal idiocy. Maybe showcasing some of their blunders would help us to hold them accountable—and, if we could complete it in time, it might help us to avoid similar mistakes in the future. Here are some of the fine verbal specimens that would surely be on display when it opened.

Referring to the United States Supreme Court's decision in *Bush v. Gore,* Alec Baldwin, the sanctimonious actor and board member of People for the American Way, declared to a cheering Florida A&M crowd in March 2002, "I believe that what happened in 2000 did as much damage to the pillars of democracy as terrorists did to the pillars of commerce in New York City."

How could any thinking, feeling American say something so grossly offensive in the wake of such bloodshed and terror? How could a coddled Hollywood liberal like Baldwin so callously diminish one of the greatest tragedies of our time?

Or how about this one: "Bush is amateurish and self-serving and, frankly, it's disgusting," sniped actress Sandra Bernhard. "Everybody is covering their asses with the Enron scandal, and it was very convenient that September eleventh came along to deflect the fact that they should never have been in the White House in the first place."

You could certainly fill a wing of the museum with similar outrageous quotes by entertainers. But if I had my way it would be dominated by jaw-dropping statements from the far more dangerous liberal Washington politicians, like Representative Barbara Lee, a California Democrat.

Lee was the only member of Congress who actually voted against a congressional resolution to use military force to destroy al Qaeda and the Taliban. That's right. She's against any use of military force to hunt down and destroy the enemy we are now searching for, before they find more American targets to blow up. She actually said that she was "not convinced that voting for the resolution preserves and protects U.S. interests." In fact, she concluded, "a rush to launch precipitous military counterattacks runs too great a risk that more innocent men, women, [and] children will be killed. I could not vote for a resolution that I believe could lead to such an outcome."

What makes her position even less defensible is that one year before 9/11, Lee voted in favor of reauthorizing the Violence against Women Act because, as she said, "we must do all we can to ensure the well-being of our women and children, and make sure that the resources are there to punish the abusers and help women get out of abusive relationships." How ironic that when it came to the biggest one-day act of violence against women in American history, Lee couldn't seem to find it within herself to "punish the abusers" with F-16s and cruise missiles.

"We need to know where we're going and who we're going after," Lee told the *Los Angeles Times*. "We need to know how to bring these perpetrators to justice. Military action is a one-dimensional strategy. What I'm saying is that we need a multidimensional strategy rooted in foreign policy."

Of course, this is all abundantly disingenuous: not one of her objections is legitimate, and it's hard to believe she isn't aware of it. Lee charged that we hadn't defined our enemies, and that President Bush was following a one-dimensional strategy involving a military response alone. Yet of course shortly after 9/11 the president had made it quite clear who our enemies were. "The enemy of America is not our many Muslim friends. It is not our many Arab friends. Our enemy is a radical network of terrorists and every government that supports them. Our war on terror begins with al Qaeda, but it does not end there."

Bush also warned that this would be like no other war we'd ever fought. It would not be like the Persian Gulf War or the air war above Kosovo. He explained that it would not involve just one battle but would be a "lengthy campaign." Some of it would be highly visible on TV; other parts would be covert.

As to Lee's contention that Bush was pursuing solely a military response, wasn't she listening as he articulated his multipronged strategy to shut down the complex terrorist networks? Perhaps Congresswoman Lee was daydreaming when the president said, "We will direct every resource at our command—every means of diplomacy, every tool of intelligence, every instrument of law enforcement, every financial influence, and every necessary weapon of war—to the disruption and to the defeat of the global terror network."

This wasn't just idle talk. Bush, with the cooperation of foreign allies, immediately froze the bank accounts and other assets of the terrorist network. And our intelligence and law enforcement services went into action and brought many terrorists into custody, doubtlessly averting further attacks on our own soil.

In addition, President Bush established an Office of Homeland Security to "oversee and coordinate a comprehensive national strategy to safeguard our country against terrorism and to respond to any attacks that may come."

Lee wasn't the only official making ridiculous statements. Another one who will certainly be featured in the Museum of Modern Left-Wing Lunacy is Representative Dennis Kucinich, a Ohio Democrat.

To his credit, Kucinich initially voted for the congressional resolution authorizing force. But soon he began backpedaling. He began publicly and provocatively attacking the president, the vice president, and the nation's efforts to fight and win the war on terrorism. In a February 17, 2002, speech in California, Kucinich offered "A Prayer For America."

"The trappings of a state of siege trap us in a state of fear, ill-equipped to deal with the Patriot Games, the Mind Games, the War Games of an unelected President and his unelected Vice President," Kucinich declared. "Let us pray that our country will stop this war."

Why in the world would a sitting member of Congress seek to undermine the very legitimacy of the American president during wartime? Unfortunately, that was just the beginning. Kucinich also accused the president of the United States of authorizing "the bombing of civilians in Afghanistan," the "repeal of the Bill of Rights," "withdrawal from the Geneva Convention," "assassination squads," and shedding "the blood of innocent villagers in Afghanistan."

In no way is that the Bush administration's policy or practice in the Afghan theater or anywhere else in the world. The whole thing was complete fabrication—and downright infuriating. So we had Kucinich on *Hannity & Colmes*, and I confronted him. I asked him whether he truly believed that we were targeting civilians in Afghanistan. "That's an outright lie, Congressman, an outright lie. And you know it."

"You are mischaracterizing that speech," Kucinich shot back.

"That's what it says. I'm reading it verbatim."

"I am telling you that you are mischaracterizing it."

"I'll read it."

So I did.

"Wait a minute," the congressman insisted. "The truth is that civilians have been bombed. That's a fact. You can't dispute that."

There is, of course, no evidence to support this charge. Had this guy completely lost it?

"Nobody *authorized* that," I responded. "We don't *target* civilians, Congressman. You know better than that."

Apparently not.

Georgia congresswoman Cynthia McKinney has charged that President Bush had prior warning of the 9/11 terrorist attacks and did nothing to prevent them. "Persons close to this administration are poised to make huge profits off America's war," she said on a Berkeley, California, radio show. McKinney also made similar assertions on the House floor without any evidence to back up her claim.

Not long after McKinney made her claim, other Democrats tried to contend that President Bush had prior knowledge of the 9/11 attacks, after incomplete information from a memo out of the FBI office in Phoenix was leaked to the press. Democratic leaders like Tom Daschle, Dick Gephardt, and Hillary Clinton started demanding an answer to the question "What did the president know and when did he know it?" The *New York Post* ran the headline "Bush Knew."

After a few days the story was debunked when the FBI agent from Phoenix, Kenneth Williams, told Congress that the memo was marked "routine" and that he knew it would take a few months to rise up in the ranks of the FBI. His memo, which raised concerns about some flight schools where terrorists could learn to fly, was not specific in any way. He also told Congress that he never imagined that these terrorists would hijack planes and crash them into buildings. Within days Democrats backed off this claim.

Even still, the lunacy of congressmen and Democratic leaders like Lee, Kucinich, and McKinney, pales in comparison to that of former president Bill Clinton. On November 7, 2001, Clinton seemingly blamed the vicious terrorist attacks on you and me and all Americans.

"Those of us who come from various European lineages are not blameless," Clinton told a student audience at his alma mater, Georgetown University. "Indeed, in the first Crusade, when the Christian soldiers took Jerusalem, they first burned a synagogue with three hundred Jews in it and proceeded to kill every woman and child who was Muslim on the Temple Mount. The contemporaneous descriptions of the event describe soldiers walking on the Temple Mount, a holy place to Christians, with blood running up to their knees. I can tell you that that story is still being told today in the Middle East, and we are still paying for it."

Of course I'm not going to defend the Crusades. But for crying out loud, that was hundreds of years ago. Just because the Turks once invaded Europe, that doesn't give us license to attack the Turkish people today. The French don't get a free pass to kill Germans because the Germans once occupied their country. Koreans don't get to kill Japanese because the Japanese once occupied their country. How could a former president suggest that Muslims are somehow justified in killing innocent Americans because of the Crusades? It's not just untrue—it's unconscionable.

But Clinton went further: "Here in the United States, we were founded as a nation that practiced slavery, and slaves were quite frequently killed even though they were innocent," the former president continued. "This country once looked the other way when significant numbers of Native Americans were dispossessed and killed to get their land or their mineral rights or because they were thought of as less than fully human, and we are still paying the price today. Even in the twentieth century in America people were terrorized or killed because of their race. And even today, though we have continued to walk, sometimes to stumble, in the right direction, we still have the occasional hate crime rooted in race, religion, or sexual orientation. So terror has a long history."

Yes, slavery is a terrible stain on our history. That's absolutely true. But for heaven's sake, we fought a bloody civil war to end slavery more than one hundred years ago. We've been fighting to end the scourge of racism ever since. That's no justification for radical Islamic terrorism.

Then, in April 2002, during a speech in Austria, Clinton revealed even deeper moral confusion. He stated that the gap between rich and poor must be reduced to make the world safer. If not another apology for terrorism, what was his point? As a leftist, he simply can't escape viewing the world through the myopic lenses of economic determinism. There will always be poor in the world, but poverty is hardly the cause of terrorism, any more than the Crusades or American slavery are.

As we've seen over the past few chapters, liberal policies have undermined the CIA, allowed an explosion of illegal immigration, and radically downsized our military forces. Along the way, liberals have turned the full force of their rhetorical firepower against anyone—particularly conservatives—who opposed them.

Threat: Sleeper Cells

As I write this, the number one threat to our homeland security comes from "sleeper cells"—foreign terrorists who have carefully burrowed themselves into our free and open society and quietly go about their business until their leaders activate or "awaken" them with orders to carry out another horrific attack.

Most of the terrorists who attacked the World Trade Center and the Pentagon—and would have attacked the White House or Capitol building—were "sleepers." They lived among us: rented apartments, obtained driver's licenses, obtained cars, attended flight schools, ate at restaurants, went to strip clubs, and moved about with little or no fear of being noticed, much less captured. Though the Justice Department under John Ashcroft's leadership has done a remarkable job of rounding up these terrorists, many certainly remain at large. The question our law enforcement officials ask themselves every day, therefore, is: How do we find, catch, and imprison them before they strike again? It is a challenge I've sought to underscore from the earliest hours of the crisis.

"Sleepers have been here for years [and] may well be planning the next level, a second tier of attacks," Lt. Col. Oliver North said on *Hannity & Colmes* just two days after the terrorists struck. "The vulnerability that we face is not just from the residuals of those who tried to carry out the bombings on Tuesday and failed because their flights were grounded. We also have that second tier of a relatively unsophisticated attack with an eighteen-wheeler full of forty thousand pounds of ammonium nitrate and diesel fuel. We've got the FBI looking into some of these student cells. I remind you that the terrorists who tried to kill my family and me in February of 1987 got their orders through the People's Committee for Libyan Students, and we know that many of these youngsters have been in American schools, where they don't get an education in American democracy and freedom. What they get is ideology that backs them up and engineering skills that allow them to build these bombs."

Ollie is absolutely right. Sleepers can hit us in any number of ways—when and where we least expect it. Car bombs. Truck bombs. Suicide bombings, like those Israel has suffered through. Shootings; kidnappings; hijackings; cyber-warfare and devastating computer viruses; anthrax or other biological and chemical attacks poisoning our water supplies; demolition of our dams, bridges, and tunnels; and attacks against our 103 nuclear power plants.

In our free and open society, the threats are real and the targets are many. Were they successful and severe, a rash of such attacks could catch us by surprise, rattle our sense of confidence and security, and trigger a dramatic public health disaster or an economic crisis.

Top U.S. officials, including the attorney general, the FBI director, the Homeland Security director and the defense secretary, say that sleeper cells of terrorists are serious threats and we must be ready to counter them for the foreseeable future.

"I think it'll take a period of years," said Defense Secretary Donald Rumsfeld in a speech at the National Defense University, warning that the threats will intensify if terrorists get their hands on weapons of mass destruction. "These attacks could grow vastly more deadly than those we suffered" in 2001.

Some complain that the FBI and other law enforcement officials shouldn't be given new powers to hunt down these terrorists in our midst. They're certainly within their rights to raise concerns about civil liberty protections—and I take a backseat to no one when it comes to championing these rights. But the problem is that some seem to routinely underestimate the magnitude of the threats we face. They don't seem to understand why we urgently need to remove certain legal handcuffs that have made it far too difficult to trace, track, and trap terrorists.

Example: Liberals made it tougher in the 1990s to track financial contributions flowing into terrorist groups. "The Clinton-Gore Administration shut down a 1995 investigation of Islamic charities, concerned that a public probe would expose Saudi Arabia's suspected ties to a global money-laundering operation that raised millions for anti-Israel terrorists," wrote Jerry Seper, the *Washington Times* premiere investigative reporter, in the spring of 2002. "Former federal prosecutor John J. Loftus said four interrelated Islamic foundations, institutes and charities in Virginia with more than a billion dollars in assets donated by or through the Saudi Arabian government were allowed to continue under a 'veil of secrecy.'"

The Bush administration, on the other hand, has been fully investigating the financing of global terrorism. Seper continued: "Federal agents last week [March 2002] began a new investigation, known as 'Operation Green Quest,' into the funding by charities of suspected terrorists, raiding 14 Islamic businesses in Virginia. Agents from the U.S. Customs Service, Internal Revenue Service, Immigration and Naturalization Service and FBI, coordinated by a Treasury Department counterterrorism task force, seized two dozen computers, along with hundreds of bank statements and other documents."

In congressional testimony on February 24, 1998, terrorism expert Steven Emerson warned that sleeper cells of radical, violent, anti-Western Muslims riddle American society and have gone unnoticed, uninvestigated, and unprosecuted for years.

With eerie prescience, Emerson testified before members of the Senate Judiciary Committee five years after the first World Trade Center bombing. "The foreign terrorist threat in the United States is one of the most important issues we face as a society today," he told the senators. "With the advent of chemical and biological weapons, we now face distinct possibilities of mass civilian murder the likes of which have not been seen since World War II.

"The specter of terrorism carries with it the threat of violence aimed at targets merely because of their religious, ethnic, or national identities," he added. "The threat of terrorism—particularly in the age of instant telecommunications—also carries a major psychological dimension through an electronic multiplier effect that has the ability to inject fear and fright into the hearts and minds of tens of millions of Americans."

Three and a half years before disaster struck, Emerson urged the federal government to focus on the threat of foreign terrorists operating on American soil. Tragically, he found little if any interest.

Now, of course, he is sought out by media from all over the country and the world, as well as by congressional and administration officials. His book—*American Jihad: The Terrorists Living among Us* (Simon & Schuster/Free Press, 2002)—is a must-read for anyone interested in understanding just how wide, deep, and far radical Islamic sleeper cells have wormed their way into our society. It should be clear to everyone that if we don't root out these cells we face the almost certain threat of further attack here in the United States.

Threat: Airborne Attacks

Once you understand the threat of sleeper cells, you'll begin to understand the importance of getting far more serious about aviation security.

Mary Schiavo served as inspector general for the U.S. Department of Transportation from 1990 through 1996. After she left government she wrote a book called *Flying Blind, Flying Safe,* full of warnings about threats to U.S. aviation security.

Schiavo described a 1995 study designed to test the effectiveness of various U.S. airport security teams at detecting bombs being smuggled onto commercial planes. The results were horrifying. New York's Kennedy Airport and Washington's Dulles detected the bombs a mere 56 percent of the time, Boston's Logan Airport only 23 percent, Los Angeles's LAX an appalling 10 percent.

Schiavo also noted that until the late 1990s, "U.S. airlines were not required by law to x-ray passenger baggage," and that overall U.S. aviation security procedures were dangerously lax. She concluded that "it's probably only a matter of time before the security practices used on international flights originating in the U.S. are adopted on domestic flights as well. I hope it does not come about because of a senseless and horrible act of domestic terrorism, but with seventy attempts on domestic U.S. aviation in the first half of 1997, the future does not look good."

Tragically, Schiavo's warnings went unheeded. During the 1990s, the Clinton-Gore team talked tough but did almost nothing to make U.S. aviation truly safe from terrorism.

In July of 1996, for example, just one week after the tragic crash of TWA Flight 800 near Long Island, during the run-up to the fall presidential elections, President Clinton promised tough new airplane and baggage screening measures, vowing that every flight would be thoroughly checked for terrorists and the tools of terrorism.

"Every plane, every cabin, every cargo hold, every time," Clinton said at John F. Kennedy Airport. "Whatever needs to be done, we will do it."

He announced that Vice President Gore would lead a new aviation security commission and come up with new security requirements within forty-five days.

On August 6, 1996, Clinton sounded even more determined. "We will not rest in our efforts to track down, prosecute, and punish terrorists, and to keep the heat on those who support them. And we must not rest in that effort," he said. "The second part of our strategy is to give American law enforcement the most powerful tools available to fight terrorism without undermining our civil liberties.

"As any of you have flown in recent days will have noticed, we're doing more hand searches and machine screening of luggage," he continued. "We're requiring preflight inspections of every plane flying to or from the United States, every plane, every cabin, every cargo hold, every time."

The final Gore Commission Report on aviation safety and security was released on February 12, 1997. Among its recommendations:

★ "Develop uniform performance standards, subject to FAA approval, for the selection, training, and re-certification of

X-ray screeners at airports. The consortium should also develop standards for screening security companies."

★ "Subject airline and airport employees to criminal background checks and mandatory fingerprint checks by the FBI."

★ "Use [an] automated passenger profiling system. The FBI, CIA, BATF [Bureau of Alcohol, Tobacco, and Firearms] should conduct research into known terrorists, hijackers, and bombers to develop profiles based on facts. Then, the consortium should develop a system by which airlines can routinely cross check passenger lists against law enforcement information in a way that won't compromise intelligence sources or civil liberties."

Clearly, Clinton and Gore knew about the serious threats to U.S. aviation. They talked tough; they had meetings; they issued reports; and they asked Congress for more money. Gore's report even boasted that he had visited Washington's Dulles International Airport personally in the summer of 1996, "saw airport and airline operations first-hand," and "discussed issues with front line workers."

In short, to their credit, they took responsibility for U.S. aviation security.

There was just one problem: while many of their recommendations were on the right track, they were never transformed into solid, effective, real world results.

Among other things, for example, we learned that despite the Clinton-Gore rhetoric, hardly any planes and bags were given thorough security checks. "According to industry experts," a *Boston Globe* editorial noted on October 11, 2001, "no more than five percent of all luggage checked at U.S. airports gets inspected by such [explosive-device detection] equipment. The percentage is likely to fall as restrictions on the number of carry-on bags lead to more luggage being checked."

What's the problem?

"The slowness of installing and utilizing the devices can be blamed on the federal government's half-hearted approach and the reluctance of airlines to take on the expense of operating and maintaining the machines," the *Globe* noted. "The government is paying for the devices, but on a schedule that is not slated to have all baggage checked until 2017. That's right: 2017."

On September 24, 2001, in the wake of the attacks in New York and Washington, I interviewed former inspector general Schiavo on *Hannity & Colmes*.

"Mary, I've got to tell you something," I began. "I think America's in a debt of gratitude to you. You have been sounding an alarm bell about airline safety for over a decade. I bet this is one case [where] you wish you were wrong, but you were not."

"I wish I was very wrong on this," she conceded. "I would give all I have to be wrong on this, but I and my former employees at the Office of Inspector General and many others had warned the FAA for well over a decade that problems were coming."

With radical Islamic sleeper cells in America today, we continue to face the threat of airborne attacks. We need to get serious about airport and airplane security. We need real baggage checks and background checks. We need far more armed federal marshals on our planes. And I believe that airline pilots should be trained in the use of handguns and armed.

In many other ways the Bush administration has moved in the right direction since 9/11. But they must move far more aggressively. The administration, for example, has opposed proposals to arm pilots—a position I think is wrong, and dangerous.

We also need to get serious about private aviation security. I travel by air quite a bit, and more and more often I fly on private planes when

I give speeches. What's totally amazed me is that there is absolutely no security if you fly on a private plane. No x-ray machines, no metal detectors, no baggage checks, no requirement to show a driver's license. Why not? Sometimes I'm flying on a Learjet over New York City, coming home from a speech at one or two o'clock in the morning, and it dawns on me: Who's keeping us safe from kamikazes on private planes? What's to keep a terrorist from chartering—or hijacking—a Learjet, filling it with explosives, and nosediving into Manhattan or the White House?

Now consider this: There are eighteen thousand private airports in America, some two hundred thousand private planes, and more than a half million private pilots. But as I sit here writing this, little or nothing is being done to ensure the safety and security of private aviation, or innocent Americans on the ground.

As of May 2002, when word began leaking out of possible threats involving private aircraft, the public began to sit up and take notice. We can only hope the government will follow suit.

Threat: "Dirty Nukes"

"For a few harrowing weeks last fall, a group of U.S. officials believed that the worst nightmare of their lives—something even more horrific than 9/11—was about to come true," reported *Time* magazine in March of 2002. "In October an intelligence alert went out to a small number of government agencies, including the Energy Department's top-secret Nuclear Emergency Search Team, based in Nevada."

What was so terrifying?

"The report said that terrorists were thought to have obtained a 10-kiloton nuclear weapon from the Russian arsenal and planned to smuggle it into New York City," wrote Massimo Calabresi and Romesh Ratnesar, adding that the information "tracked with a report from a Russian general who believed his forces were missing a 10-kiloton device."

How deadly would such a nuclear device be, particularly if it were left in a car or truck or suitcase? "Detonated in lower Manhattan, a 10-kiloton bomb would kill 100,000 civilians and irradiate 700,000 more, flattening everything in a half-mile diameter."

When the *Time* report broke, Alan and I interviewed Representative Curt Weldon, a Pennsylvania Republican, a senior member of the House Armed Services Committee, and an expert on Russia. I asked him point-blank, "Is it a strong possibility that one day, in an American city, we're going to turn on the Fox News Channel or local news [and] hear that a nuclear weapon has gone off in this country?"

"Well, as unfortunate as it is, there's much greater probability of that than there's ever been in the past," Weldon responded. "It may not be an actual nuclear bomb. I mean, in talking about miniaturized nuclear weapons today, small atomic demolition munitions, tactical nukes, there are thousands of them around the world. But what I think is a very real probability would be what we call a 'dirty nuke,' and that would be a conventional weapon with nuclear waste or nuclear material wrapped around it. That would not have the same devastating impact as a nuclear bomb, but it certainly would cause a psychological havoc."

The congressman described his discussions with Alexander Lebed, a top Russian general, who "was assigned by [then president Boris] Yeltsin to account for a hundred and thirty-two small atomic demolition munitions. These are commonly referred to as suitcase nukes. [Lebed] said, 'Congressman, I used all of the leverage I had as a president's adviser. We could only locate forty-eight.' Which meant that there were over eighty small atomic demolition devices with a capacity of one to ten kilotons that they just could not locate." Some people, including Russian President Putin, have since disputed this, but what if they are wrong? Nobody has given us a full accounting of these weapons.

Worse, Weldon told us that in the 1990s, the Clinton-Gore

administration "basically ignored violation after violation by Soviet officials." He said "these devices are not allowed to be transferred to unstable nations," but the United States had "caught Russian entities transferring these to Iraq three times," and all told, the United States had caught chemical, biological, and nuclear weapons technology leaving Russia thirty-eight times.

Threat: Ballistic Missiles, Weapons of Mass Destruction, and the Axis of Evil

"Our cause is just, and it continues," President Bush declared in his eloquent State of the Union address on January 29, 2002. "Our discoveries in Afghanistan confirmed our worst fears and showed us the true scope of the task ahead. We have seen the depth of our enemies' hatred in videos, where they laugh about the loss of innocent life. And the depth of their hatred is equaled by the madness of the destruction they design. We have found diagrams of American nuclear power plants and public water facilities, detailed instructions for making chemical weapons, surveillance maps of American cities, and thorough descriptions of landmarks in America and throughout the world."

President Bush made it clear that America's first goal would be to "shut down terrorist camps, disrupt terrorist plans, and bring terrorists to justice." We're well down the road to doing just that.

"Our second goal," the president continued, "is to prevent regimes that sponsor terror from threatening America or our friends and allies with weapons of mass destruction. Some of these regimes have been pretty quiet since September the eleventh. But we know their true nature."

The president put three countries on notice: North Korea, Iran, and Iraq.

"North Korea is a regime arming with missiles and weapons of mass destruction while starving its citizens," the president said firmly. "Iran aggressively pursues these weapons and exports terror, while an unelected few repress the Iranian people's hope for freedom. Iraq continues to flaunt its hostility toward America and to support terror. The Iraqi regime has plotted to develop anthrax, and nerve gas, and nuclear weapons for over a decade. This is a regime that has already used poison gas to murder thousands of its own citizens—leaving the bodies of mothers huddled over their dead children. This is a regime that agreed to international inspections—then kicked out the inspectors. This is a regime that has something to hide from the civilized world."

Crisp moral clarity. "States like these, and their terrorist allies, constitute an axis of evil, arming to threaten the peace of the world," he said. "By seeking weapons of mass destruction, these regimes pose a grave and growing danger. They could provide these arms to terrorists, giving them the means to match their hatred. They could attack our allies or attempt to blackmail the United States. In any of these cases, the price of indifference would be catastrophic."

What, then, would the United States of America do to counter such threats? "We will work closely with our coalition to deny terrorists and their state sponsors the materials, technology, and expertise to make and deliver weapons of mass destruction," the president announced. "We will develop and deploy effective missile defenses to protect America and our allies from sudden attack. And all nations should know: America will do what is necessary to ensure our nation's security." Including attack and invade foreign countries, if necessary.

Why? Because "history has called America and our allies to action, and it is both our responsibility and our privilege to fight freedom's fight."

President Bush received a thunderous standing ovation, and it's no wonder. In straightforward, honest, passionate terms, he had clearly explained the threats against us, accurately defined them as evil, and confidently outlined America's course of action. And Americans—and freedom-loving people around the world—embraced the man and his message.

Except, that is, for certain liberals.

Former President Jimmy Carter soon lashed out at President Bush's "axis of evil" speech. In a talk about terrorism to students at Emory University, Carter called Bush's remarks about North Korea, Iraq, and Iran "overly simplistic and counterproductive" and said, "I think it will take years before we can repair the damage done by that statement."

This surprised me, even coming from a liberal warhorse like Carter. What is it about Iran, for example, that the former president doesn't see as evil, as a threat? It was during his presidency, after all, that Iran took American citizens hostage for 444 days, humiliated America before the entire world, and funded, trained, and armed radical Islamic terrorists to attack Americans and Israelis all over the world. It is Iran that is building weapons of mass destruction and the missiles to fire them at Israel, NATO, and eventually the United States, and that vows to spread its vision of radical Islam across the entire planet, no matter how many people are murdered along the way.

How is it, then, that Jimmy Carter—a man for whom, in many ways, I have great respect, especially as a Good Samaritan ex-president—cannot see the threat before us?

A week after Carter's criticisms, and a month after President Bush's powerful speech, Tom Daschle launched his own barrage of public criticisms. He accused President Bush of seeking a military "expansion without at least a clear direction."

What could be clearer than these urgent threats: sleeper cells, airborne attacks, dirty nukes, ballistic missiles, weapons of mass destruction—chemical, biological, and nuclear? What could be clearer about the threats posed by Iran, Iraq, and North Korea, not to mention other radical Arab and Islamic states, Communist China, and even a nuclear-armed Russia, were she ever to fall back into the hands of Stalinesque anti-Westerners or fascist Russian nationalists? What could be clearer about the urgent need to hunt our enemies down and wipe them out before they destroy civilization as we know it?

Daschle, as you'll recall, voted *against* going to war with Iraq in 1991. He preferred to dither, doodle, dodge, and demagogue. He preferred to wait, when waiting was the most dangerous course of action. But he was dead wrong. I've interviewed Khidir Hamza, an Iraqi nuclear scientist who spent two decades building bombs for Saddam Hussein. I've read Hamza's chilling book, *Saddam's Bombmaker.* When the Gulf War began, Hamza reveals, Iraq was just months away from completing its first nuclear bomb. Operation Desert Storm averted a possible nuclear disaster. In 1991 President George Bush and our brave military forces set back Iraq's terrifying nuclear program. Unfortunately, during the Clinton-Gore administration, weapons inspectors were kicked out of Iraq. Today Saddam Hussein could be between one and three years away from finishing two or three nuclear bombs, Hamza told me. It's an assessment James Woolsey—Clinton's own CIA director—confirmed in an on-air interview with me.

Can there really be any doubt that when Saddam Hussein gets these terrible weapons, he will use them? He may attack Israel, our great friend and only democratic ally in the Middle East. He may attack Saudi Arabia. He may attack the United States directly. But we can be sure that he will attack us either directly or through terrorist surrogates he sponsors—unless we destroy him first. Clearly we must bring down Hussein's regime and destroy his military capabilities as quickly and decisively as we possibly can. If the likes of Daschle can't see that, they have no business leading the Senate, never mind the nation.

Unfortunately, Daschle offered other gratuitous criticisms.

"I don't think the success has been overstated," Senator Daschle said of U.S. military operations in Afghanistan, "but the continued success, I think, is still somewhat in doubt."

Senator Robert Byrd, a West Virginia Democrat, echoed Daschle's gratuitous skepticism, telling Pentagon officials charged with winning the war on terrorism that they should not expect "blank checks to be written" to fund the war effort. Who said anything about "blank checks"? Was Senator Byrd suggesting that the American people should shrink from their commitment to fund this war of self-defense, with our brave young men already in combat on the front lines?

Byrd also publicly declared that "we seem to be good at developing entrance strategies, [but] not so good at developing exit strategies." Perhaps Byrd doesn't yet have a full grasp of the long war against terrorism before us. But it certainly sounds like he was seeking to score political points by asking a question no one can yet answer. The truth is, the war on terrorism is like no war we've ever fought: its end cannot be measured precisely—but that is no reason to impugn its crucial importance to our security as a nation.

Next, Senator Kent Conrad, a North Dakota Democrat and chairman of the Senate Budget Committee, accused conservative Republicans of "bootstrapping this operation into adopting the dramatically higher defense spending they'd been proposing before this ever happened. . . . That's the budget tactic they're using."

Of course conservatives are pointing to the crisis of three thousand Americans being killed by a global terrorist network, the threat of more attacks, and a war of self-defense to begin rebuilding America's radically downsized military. That only makes sense. What doesn't make sense is the liberal conclusion that a military buildup in this environment would be anything but mandatory.

Moreover, why do liberals so bitterly resist building a missile defense shield in an age of such terrifying technology and radical regimes? Why do they cling to their willful blindness about these emerging catastrophic threats? A series of recent reports—the 1998 Rumsfeld Commission Report on the rapidly growing ballistic missile threat, the 1999 Cox Commission Report detailing Chinese espionage, nuclear weapons, and ballistic missile programs, and the 2002 unclassified CIA report "Foreign Missile Developments and the Ballistic Missile Threat through 2015"—have made the threat chillingly clear. They outline how some countries already have the potential to launch a serious nuclear missile attack on the United States. Others will have the same capacity within five to fifteen years. Why not augment our defensive capabilities? If we wait, history is clear: we will weaken, and we will fall behind. Yet year after year, liberals like Tom Daschle, Ted Kennedy, and Joe Biden stand in the way of urgent development and deployment of such vital defenses.

When we think of what kind of world we would like to leave our children, do we have any choice but to remain the world's only superpower, with the best defense forces money can buy?

SIX

THE PLEDGE, THE DECLARATION, AND PATRIOTISM

One of the unintended consequences of 9/11 was that it forced us all to take stock of our values—to make some hard-nosed choices about who we are, what we believe, and what we choose to teach our children and pass on to future generations.

Most of us instinctively rediscovered our deep and abiding love for our families, friends, and neighbors, our devotion to and love of our country, and our devout faith in a loving, holy God. Amid all the pain, sadness, and horror, we reaffirmed our love, patriotism, and faith. And we did so unashamedly.

We began flying American flags on our homes and cars and wearing pins of Old Glory on our lapels. We began attending church and synagogue for prayer and vigils. We began gathering in schools, fire halls, community centers, and VFW posts to express our solidarity. School kids began saying the Pledge of Allegiance again, singing Irving Berlin's great hymn of the twentieth century, "God Bless America," and decorating their schools with red, white, and blue flags, banners, and bunting.

For all the cynicism and divisiveness that seemed to dog us in the 1990s, suddenly we were brought together in a way that harkened back to the 1940s and World War II. We were all proud patriots again—with a few exceptions.

For many years now this country's values have been under attack by a persistent cadre of people eager to remove God and prayer from our public schools, denigrate our history and flag, and assault our culture and traditions. And sadly, September 11 didn't jolt them back to their senses. This fringe movement opposes overt displays of patriotism, especially in our schools and other public facilities, from waving the flag to reciting the Pledge of Allegiance to singing the national anthem and "God Bless America." But in many cases it's more than just the expressions of loyalty to the nation that rankle them. They also bristle at the Declaration of Independence and what they seem to think it represents.

In this chapter we'll examine this phenomenon—with special attention to attacks on the Pledge and contempt for the Declaration. We will examine the real reasons behind the opposition of these individuals, and I believe it will become clear that while they often claim to be merely holding up their side of the public debate, in truth their motivation is of a different order entirely. Too often what drives them is a basic revulsion for what this nation stands for, and that is tragic—and ironic, considering that in many nations they wouldn't have the freedom to register such dissent.

I PLEDGE ALLEGIANCE

Here are some choice snapshots from a variety of locations around the nation that illustrate the nature and magnitude of the problem.

Snapshot: Madison, Wisconsin

On Monday, October 8, 2001, liberals running the Madison Metropolitan School District voted three to two to ban schools from leading children in the Pledge of Allegiance.

They didn't just ban the Pledge, though. They also banned schools from singing the words to "The Star Spangled Banner." Instrumental versions were fine, they said. But the school board made it crystal clear: using the words of America's national anthem, even during a time of war, was forbidden—and that was final.

"We do have staff members that are as adamantly opposed to the national anthem as they are to the Pledge," said the superintendent of Madison's schools.

"Indoctrination leads to totalitarianism," one Wisconsin educator said, supporting the school board's actions, "and we're approaching that moment."

"I hope the good sense of teachers in the classroom will temper whatever jingoistic attitudes there are," said a school board member supporting the ban, worrying that a "flag-waving" approach to education would be harmful to children.

"Mandating patriotism is a really scary thing," said a first-grade teacher in Madison, refusing to lead her class in the Pledge. "It leads to nationalism and ultimately to fascism."

This attack on the Pledge quickly gained national attention. I certainly shone my spotlight on the controversy on radio and television, as did conservative and liberal talk-show hosts, columnists, and editorial writers all over the country. Two thousand incensed citizens called district leaders to protest. Nearly twenty thousand e-mailed. Others wrote letters to the editor, called radio talk shows, and organized neighborhood opposition to the decision. Some twelve hundred parents, students, and residents showed up at a school board meeting to argue against the ridiculous decision.

Leading children in the Pledge of Allegiance "makes our country as bad as Osama bin Laden [by setting up] a war between the believers and the infidels," insisted Annie Laurie Gaylor, head of the Freedom from Religion Foundation, based in Madison. Gaylor is an avowed atheist. She said on *Hannity & Colmes* that she refuses to let her sixth-grade daughter say the Pledge of Allegiance because it includes the phrase "under God." Moreover, she thinks what the Madison school board did was exactly right.

"I think that religious patriotism is very dangerous," Gaylor told me. "And when you combine the idea of country and God together, this is the most incendiary mix possible." She added that she believed the terrorist attacks on the United States were "faith-based," and an example of what happens when religion and politics are mixed.

"Are you against 'under God' in the Pledge of Allegiance?" Ann Coulter, a conservative constitutional lawyer, asked Alan on the same show. "Yes, I am, as a matter of fact," he said.

Fortunately, there was a public outcry against the school board's actions. One Madison parent told the board that "in your great zeal to protect the few, you have stifled the expression of the majority," adding that the school board had behaved like "arrogant, elitist, heavy-handed radical leftovers."

It was a great point, and it appears that this parent was speaking for most of Madison, and most of the country. In the end—under great public pressure and after more than eight hours of raucous debate and passionate chants of "USA, USA, USA"—the Madison school board voted six to one in favor of lifting the ban and letting schools lead kids in saying the Pledge or singing the national anthem.

Snapshot: Sacramento, California

In late September 2001, the children of Breen Elementary School, near Sacramento, California, were looking for a way to express their love of God and country and to help the families of September 11 victims. So with the help of parents and teachers they raised nearly $4,000, held a rally to honor the policemen and firemen who risked and lost their lives, and put up a sign on their school grounds that declared "God Bless America." This patriotic sign was a simple, heartfelt, and innocent expression of patriotism. But certain liberals didn't see it that way.

On October 3, 2001, the American Civil Liberties Union sent a letter to school officials demanding that they take the sign down immediately. The ACLU called the sign a "clear violation of the California and United States constitutions, as well as the California Education Code" and communicated "a hurtful, divisive message."

Thankfully, school officials refused to back down. "I would like someone to explain how 'God Bless America' hurts anyone," said the president of the Rocklin Unified School District board of trustees, adding that he was "disgusted" by the ACLU demand.

It was a great question, and it received this predictable and wholly unconvincing answer from Margaret Crosby, a lawyer for the Northern California branch of the ACLU: "By displaying a religious message, the Breen Elementary School is dividing its young students along religious lines." Furthermore, she said "school officials are hurting and isolating their schoolchildren of minority faiths when they should be supporting them and the values of pluralism and tolerance."

Kevin Brown, the superintendent of Rocklin Unified School District, exposed the absurdity of Crosby's position on *Hannity & Colmes.*

"Well, there's a backdrop to this issue, Sean," Brown told me. "When the tragedy happened in New York on September the eleventh, the student body wanted to get involved and help out, and they developed a program they phrased 'Coin for Courage.' They went about raising money to help support the relief efforts. They also learned the song 'God Bless America,' and as part of this patriotic, philanthropic endeavor, 'God Bless America' was put up on the school marquee in support of this civic activity."

Isn't this exactly what we want our kids to be learning and doing in our public schools?

Far too many liberals demand that "one nation under God" be ripped out of the Pledge or the Pledge banned altogether. They want "In God We Trust" erased from our coins. They want the Ten Commandments ripped off the walls of public buildings. What they fail to acknowledge is that these references to God are not intended to promote any particular religion, or even religion in general. They recognize and reinforce the historical and foundational principles of our great country.

Those who oppose these references are in a distinct minority, yet they seek to impose their views on the rest of us. What we have here is the tyranny of the disgruntled few. In this case in California, for example, the ACLU launched its attempt to ban "God Bless America" from an elementary school because one person—just one person—complained.

"I had a phone call from a parent who took exception to the phrase and felt we were in violation of the Constitution and asked that it be taken down," Brown told me. "I respectfully disagreed with her and her position . . . and she in turn then notified the ACLU and various media sources."

As Superintendent Brown made clear, they were not professing to endorse religion or promote or establish religion in any way. He also pointed out that the phrase "God Bless America" has been supported in other court decisions as a patriotic statement. And he added that members of Congress themselves stood on the Capitol steps, hand in hand, arm in arm, and sang "God Bless America" on national and worldwide television just days after September 11.

If it's good enough for America's leaders, then it should be good enough for America's schoolchildren.

Snapshot: Denver, Colorado

Check out this headline: "DEMOCRATS KILL REQUIREMENT FOR PLEDGE OF ALLEGIANCE."

I kid you not.

It was from the Associated Press—dateline: Denver—February 5, 2002. I remember reading it at the time and thinking that if it weren't so outrageous, it might actually be funny. Colorado Senate Democrats had rejected a Republican bill to help schoolchildren learn more about their country, their flag, the threats to their freedom, and the need to be united in defense of liberty.

But that wasn't all. Nine days later there was more news from Denver: "FLAG-DISPLAY MEASURE KILLED."

That was a *Rocky Mountain News* headline on February 14, 2002—a little liberal Valentine to the country. Sure enough, Colorado Democrats had killed a bill protecting the right of Coloradans to display the American flag in their workplaces and other public places.

The bill had been written in response to an incident in October, when the head of the Boulder Public Library prohibited employees from flying a 10- by 15-foot flag at one of the library's entrances. Local media outlets reported that library officials didn't want to offend anyone who didn't share such expressions of American patriotism, fearing that it might compromise the institution's "objectivity." Once again, though, public outrage eventually forced the library to put the flag back on display.

What was particularly offensive about this incident was that days later the library had no qualms about displaying something a little less mainstream: a collection of "brightly colored penises attached to a clothesline."

"If it hadn't been for the flags, visitors to the city's library and museum probably would have missed the penises. But now they are seeing plenty of both," reported the *Denver Post.*

Officials, of course, strenuously denied any connection between the two issues, but one couldn't help but wonder. "Somehow or another, the two issues were linked and misinterpreted," a library employee told the *Post.* "They thought we'd do penises but not flags, and that's not the case."

Representative Tom Tancredo, a Colorado Republican, was so disturbed by these events that he introduced legislation in Congress that would cut off federal funds from any government institution or private or public company that banned the display of Old Glory.

"If you are here in this country and you are somehow offended by this flag, I really and truly have only one message . . . get the hell out," Tancredo told reporters.

Many people shared the his anger, and I felt it was time to confront those that were attacking the flag, so I invited Colorado State Senator Ken Gordon, the Democrat who helped lead the charge against the Pledge of Allegiance and the flag-display bill, to appear on *Hannity & Colmes.*

"Senator Gordon," I said, "I'm glad you're actually taking this position because this is now the face of the Democratic Party, not only in your state but in the country. The Democratic Party in America is the party against the Pledge of Allegiance. I want all of America to know that's what you represent, taking the Pledge out of America's schools."

"You know that's demagoguery," Senator Gordon shot back.

"No, that's a fact."

"You know, whenever we're under stress, we do things like [putting] the Japanese in internment camps during the Second World War," Senator Gordon added moments later. Comparing the Pledge of Allegiance by schoolchildren during wartime to Japanese internment camps is just the kind of perverse thinking that drives so much of the Left's agenda. Only this bizarre mindset could envision such an illogical leap from patriotism to xenophobia. Yet that is the theme running through many of the incidents described in this chapter: patriotism is a destructive force that necessarily leads to intolerance and oppression of minorities and foreigners. It is this type of thinking—not their criticisms of government policy—that leads many conservatives to conclude that some extreme leftists are unpatriotic.

"Hey, wait a minute, Ken," I said, "you're going nuts here."

"I am a proud Democrat," Senator Gordon told me.

That statement speaks for itself, does it not?

Snapshot: The Olympics, Salt Lake City, Utah

On Tuesday, February 5, 2002—just a few days before Opening Ceremonies of the 2002 Winter Olympic Games in Salt Lake City—I got an interesting phone call on my radio show from Curt Kellinger, a New York Port Authority police officer who was in the thick of the battle on the day the terrorists attacked. He was a first responder and helped rescue people throughout the day. When the first tower went down, he was on the fortieth floor of the second tower. Tragically, he lost his partner on September 11. By God's grace, Officer Kellinger survived. He is, by every definition, a hero.

But on the day we spoke, Officer Kellinger had a problem. Athletes on the U.S. Olympic Team had heard that an American flag had been recovered at the World Trade Center site. They were right: it turned out there was a flag flying in front of the center that dreadful Tuesday morning. A tattered American flag had been recovered three days after the attack, and Officer Kellinger was keeping it safe in honor of all those who were lost that day. Initially there was a plan to burn the flag, but Officer Kellinger wanted to preserve it—the only flag flying over the trade center on 9/11—and his efforts paid off when he convinced them not to burn it.

Now the American athletes were asking if they could carry that flag into the Opening Ceremonies. That sounded fine to Kellinger, but not to the International Olympic Committee. Incredibly, the IOC decided not to let the U.S. athletes bring the flag into the stadium—because, they said, it was "too political."

This is absurd. Our American flag does not represent American interests alone; it is a symbol of freedom and represents the struggle of all civilized societies against tyranny and oppression in general and specifically the darkness of terrorism. The flag is hardly threatening to nations attending the Olympics but should serve to unify them, especially in this time of war. As Steven Push of Families of September 11 noted, "This is not a political issue. It's a humanity issue."

Officer Kellinger agreed. He told me, "The politics of all this is just beyond my comprehension. If our team carried that flag in, who in the entire planet would be insulted?"

As Officer Kellinger told the story of the IOC's position on my radio show, my listeners and I got angry—very angry. But more importantly, my listeners started to react. They called IOC headquarters and registered their protest. All I did was give out the number. My friend the Internet columnist Matt Drudge was listening, too. He picked up the story, punched out an article, and quickly posted in on his web site. That alerted millions more. Then the news wires picked up the story, along with media outlets in Salt Lake City and around the country.

As the pressure intensified, the whole thing exploded in the IOC's face. They backed down and agreed to let the flag fly. It seemed like a victory for the good guys—but the final chapter had yet to be written.

Two days later, I got another call—off the air—from a source within Kellinger's department, alerting me that Officer Kellinger's boss had called him on the carpet and reprimanded him for calling my radio show and taking the case public. He was told he couldn't escort the flag out to the Olympics. Officer Kellinger was being punished for standing up for what was right, and now he needed some help. All I did was tell my radio audience the story, give out the Port authority's phone number—and the rest, as they say, is history.

My audience began calling Port Authority officials and demanding justice. I had sources on the inside calling me and telling me the PA phone lines were melting down. We learned that Port Authority Chairman Jack Sinagra was forced to review the whole situation. The PA reversed itself within twenty-four hours, and Officer Kellinger and his heroic colleagues traveled to Utah and escorted the flag into the stadium, along with representatives of the New York Police and Fire Departments.

It was a remarkable turn of events, and it turned out well. That flag did fly at the Opening Games. That man *did* honor his country and his colleagues. The world did see Old Glory, tattered but undefeated. That full-color photo of the flag, Officer Kellinger, and the heroes that accompanied him did wind up on the front page of the *New York Times,* a happy ending to a wild story. But if a bunch of liberal bureaucrats all hot and bothered about political correctness had had their way, it never would have happened.

FROM APATHY TO DISDAIN

I respect the right, but not the wisdom, of liberals to object to the Pledge and other displays of good old-fashioned American patriotism. That said, I don't want them imposing their repressive views on our schoolchildren. And here is a pungent irony: it is the Left that is narrow-minded and intolerant on these matters, not conservatives.

It seems undeniable that a great number of people in this country, from all walks of life, lack a fundamental appreciation for this republic and the unique freedoms it offers. Some of this can be explained by simple disengagement, but there's often more to it.

As an example of the prevalence of apathy and ignorance about America's heritage of freedom, let me tell you a story. While I was working on this book, there was a little item about me in Jim Mullen's "Hot Sheet" column in *Entertainment Weekly* magazine. Mullen makes his living writing about who's hot and who's not, who's up and who's down, and one day he mentioned some of us folks at Fox.

"Greta Van Susteren . . . has the bags under her eyes removed and it's news," wrote Mullen. "Sean Hannity has his brain removed and no one mentions it."

It was harmless liberal sniping, and I got a kick out of it. So I invited Mullen onto my radio show for some fun, and being a good sport, he accepted. Little did he know that I was actually working on this chapter and thinking about the whole issue of the Left's disdain for the Pledge, so I figured I'd do a little experiment with him.

"If I asked you how to say the Pledge of Allegiance, I'm sure you could do it, right?" I asked Mullen on the air after we'd bantered around a bit.

"Probably not," he said. "It's been forty years."

"Let me hear you do it. Let's go."

"No. That's not a question I'm calling up to answer."

"No, no, no, come on, Jim, come on. Let's just say the Pledge of Allegiance so our country knows you're not a left-wing wacko."

Then Mullen tried to turn the tables.

"You tell me who is in the movie *In the Bedroom.*"

"Marisa Tomei and Sissy Spacek," I said.

"Very good. Very, very good."

"Now you say the Pledge of Allegiance or I'm not answering any more of your questions," I joked.

"Well . . ."

"Say the Pledge of Allegiance."

"And would I do that why?"

"You can't say the Pledge of Allegiance, can you?"

"You know, I don't know," Mullen told me. "But I'm not going to do it for you. I don't understand why that's a question. What does that got to do with anything?"

"And you're writing about my brains being removed?"

We both got a laugh out of it. But it was also instructive. I can't tell you how many times I've sent one of my radio producers out on the streets of New York on a Friday afternoon (we do man-on-the-street segments most weeks on my radio show) to interview people and see if they can recite the Pledge—and they can't. They don't even know the most basic elements of Civics 101. It makes me wonder: How we are supposed to remain "one nation" and "indivisible" if we don't teach the next generation the basics of good citizenship and respect for the traditions of our country?

DEEP-ROOTED DISDAIN

In the summer of 2001, a Tennessee state legislator by the name of Henri Brooks ignited a national controversy by refusing to recite the Pledge of Allegiance in the state capitol because she insisted the American flag was a symbol of racism.

Her move was quickly endorsed by Julianne Malveaux, a left-wing syndicated columnist, who told the *Washington Times*, "it's ridiculous for black Americans to recite the Pledge of Allegiance because its words are nothing but a lie. Just a lie."

How could I let that go? We immediately invited Julianne on *Hannity & Colmes* so I could question her about her outrageous comment.

"You actually said that?" I asked her, citing the *Washington Times* quote.

"Absolutely. I did say that. I stand by that. I consider Representative Brooks one of my heroes, quite frankly. I think she's a woman of courage."

"All right," I said. "Let me ask this question then. Do you not say the Pledge of Allegiance yourself?"

"I do not," she told me.

"How long has that been going on?"

"Probably since I was eleven or twelve years old."

"Eleven or twelve years old?"

"Absolutely. That's when I began to learn history and to understand the nature of our nation's inequalities and really to be stunned by them . . . and to look at these words, which are a promise, and to see how far we've come—you know, what the big gap is between the promise and the reality. I can't say a lie. I'll tell you something, Sean. It gets caught up in my throat like sawdust, and it won't come out."

"You know what's sad about this, Julianne? First of all, you talk about the promise [and the] reality. I see Julianne Malveaux as somebody who's very successful, has a nationally syndicated column, appears regularly in *USA Today*. She's often quoted in newspaper articles. She's often on television. I think America has been a good country for you, providing you opportunity and the freedom to even say the things you are saying tonight on a national television network. I think America has been pretty good to Julianne Malveaux."

"And I think I've been pretty good for America," she responded.

The problem, I told her, is that "young kids are going to hear you tonight, and what you're saying is 'America is this, America is that,' and what's sad is you are not telling them this is the greatest, freest, single-best country, with more opportunity that God ever gave man, and if you work hard and study and develop marketable skills, you will be a success and you can't fail." Why wasn't that her message?

This is a debate I've had with liberals for years, but I have to admit that after the terrible events of 9/11, I thought the debate would have changed forever. I was wrong.

In March of 2002, for example, I interviewed Bernie Ward, a left-wing radio talk-show host on KGO in San Francisco, about whether it made sense for teachers to lead children in saying the Pledge of Allegiance. I pointed out that, while some children of the 1960s counter-culture despise this country and the values for which it stands, most American parents want their children to say the Pledge of Allegiance and develop a deep love and respect for this country, even if we're not perfect.

"Do you know what they understand, Bernie?" I asked him. "That this is the greatest best country God ever gave man. You don't disagree with that, do you, Bernie?"

"God, you are so full of it," he shot back.

I kept at it, trying to get him to agree, just as a starting point, that America is the greatest country in the world. But he wouldn't do it. He kept hemming and hawing and interrupting me and asking me which is more patriotic: to vote or to say the Pledge. Both are acts of patriotism, of course. But Bernie wouldn't budge.

"You have a radio show," I finally told him. "You invite me on as a guest. I'll answer your questions. But you're on my show now. You can answer my question." So I asked one more time: "Is this the greatest, freest, best country God gave man, Bernie?"

"No," Ward finally announced. "Absolutely not."

"There you go," I said. "I want everybody in America to look at you. This is what's wrong with liberal America today."

The sad thing is, Bernie Ward is not alone. If indeed these types love America, they have a curious way of showing it.

DISDAIN ON THE BENCH

The most outrageous assault on the Pledge of Allegiance—and, arguably, on the moral underpinnings of our country—took place on June 26, 2002, just as this book was going to press. On that date, a

three-judge panel for the 9th Circuit Court of Appeals held that reciting the Pledge of Allegiance in public schools is unconstitutional
because the two words "under God" added by Congress in 1954 violate
the First Amendment Establishment Clause.

The plaintiff in the lawsuit was Michael Newdow, a doctor and
avowed atheist from Sacramento, California. He argued that the
teacher-led pledge violated his second-grade daughter's constitutional
rights, even though neither she nor any other students were required
to participate in the recital. According to Mr. Newdow, just having to
"watch and listen" to other students voluntarily state the Pledge
infringed on his daughter's rights.

Then, in an utterly bizarre turn of events, Judge Alfred Goodwin,
one of the two judges on the three judge panel, issued a stay against his
own ruling pending appeal to the entire 9th Circuit panel of judges. In
a telephone interview a few days after the ruling, however, the judge
was unapologetic. "It's not as far out as a lot of headline writers seem
to think," he said. But perhaps revealing more than he intended to
about his mind-set, he added, "I knew it would be an attention-getter."

That's an understatement. Almost immediately the Senate—
including every single Democrat—voted to distance themselves from
the horrendous ruling. In two successive resolutions—one on the very
day of the ruling and the other the next day—they voted 99 to 0 (only
the ailing Jesse Helms was unable to vote) to condemn the ruling and
to affirm their support for the words "under God." Also on the day of
the ruling members of the Senate recited the Pledge on the Capital
steps. The House passed a resolution condemning the 9th Circuit's
decision by a vote of 416 to 3. President Bush himself called the ruling
"out of step with the traditions and history of America."

Of course, the decision was preposterous and completely out of
phase with the framers' original intent. The Establishment Clause was
intended merely as a prohibition against the federal government establishing a national religion. It was not a bar to state government action,

much less to subsidiary entities like the public schools. But even more important, reasonable people would hardly conclude that such a voluntary recital in public schools remotely constituted an establishment of religion.

As of this writing, though, there is a bright side to this ruling, which is that it underscores just how far out of step liberalism has become with our founding traditions. Had there not been such an overwhelming reaction against the court's ruling, it is doubtful that Democrats would have scrambled so fast from their sacrosanct "separation of church and state" perch. Maybe they sense that the public has just about had it with their aversion to God in the public square.

Republicans would do well to keep this issue in the public eye through the fall 2002 elections. The ruling illustrates the critical importance of electing Republicans to the Senate (and elsewhere) who believe that the Constitution ought to be interpreted according to its original intent. Perhaps this will help Republicans demonstrate the high stakes in retaking the Senate majority so they can put an end to Democratic Senator Leahy's persistent obstruction of President Bush's judicial nominees. With any luck, by the time this book hits the shelves the 9th Circuit will have reversed its three-judge panel's regrettable ruling.

A GREAT CLASH OF VALUES

In 1977 Democratic Governor Michael Dukakis of Massachusetts vetoed a bill requiring public school teachers to lead children in the Pledge of Allegiance. When then vice president George Bush criticized his veto during the 1988 presidential campaign, Dukakis and his supporters went ballistic. They charged that Bush was impugning Dukakis's patriotism, and called the debate over the Pledge a "frivolous" issue.

But Bush wasn't questioning the governor's patriotism. He was questioning the governor's values. He was asking the country if it really wanted a leader who opposed teaching schoolchildren the value of pledging allegiance to a flag, a country, and a set of ideas and ideals that distinguish our nation from all others. When voters learned about and evaluated Dukakis and his left-wing ideology, his early seventeen-point lead evaporated almost overnight, and George Bush won the presidency in a landslide.

In 1984 a liberal protestor named Gregory Johnson burned the American flag outside the Republican National Convention. He was arrested, tried, convicted, and fined $2,000 for desecrating the symbol of our country. But sure enough, his liberal pals at the ACLU sued. They took the case all the way to the Supreme Court. Incredibly, on June 21, 1989, the liberal-leaning Court overturned Johnson's conviction, claiming there were First Amendment considerations.

So Congress passed a law making it a federal offense to desecrate the flag. But on June 11, 1990, the Court overturned that law. Next, Congress tried to pass a constitutional amendment protecting the flag from desecration. Although 84 percent of Senate Republicans voted in favor of the amendment, a stunning 64 percent of Senate Democrats voted against it, killing it in the cradle. Among those voting against protecting our flag: Al Gore, Joe Lieberman, and Tom Daschle.

Should we be questioning the patriotism of such men? No. But we *should* be questioning their values and qualifications for leading America and advancing the cause of freedom at home and around the world.

On the other hand, there are certain liberals whose patriotism is, I believe, open to legitimate question. After all, patriotism means loving your country, and there is precious little evidence of it from some of these people. I'm not afraid to challenge their level of patriotism or lack of it. And I'm not trying to suppress their free speech by saying so—though these types often cite the First Amendment as a specious diversion from their shameful behavior. No, this is not about their right to denigrate America; they have that right and I would never take it away from them. But likewise, they're not going to rob me of my right to expose them. When you consider how many people have fought under our flag and have died in the service of their country, the least we can do is hold out this flag as a sacred memorial to them. Liberals can still yell at the flag and curse at the flag, and they don't have to salute the flag or even pledge allegiance to it, but to honor those who served under it—they ought not be allowed to burn it.

These types refuse to recognize, and fail to appreciate, what we've accomplished as a people. They have no interest in teaching children about the greatness of America, that for all our faults we have been a beacon of freedom, progress, and hope for millions of people around the world. Indeed, as we have seen, some would rather burn the American flag than pledge allegiance to it.

They reject the notion that since its inception America has been a beacon of freedom for the rest of world. As we'll see in the next section (and again in the following chapter), they appear more ashamed than proud of our heritage and are doing what they can to make sure that our public schoolchildren see things the way they do. And they reserve particular hostility for the Declaration of Independence, astonishingly enough—for reasons we'll explore (and challenge) after considering a few examples.

THE DECLARATION OF INDEPENDENCE

In March of 2002—just six months after President Bush led America into war—the American Red Cross prohibited a group of public school children from singing about the Declaration at a Red Cross event. It also prohibited the seventh and eighth grade students of Orange County High School of the Arts from singing its "Heroes

Trilogy," a medley of "America the Beautiful," "God Bless America," and "Prayer of the Children."

Red Cross officials deemed such songs too political and too religious. They worried that such historical, patriotic songs in a time of war might offend someone's sensibilities. The whole thing was absolutely ridiculous and offensive—a textbook example of liberals hijacking American values at the expense of our children.

"The dispute centers only on our sensitivity to religious diversity and a preference for a music program that would be inclusive and not offend different populations participating in this event," read an official statement from the Red Cross.

Translation: Americans literally gave of their own blood so the Red Cross would have adequate supplies in case of more terrorist attacks against innocent American citizens, yet the Red Cross refused to allow American schoolchildren to sing about the Declaration of Independence and "God Bless America."

"We wanted songs representative of all races, all creeds," added a spokeswoman for the Orange County chapter of the Red Cross. "We are not a religious organization. We have to be neutral and impartial in all situations."

How would permitting the kids to sing these songs compromise the Red Cross's neutrality? Besides, shouldn't schoolchildren be free to sing about God and country in the presence of a nonreligious civic group? What is really so offensive about that anyway? This is what I mean in complaining about elitists who are hostile to our values. They don't merely want to protect neutrality and pluralism; they want to suppress the expression of our values. That's what they mean by tolerance—free rein to all views but those of the Judeo-Christian persuasion.

"The Red Cross is teaching these kids that some values can only be held privately and they have to be someone else in public," said Cherilyn Bacon, the singing group's director. "We have never had a complaint about the medley. People have cried when they heard it. I think the Red Cross is taking the issue too seriously."

She's absolutely right. Unfortunately, the Red Cross dug in its heels. So the students reluctantly decided to cancel the show rather than have their patriotic expressions scrubbed from their performance.

"I don't understand why we can't honor the heroes of September eleventh the way we want to," Nicholas Baragno, thirteen, told the *Orange County Register.*

"I just wanted to tell the heroes of September eleventh how much we appreciated what they did for the country," added Klarissa Mesee, fourteen.

THE WAR ON THE DECLARATION—CONTINUED

This was not an isolated instance of political correctness run amok. It was part of a pattern—of the Left's concerted attack on American history and culture.

In the first few months of 2002, for example, Florida legislators debated a bill that would institute a "Celebrate Freedom" week during the last week of every September. During such a week, students would study the founding documents of our country and recite the Declaration of Independence. A Florida state senator—a Democrat—told a local newspaper that students might be offended by reciting the Declaration, since minorities and women were discriminated against at the time it was written. A lawyer with the ACLU warned that the bill would violate the separation of church and state. Another Florida Democrat insisted that "September 11 has been used as a catalyst or an excuse for a whole lot of bad legislation." A liberal columnist warned that conservatives were trying to "turn the state's educational system into the PTL Club." Another liberal columnist wrote an article whose headline read, "RELIGIOUS RIGHTS ACTING LIKE U.S. VERSION OF THE TALIBAN." Yet another Florida Democrat wanted a provision in the bill allowing students to opt out of reading the Declaration of Independence.

Florida isn't the only place where this battle rages. Since 1989, conservatives in the New Jersey legislature have been trying to pass a bill requiring schoolchildren to memorize and recite each morning a passage from the Declaration of Independence:

> We hold these truths to be self-evident, that all men are created equal, that they are endowed by their Creator with certain unalienable Rights, that among these are Life, Liberty and the pursuit of Happiness.—That to secure these rights, Governments are instituted among Men, deriving their just powers from the consent of the governed. . . .

Understandably, these lawmakers are concerned that too few kids know much about our founding. They're concerned that public schools today don't competently teach American history and that our MTV generation has little understanding of or appreciation for the patriots who sacrificed their lives so that we might live free.

Yet as surely as the sun rises each morning over the Jersey Shore, Garden State liberals have been fighting this bill tooth and nail and defeating it every year. Most recently, in June of 2001, the bill was defeated 39 to 38.

Some liberals have attacked the Declaration as sexist. Others have charged it's racist. Still others object to its reference to the Creator. "I would never allow my grandchildren to stand in class and repeat these words," declares New Jersey State Senator Wayne Bryant, a Democrat from Camden. "It's another way of being exclusionary, unfeeling, insensitive to a large majority of the population."

This is the founding document of the United States of America we're talking about. Of course the Founders weren't perfect, but they were brilliant and courageous in their foresight. They enshrined a vision of our country's highest ideals, ideals that would in time open the doors of true liberty and equality for all people, including women and minorities. For this they are to be celebrated and admired.

"This does not apply to me as a woman; this does not apply to me as a minority," insisted New Jersey Assemblywoman Bonnie Watson Coleman, also a Democrat. "In our hearts we know this is meaningless."

How far we've fallen from our sense of mission, our priorities, our awareness of history, when an elected representative in a state that was part of the original thirteen colonies can describe the Declaration of Independence as meaningless.

Of course its principles and values apply to women and minorities. In 1776 our Founders—many white, slave-owning men to be sure— set a standard higher than even they themselves could reach. But it has been the standard for which we've been striving ever since. It's been our North Star during times of moral fog and confusion. Indeed, it continues to be an inspirational guiding light today, not just for Americans but for people all over the world.

Still, I've interviewed many liberals on radio and television, and I can tell you from personal experience that they routinely reject Thomas Jefferson and his Continental colleagues as nothing more than a bunch of dead white bigots.

In June of 1999, for example, Alan and I interviewed New Jersey Assemblyman Michael Patrick Carroll, author of the Declaration bill, and Gloria Allred, a renowned feminist attorney. Gloria is smart and savvy, but she's also an absolute caricature of a left-winger. Alan began by asking her point-blank what's wrong with having kids recite a portion of the Declaration every day.

"Well, what's right about it?" Gloria replied. "I mean, you were right, Alan, when you suggested that at the time of the writing—[and] still today in 1999—women do not enjoy full and equal rights under the United States Constitution."

"I don't want to change history," she added a few moments later, "but I do want our living history to be different for our daughters. I do want our daughters to not be second-class citizens but to enjoy equal rights under the law. . . . Why don't we add a sentence to all of that and say we hold this truth to be self-evident in 1999 that girls are equal to boys."

I was dumbfounded. Apparently Gloria still sees America as inherently sexist and unfair, despite all the progress women have made over the last two hundred years. Apparently she doesn't realize that the Constitution actually *does* guarantee the equal treatment of men and women. "You're almost implying that the country was not worth form-ing," I told her. "You wouldn't be here debating this today if it weren't for the mechanism that they put in place to right wrongs and injustices like we've been able to do. Don't you see the fault in your argument?"

"No, I don't at all," she insisted, admitting that she understood the practical reasons the Founders set up the country the way they did but conceding no ground on her disagreement with the basic premise that they were great men who created a great nation despite the flawed times in which they lived. Like many feminists, she appears to see everything, including our founding, through the lenses of gender and racial adversity.

"The purpose is once again to assert white male privilege and dominance in this country," Gloria went on to say, ripping the idea of reciting the Declaration of Independence.

"Maybe we could settle this whole thing out of court," Alan inter-jected, talking to Representative Carroll. "What if we were to change it to say, 'all people are created equal'? Michael, do you have a problem with that?"

"Well, yeah, I do," Carroll responded, "because again it changes the Declaration. It goes back and in effect makes the Declaration po-litically correct."

That's exactly it. Modern liberal elitists simply won't leave history alone—they insist on conforming it to their own liking. Because they are ashamed of our past, they want to modify it and in the process delete essential features of it, including the Declaration.

"This smacks of the idea that children are empty sacks that need to be filled," Susan Mintz, the superintendent of schools in Medford Township, New Jersey, once told a *New York Times* reporter. "It seems as if the bill's proponents are looking at injecting this rote knowledge as a vaccine against something," she said, adding that "it's a little scary. If you come out against this bill you're un-American. Your patriotism is in question. That smacks of something in history, too."

Young children aren't being taught the stories of the men and women who built this country from the ground up. They aren't learning about the bravery and sacrifice that exemplified the character of our Founders and our greatest civic, military, and political leaders over the past two hundred–plus years. Sadly, public educators are too often teaching our children only the negative aspects of our history and completely ignoring the essential truth that America is unique—in a positive way—and has been and remains a model for other nations. This is a matter that needs to be corrected because it is unhealthy for an entire generation of people to be infused with utterly false and slanderous notions of America.

THE REASONS BEHIND THE RHETORIC

There are several reasons, beyond their rhetoric, that the Left fiercely resists teaching America's children the Declaration of Independence in our public schools today. Here are just three:

First, liberals absolutely abhor and militantly reject the Founders' belief in absolute truth. America's Founders believed deeply in certain fundamental truths about life, liberty, and the nature of man. In fact, they believed—they weren't just inserting lofty-sounding but meaningless platitudes in the document—that such truths were "self-evident."

By sharp contrast, the Left embraces moral relativism with an arrogant tenacity. The existence of absolute truths would mean that liberals couldn't ignore certain "unalienable rights," such as the supremacy of the right to life, because it would mean they weren't free to amend them at their whim.

When everything is relative, the distinctions between right and wrong and good and evil are obviously blurred. This suits the dogma and purposes of the Left. Yet nothing could be further from the expressed beliefs and intentions of the Founders—which is precisely why the Left omits those history lessons and lobbies for the abandonment of any fixed standards.

Second, liberals flat-out reject the Founders' belief that we were "created" and "endowed by our Creator" at all, much less with unalienable rights. To teach children that we were "created equal" requires teaching them that we were created in the first place. And teaching children that there is a Creator—an all-powerful, supernatural God—is abhorrent to the Left. This was routine in public schools prior to two Supreme Court decisions in the early 1960s.

The existence of God means the existence of absolute truth and fixed moral standards. Moreover, acknowledging the existence of God means conceding that the federal government is not the highest authority.

Third, and perhaps most prevalent, liberals condemn the Founders for preaching equality while refusing to end the hideous inhumanity of slavery. This charge, in which the Founding Fathers are dismissed as bigots and racists, has been repeated often by the Left. For this reason I'll spend some time addressing it.

In declaring independence from England and in adopting a Constitution, the Founders believed it was critical that the colonies (later the states) act unanimously. And the truth is that the Founders struggled with the issue of slavery when debating both the Declaration and the Constitution. In autobiographical notes penned in 1821, Thomas Jefferson, who wrote the first draft of the Declaration of Independence, recalled that when the Congress was considering the Declaration, "[t]he clause . . . reprobating the enslaving the inhabitants of Africa was struck out in [compliance] to South Carolina and Georgia, who had never attempted to restrain the importation of slaves, and who on the contrary still wished to continue it."

In October 1787, James Madison, perhaps the most important contributor to the Constitution, wrote to Jefferson about the debate at the Constitutional Convention over slavery: "Some contended for an unlimited power over trade including exports as well as imports, and over slaves as well as other imports; some for such power, provided the concurrence of two thirds of the power, with an exemption of exports and slaves, others for an exemption of exports only. The result is seen in the Constitution. S. Carolina & Georgia were inflexible on the point of slaves."

And the result Madison referred to was the framers' attempt to limit the institution of slavery in the Constitution itself. Article I, Section 9 of the Constitution empowered Congress to abolish the importation of slaves by 1808. Moreover, Article I, Section 2 effectively reduced the number of slave state congressmen who could serve in the House of Representatives—thereby limiting the influence of the slave states in Congress—by counting slaves as "three fifths of all other persons" for purposes of apportioning representation.

This three-fifths language has understandably been the subject of great controversy over the years. But what has usually been absent from the discussion is the fact that commentators at the time saw the framers' efforts as an important first step toward eventually abolishing slavery. For example, in the fall of 1788, Philadelphia's *Independent Gazetteer* published several essays about the Constitution, including this observation:

The importation of slaves from any foreign country is, by a clear impli-cation, held up to the world as equally inconsistent with the dispositions and the duties of the people of America. A solid foundation is laid for exploding the principles of Negro slavery, in which many good men of all parties in Pennsylvania, and throughout the union, have already concurred. The temporary reservation of any particular matter must ever be deemed an admission that it should be done away. This appears to have been well understood.

In addition to the arguments drawn from liberty, justice, and reli-gion, opinions against this practice, founded in sound policy, have no doubt been urged. Regard was necessarily paid to the peculiar situa-tion of our southern fellow-citizens; but they, on the other hand, have not been insensible of the delicate situation of our national character on this subject.

Slavery continued to haunt the Founding Fathers after the adop-tion of the Constitution. In March 1790 Thomas Paine, who helped foment the American Revolution with his widely read pamphlet "Common Sense," wrote to Dr. Benjamin Rush (himself a signer of the Declaration): "I wish most anxiously to see my much loved Amer-ica—it is the country from whence all reformations must originally spring—I despair of seeing an abolition of the infernal traffic in Negroes—we must push that matter further on your side [of] the water—I wish that a few well instructed Negroes could be sent among their brethren in bondage, for until they are able to take their own part nothing will be done."

And, of course, some seventy years later, the issue came to a head. From 1861 to 1865, fellow countrymen, friends, and even relatives took up arms against each other in the bloodiest war in American history—in which the fate of both the Union and slavery were decided.

Slavery will always be a deplorable stain on our history. Without the principles enunciated in the Declaration of Independence and adopted by the colonies, however, there would have been no American Revolution, no United States, no Constitution, and no war to end slavery. The Declaration is a document that celebrates liberty. Its authors and signers deserve our praise and thanks, *not* our disdain, for they put in place the ability to correct wrongs and injustices so that future generations would proudly want to say the Pledge of Allegiance.

[SEVEN]

SETTING PARENTS FREE

Too many of our public schools have become liberal indoctrination centers, cultural battlegrounds, and poorly performing graduation factories.

Modern liberal elitists, since the 1960s, have largely taken control of our educational establishment. Motivated by an aversion to many of the traditional values and principles upon which this nation was founded (and to Western civilization in general), they deemphasize and distort them in their revised versions of history. Instead of proudly acknowledging our heritage, they apologize for it. Where fair-minded students of history see America as a grand and noble experiment, they see it as racist, sexist, homophobic, and unjust.

The Left seeks to extinguish virtually all references to God, Judeo-Christian beliefs, and the Bible in our public schools. And tried-and-true educational techniques are frequently replaced with unproven experimental teaching methods.

This has all contributed to a rapid decline in the quality of education our students receive.

Sure, there are great schools and great teachers out there. But overall, K–12 education in America is an unmitigated disaster. It's appalling, immoral, and unjust—especially in our inner cities—and the only way to really fix it is to get radical: set parents free to choose the schools and teachers and systems that work best for their kids. That's not going to be easy. In fact, it's going to take a minirevolution to make it happen. But that's exactly what we need.

Too many children in our country are being cheated. Too many are being warehoused. Too many are being denied their civil right to a decent education and a shot at the American dream. And I, for one, cannot sit by and watch the destruction of another generation's future.

If we as a nation truly solve our educational problems—if we ensure that all our kids are free to go to schools where they will really learn to read, write, think, do math and science, and understand the difference between right and wrong—we'll go a long way toward solving a wide range of other social problems, from drug use and crime to teen pregnancy and welfare dependency. But if we continue to trap kids in dirty, dangerous, dilapidated, drug-infested schools, we'll be playing Russian roulette with six bullets.

A NATION AT RISK

The crisis in American education isn't new—and that's what's so infuriating. In April of 1983, a landmark study entitled "A Nation at Risk" was presented to President Reagan and to the American people by the National Commission on Excellence in Education. Its findings were startling. Its conclusions were sobering.

"The educational foundations of our society are presently being eroded by a rising tide of mediocrity that threatens our very future as a nation and a people," the report began, adding that "if an unfriendly foreign power had attempted to impose on America the mediocre educational performance that exists today, we might well have viewed it as an act of war."

Worse, the report found that the gains in student achievement we'd made in the 1950s and early 1960s—in response to the urgent needs of the Cold War to outperform the students of the Soviet Union and other Communist countries—had long since been squandered by an educational bureaucracy that no longer placed an emphasis on high standards and world-class achievement.

"We have, in effect, been committing an act of unthinking, unilateral educational disarmament," the report concluded.

Liberals say we're not spending enough money to solve the problem. But that's simply not true. We've invested hundreds of billions of dollars in "reforming" our public schools over the past two decades, and we're spending more today than at any time in our history. Adjusting for inflation, we spend about 70 percent more on education today than we did when "A Nation at Risk" was being researched. Federal spending on education alone has nearly doubled since the 1980s. During the 1999–2000 school year, combined federal, state, and local spending on kindergarten through twelfth grade education hit $389 billion—about $100 billion more than we spent on defense—and in constant dollars, average per pupil spending on K–12 education soared from $3,367 in 1970 to $6,584 in 2000.

The question isn't whether we're spending enough money. We are. The question is whether we're seeing dramatically improved results as a result of our investment. The painful truth is, we aren't. In fact, the results have been disastrous.

In 1998 former education secretary Bill Bennett assembled a team of education experts to review the state of American education fifteen years after the release of "A Nation at Risk." What they found was depressing. In a new report, "A Nation Still at Risk," Bennett and his team found that since 1983:

★ "More than 10 million Americans have reached the 12th grade without having learned to read at a basic level."

★ "More than 20 million have reached their senior year unable to do basic math."

★ "Almost 25 million have reached 12th grade not knowing the essentials of U.S. history. (And those are the young people who complete their senior year.)"

★ "In the same period, more than 6 million Americans dropped out of high school altogether."

★ "In 1996, 13 percent of all blacks aged 16 to 24 were not in school and did not hold a diploma."

★ "Seventeen percent of first-generation Hispanics had dropped out of high school, including a tragic 44 percent of Hispanic immigrants in this age group [aged 16 to 24]."

How is this possible? How have we let things get so bad?

THE URBAN EDUCATION ABOMINATION

Actually, it's worse.

Here in New York City, where I work each and every day, the public school system is an absolute abomination. Sure, there are some great schools. But the grim truth is that hundreds of thousands of children in this city are being locked into institutionalized failure.

Last year, for example, 36 percent of the students in the city's high schools failed to meet the state's English and math standards. Worse, 56 percent of the children in the city's elementary schools and 77 percent of the kids in the city's middle schools failed to meet those standards. At one school in the Bronx, an unbelievable 73 percent of the kids flunked basic reading. The year before, 60 percent had flunked. And as if all that weren't bad enough, city and state education officials didn't seem to have a clue about what was going wrong.

"Is it teaching?" asked state Education Commissioner Richard Mills. "It is teaching practice? Is it the material? Is it the work students are doing? What are they reading? What are they writing? What kind of math problems are they doing?"

What are these people doing with our tax dollars if they don't even know the answers to these questions?

For one thing, they're sending a record number of these kids to summer school. During the summer of 2001, for example, nearly one in three students in the New York City public schools—almost 330,000 kids, at a cost of some $175 million—were required to attend summer classes because they couldn't pass basic proficiency tests during the regular school year. But even that hasn't done much good. In recent years, school officials have actually held back a record number of students because they couldn't pass their tests even at the end of summer school.

In New York as well as nationwide, we also have an incredibly serious teacher quality crisis. Sure, many teachers around the country are first-rate. But far from all of them are. I remember a report back in the late 1980s indicating that almost one in five young people applying to become public school teachers were actually flunking their certification exams, even though the exam itself was believed by critics to be too easy to begin with, so that even those who pass aren't exactly up to snuff.

There was an almost unbelievable story in the *New York Post* not long ago about a Brooklyn social studies teacher who wrote a series of letters to the editor defending teachers against the charge that they weren't doing a good enough job. There was just one problem: the letters were chock-full of spelling errors. The teacher even misspelled the name of the course he taught, "socail studies," the *Post* reported, though he'd passed the state licensing exams. What was the teacher's defense when informed of all his misspellings? "It's just my personality," he said. "Sometimes, I just get overexcited, don't read over my work, and my shortcomings come out. But as far as my own flaws go, my own writing doesn't reflect how I teach in the classroom."

It's not just New York, of course. This educational abomination is evident in cities all over this great country, and it infuriates me. Who will stick up for these kids? Who will see that they have a chance in life? Who will be their advocate when the very school system designed to help them is their worst enemy?

JOE CLARK IS RIGHT

You think I'm critical of urban education? You should meet Joe Clark. The African-American former principal of Eastside High School, an inner city school in Paterson, New Jersey, Clark is practically a legend in the history of modern public schools. Almost single-handedly he battled the entire liberal public school establishment in his attempt to drive drug-pushers and gang-bangers and other deadbeats from the high school he ran. He fought to raise standards. He fought to inspire teachers and students. He fought to give parents and their children and their community some hope where most hope had been lost. His story was so inspiring that it was turned into a fantastic Hollywood film, *Lean On Me*. (If you haven't seen it, go rent it today.) But that didn't stop the powers that be from getting rid of him anyway, proving that no good deed goes unpunished when it comes to the liberal education bureaucracy.

I've interviewed Joe Clark many times over the years—not just because he knows the strengths and weaknesses of public schools inside and out but also because he's a hero. He's been there. He knows how badly parents feel when they see their kids trapped in schools that stink, and he understands the moral necessity of setting those parents free.

"I want to ask Joe Clark this," I told him one night on *Hannity & Colmes*. "I'm a big supporter of vouchers. We spend three hundred and eighty billion dollars a year on education. If you have those schools competing for that three hundred and eighty billion dollar prize, you're going to see excellence in education because the parents are going to send their kids to schools where there is discipline, where there are no problems, where their kids will get a good education, and we'd see test scores go through the roof. You agree?"

"Yes. I'm a supporter of *teachers*," Clark responded. "I'm a supporter of public education. And let me just state this for the record. Teachers by and large do a good job under adverse circumstances. They're overworked, underpaid, and denigrated for everything that goes wrong. But basically, public education—especially in the inner city—is brain-dead. It's the dog that won't hunt because it's antithetical to the premise of democracy, which is free enterprise."

When Alan began to disagree about vouchers, Clark didn't back down. "I can say this to you," Clark told him, "the Ku Klux Klan must be jubilant over the fact that the lives of black individuals in the inner city are being categorically destroyed."

I thought Alan was going to have a stroke.

"And let me go one step further," Clark continued. "If private schools are good enough for Congress and the Black Caucus, then it [should be] good enough for the downtrodden in the city!"

A few months later, Clark was gracious enough to come back on *Hannity & Colmes* and clarify his case even further.

"I certainly believe in the voucher system," he told Alan and me. "I think that the government school is antithetical to the premise of democracy, which is competition. If there is no competition, there can't be any accountability." A few moments later he added that "our [government] educational system is . . . an abomination. It's the epitome of fraud and hypocrisy when you're turning out in the inner cities black American kids [who are] impotent intellectually. That's wrong."

That immediately drew a strong reaction from Nadine Strossen, the left-wing, antiparental-choice national president of the American Civil Liberties Union.

"Well," Strossen protested, "I think it's wrong to remove control of education from the public and put it in the hands of private individuals who are unaccountable and then require other people in the public to finance it."

Clark responded by turning the tables on Strossen. "I'm sure that the Ku Klux Klan is ecstatic over you left-wing liberals" opposing parental choice, Clark said, not surprisingly sparking a heated reaction.

"You want to equate the liberals with being in the pocket of the Ku Klux Klan?" Alan said, incredulous. "Is that what you believe?"

"I want to equate them with doing something diabolical," Clark shot back, "especially to black Americans in this country, yes."

Later, Clark added, "When you begin to talk about vouchers, people begin to hiss and snarl like a vampire before a cross of garlic," noting that for liberals, "it's not about the young people, about the kids, it's about the almighty dollar."

Joe Clark is right. Black and Hispanic children are being destroyed by horrifying inner city public schools. Yet rather than fight for truly equal education for all children—regardless of race, creed, or national origin—liberals whine and complain about money. They focus on saving the educational establishment rather than serving the children's interests. They insist on controlling how every single education dollar is spent in this country, and cry bloody murder if anyone suggests that a parent could spend that money better than a bureaucrat.

Moreover, liberal hypocrisy particularly abounds on the issue of school choice. Rich and powerful liberals send their own children to private schools to escape the abomination of urban education, but they refuse to set urban and minority parents free to choose good, safe, clean schools for their own children.

Bill Clinton went to a Catholic school when he was a kid. Bill and

Hillary sent Chelsea to a private school rather than a Washington, D.C., public school when they lived in the White House. Al Gore went to a private school, and Al and Tipper sent their kids to private schools when they served in government. Ted Kennedy sent his kids to private schools. So did Jesse Jackson. In fact, one out of every five members of the congressional Black Caucus send their kids to private schools, as do 40 percent of the House of Representatives and a whopping 49 percent of senators who have school-age children.

This is precisely the kind of segregation Joe Clark and other school choice advocates are battling, and the kind of hypocrisy they detest.

THE FUTURE OF HISTORY

Let's look a little deeper and see how the elitist culture is downgrading and damaging the public school curriculum. American history is a story of hope, of progress, of a great adventure in pursuit of more freedom and opportunity for every man, woman, and child. We seek to pass on its lessons to succeeding generations. It's the right thing to do.

My wife, Jill, and I have two young kids, ages three and one. As they grow up, we want them to learn about our country's past. In this way they will come to understand the incredible sacrifices of past generations that make us such a great people and nation today. They will learn about America's central role in winning two world wars, including defeating Nazism and ending the Holocaust. They will learn about America's victory over the Soviet Union, including ending that regime's iron grip on most of Eastern Europe. By understanding and appreciating what came before, my children, and all children exposed to the story of America's past, will be better prepared to contribute to their generation and generations to come.

Jill and I will probably send our kids to Catholic schools one day. But it's not just because we want them to learn theology there. We simply want them in a disciplined, safe, and morally positive environment that reinforces the values and principles we're trying to teach them at home. We're not convinced that's going to happen in our public schools. We're fortunate in that if we choose private school for our children, I earn enough to pay for it. But many parents can't. They have no choice but to accept whatever quality of education is offered by their local public school.

And the problem isn't just the attacks on the Pledge or the rejection of the Declaration in our classrooms that I discussed in the previous chapter. Our public schools are dumbing down the curriculum, lowering academic standards, rewriting history, and promoting multiculturalism—which really means demonizing Western civilization.

For example, one Monday morning in January of 2002, I woke up, headed to the radio studio at WABC, and went on-line to scan headlines on FoxNews.com, the Drudge Report, and newspaper web sites from all over the country. One story jumped out at me. It was written by Ellen Sorokin, a reporter for the *Washington Times,* and it was about how the liberals in the New Jersey Department of Education had just written a new set of history standards. Just one problem: they'd left out any mention of George Washington, Thomas Jefferson, Ben Franklin, the Pilgrims, and the Mayflower. They also banned the word *war,* preferring that teachers talk about *conflict* instead.

How in the world are you supposed to teach kids the lessons of American history if you willfully ignore its most important people and events? The answer, of course, is: you can't.

Needless to say, Sorokin's incredible article—*which you should note was written after 9/11*—was my lead topic on that day's radio show. I expressed my distress at what New Jersey was doing to its schoolchildren, and my audience was troubled (and angered) as well. So you can imagine my satisfaction when I logged on to the *Washington Times* web site the following Saturday and read Sorokin's follow-up story: "FOUNDING FATHERS GIVEN NEW LIFE IN NEW JERSEY." It seems that state Commissioner of Education William L. Librera was reversing course. Now he was insisting that the New Jersey history standards reflect actual American and New Jersey history.

"The names of these individuals must remain in the curriculum," Librera said. "We have an obligation to make sure that our schools are helping our young people understand the critical role these leaders have played in our state's and our nation's history.

Sorokin further noted that Librera "also added the names of Abraham Lincoln, Franklin D. Roosevelt, John F. Kennedy, Lyndon B. Johnson and Martin Luther King, all of whom were missing from the original revised version of the standards."

The Left has engaged in this battle in state after state, and even at the national level. During the first Bush administration, conservative education experts set up a national committee to develop solid history standards. The goal was to give states, local school systems, and textbook publishers a set of useful voluntary guidelines they could use to craft stronger, more accurate, more useful history courses. It was a good idea—until the revisionists intervened.

By the time the national history standards were released, with input from the Clinton-Gore administration in 1994, American history had been radically reconstructed to conform to the liberal agenda.

The Ku Klux Klan was mentioned seventeen times. McCarthyism was mentioned nineteen times. Students were encouraged to understand the emotional appeal of left-wing labor unions, including singing songs about the Depression and "Which Side Are You On?" But never mentioned were Paul Revere, Thomas Edison, Daniel Webster, Robert E. Lee, the Wright Brothers, Alexander Graham Bell, Henry Clay, or Jonas Salk. George Washington was mentioned only in passing.

Gary Nash, head of the history standards project, defended such omissions, claiming it was time to "bury" American education's historic approach to teaching history. "Let's let the kids out of the prison of facts, the prison of dates and names and places, and let's have them discuss really important, momentous turning points in American history," said Nash. This is unadulterated psychobabble. Just ask any serious historian how much meaningful history can be taught without reference to historical facts.

In this case, fortunately, not even the liberals in the U.S. Senate could politically defend the revisionism. The Senate passed a resolution denouncing the Clinton-Gore national history standards by a vote of 99 to 1. The resolution also provided that no federal funds would be allocated to develop such standards in the future unless "the recipient of such funds should have a decent respect for the contributions of Western civilization and United States history, ideas and institutions." Unfortunately, despite the boldness of the resolution, the federal government had already wasted an incredible $2 million dollars developing these misguided standards.

AND IT'S MORE THAN HISTORY

As Bill Bennett's 1998 "A Nation Still at Risk" makes clear, the deficiencies in our educational system transcend the subject of history. Academic inferiority has pervaded every discipline. And a foreign enemy might as well have taken over the system—because forces hostile to academic excellence have subsumed it, sapping it of its vibrancy and of decades worth of effective teaching techniques. Anything that smacks of tradition—regardless of generations of proven success—the modern educator dismisses automatically as obsolete.

Thus in 1989 the National Council of Teachers of Mathematics issued standards that rejected "computation" and "other traditional skills"—that is, basic arithmetic. The council insisted that learning these basics would stifle the students' creativity. It actually took the position that students would benefit more from trying to develop math problem-solving strategies with their peers than from having experienced teachers impart math facts and other tools to them.

We also know that frustrated parents are increasingly turning to outside programs and games—not to mention home schooling—to teach their children to read the old-fashioned way, with phonics, rather than by ineffective whole-language methods. The phonics method, which worked for years in America during our periods of greatest literacy, teaches children to sound out words so that they can learn to recognize words they have never encountered. The whole-language method, developed not by reading experts but psychologists, teaches children to memorize words instead of giving them the tools to figure the words out for themselves. While the American educational establishment still doggedly adheres to the whole-language approach, the results speak for themselves. Those learning to read with the phonics method won't be swelling the illiteracy rolls.

THE EDUCATIONAL ESTABLISHMENT'S LEFT-WING AGENDA

We should expect trouble in our educational system when we realize that the main organization representing public school teachers, the National Education Association (NEA), is a glorified political lobbying group forever advocating policies that have little to do with education and everything to do with the liberal political agenda. Indeed, if the NEA were committed to the best interests of students, it would abandon its extracurricular political activities and rededicate itself to academic excellence. It would cease its efforts to keep inner city children trapped in inferior schools, and it would endorse the concept of competition in public schools. Instead, it serves as the primary obstacle to the best opportunity for real educational reform: school choice.

"The success of America's domestic security will depend on more than metal detectors and sky marshals," wrote Bob Chase, president of the NEA on November 1, 2001. "It also will depend on the values taught in America's public schools."

Chase is right. The question is: Which values will be taught, and by whom?

Let's take a look at some of the areas in which the NEA has invested its energy and dollars in the last few decades.

NEA Goal: Disarm Our Nuclear Forces. In 1982—at the height of the Cold War—the NEA passed a resolution calling for a nuclear freeze and the dismantling of our nuclear weapons arsenal. It passed a similar resolution again in the year 2000.

NEA Goal: Disarm Our Conventional Military Forces. Again in 1982—and in 2001—the NEA passed a resolution urging teachers to teach children "strategies for disarmament."

NEA Goal: Reject English as an Official Language. In 1987—and again in 1993—the NEA passed a resolution opposed to making English the official language of the United States because the NEA sees it as an attempt to "disregard cultural pluralism" and "deprive" people of "education, social services, and employment."

NEA Goal: Encourage Mushy-Minded Multiculturalism. In 1969—and again in 1995—the NEA passed a resolution calling for "educational materials and activities" that "accurately portray cultural diversity and contributions of ethnic-minority groups" while saying nothing about strengthening the teaching of American history or culture or the contributions of Western civilization.

NEA Goal: Encourage a Radical Sexual Agenda for Children. In 1969—and again in 2001—the NEA passed a resolution stating that "it is the right of every individual to live in an environment of freely available information and knowledge about sexuality" and that sex-ed programs should cover, among other things: the teaching of "birth control," "diversity of sexual orientation" (read: homosexuality and bisexuality), "sexually transmitted diseases," "homophobia," and "incest." Adding insult to injury, the NEA believes that teachers and health professionals "must be legally protected from censorship and lawsuits."

On February 8, 2002, the NEA board approved a plan designed to make schools safe and hospitable for gay, lesbian, bisexual, and transgendered students and employees. The plan encourages school districts to enact policies punishing harassment and discrimination. It also urges schools to make materials on homosexuality available for classroom discussions.

The NEA is hardly ashamed of its activities. In one of its press releases it boasted that it will try "to provide students, education employees and the general public with accurate, objective and up-to-date information regarding the needs of, and problems confronting gay, lesbian, bisexual and transgendered students." It adds the usual sanctimonious claptrap about tolerance, by saying that this information will be "nonjudgmental in terms of sexual orientation/gender identification."

One has to wonder how most American parents would feel if they knew that this country's self-professed "largest organization committed to advancing the cause of public education" was focused on its teachers imparting "objective" information to their children about homosexuality and alternative lifestyles.

Unfortunately, the NEA is not the only negative force in education. Throughout the country we see examples of educators themselves contributing to the problem. In Novato, California, a group of parents recently filed suit against the public school district "for allowing their children to see pro-homosexual plays at school without any prior notice or parental consent." These plays are produced under a school program entitled Cootie Shots: Theatrical Inoculations against Bigotry.

The plays themselves—shown to second through sixth graders—promote homosexual themes. One of the plays shows a boy wearing a dress and talking about cross-dressing. Another strongly suggests lesbian themes, with the female character becoming involved with a princess rather than a prince.

Here's another example of the problem. There was a case in Massachusetts in 2000 in which state education officials helped teach a workshop for students as young as fourteen called What They Didn't Tell You about Queer Sex and Sexuality in Health Class. The topics included sexual positions for gays, whether to use condoms, and how to have oral sex. It was all sponsored by the state's $1.5 million commission on gay and lesbian youth.

On *Hannity & Colmes,* I interviewed Scott Whiteman of the Parents' Rights Coalition, who attended the seminar and later helped expose what was going on there.

"Scott, you were there," I began. "You're speaking from experience in what you saw and heard. Was it discussed in front of fourteen-year-old kids, [subject matter like] oral sex and the ingesting of semen?"

"Yes," he replied, adding that "one of the comments from one of the public officials after discussing oral sex was 'I hear it's sweeter if you eat celery beforehand.'"

The whole thing was absolutely disgusting, and all the more so because it was being funded by the taxpayers. But as you might expect, the Left was not perturbed.

"Why shouldn't these kids get this information?" Ellen Ratner, a liberal commentator and Fox News contributor, asked on our show that night.

Later in the show, I asked Scott to note another graphic moment in the workshop.

"Besides talking about ingesting semen in front of fourteen-year-olds, they also talked about a practice called fisting," I said. "I want parents to know what was said. I want you to explain it because they need to know how radical it was."

"Right," Scott replied. "The question was, 'What's fisting?' The answer was, 'Sticking your whole hand in the A or P of another.' And then it was given advocacy when someone said, 'Why would anybody want to do that?' And a Department [of Education] employee said that it's an experience of opening up yourself fully to someone that you want to be that close and intimate with."

Even Ratner saw the problem now. "Listen, from what I understand from the people involved in the workshop, these two people may have gone overboard. But that does not mean we should not have sex education." She refused to see the connection.

Fortunately, after the Parents' Rights Coalition exposed the workshop and state involvement, one of the two Education Department employees who helped teach it was fired and the other resigned. Education Commissioner David Driscoll admitted upon reviewing the evidence that the course "went too far" and demonstrated a "lack of good judgment and perspective."

Not surprisingly, one of the employees sued, charging in part that "the actions of Massachusetts conservative groups and of my former colleagues at the Department of Education are unconscionable."

Let me give you just one more illustration of the educational establishment's preoccupation with nonacademic issues—often silly issues—other than academic quality. The latest obsession, apart from alternative sex, has to do with two long-popular childhood games: dodgeball and cops and robbers. It seems our elitists have decided that these games are harmful to students and must be banned.

The eggheads have dodgeball in their sights because it's too violent. They say it promotes cutthroat competition and discourages inclusiveness—that great buzzword that manages to inject itself into all the Left's worthy causes. Yes, even worse than the physical violence is that the game can hurt children's feelings because when they are hit they must leave the game. Oh my.

Just in case you think I'm making this up, let me cite Diane Farr, a curriculum specialist from Austin, Texas. She said that her school district banned dodgeball in order to "preserve the rights and dignity" of all students. "What we have seen is that it does not make students feel good about themselves."

Another antidodgeball activist insists that "at its base, the game encourages the strong to victimize the weak. . . . Schools preach the values of harmony, community and cooperation. But then those same schools let the big kids loose to see if they can hit the skinny nerd in the head with a hard red rubber ball." Couldn't the same be said for most popular sports? While they don't all involve the gradual elimination of the losers from the game, they do all teach competition and survival of the fittest. The winners win and the losers lose and they have to learn how to deal with it—just as in life itself.

The old neighborhood favorite cops and robbers has also come under attack. In a surprising number of places throughout the nation, schools are suspending and otherwise punishing students for playing the game with paper guns or simply using their fingers. Some kids have been run through the criminal justice system (and sometimes ordered to undergo psychological evaluation) for shouting feigned death threats in the throes of such games of make-believe. If I hadn't read about it with my own eyes I truly wouldn't believe it.

Tragically, the Left has virtually monopoly control over our public education system. Through the NEA and its 2.6 million members, it largely determines who teaches our children and what our children are taught. As a result, America's youth have been forced to pay a high price. Reasonable people can disagree about homosexuality, dodgeball, and various teaching methods in core subjects. But what is most troubling is that the educational establishment in this country seems to spend more of its time, energy, and money trying to impose its own values on our children than it does trying to ensure a quality education for them.

On October 1, 2001, I ran across the following headline on the *Washington Post's* web site: "SEPT. II PROMPTS LESSON REVIEW; EDUCATORS RETHINK MULTICULTURALISM." At first I thought the liberal *Post* was actually reporting that some of America's most liberal educators had decided to ditch several decades of multicultural madness. I couldn't have been more wrong. "Those people who said we don't need multiculturalism, that it's too touchy-feely, a pox on them," said Judith Rizzo, the deputy chancellor for instruction in the New York City school system. "I think they've learned their lesson. We have to do more to teach habits of tolerance, knowledge and awareness of other cultures. . . . We are preparing kids for the twenty-first century. We have to teach them what is."

Here was one of the highest ranking and most influential educators in the country—responsible for the education of hundreds of thousands of children in a city that had just been brutally attacked—claiming that the lesson of 9/11 was that we Americans needed to be more tolerant of others (presumably of those intolerant enough of us to have murdered three thousand of our fellow citizens).

Four days after the *Post* story was published, Lynne Cheney, the wife of the vice president and a former U.S. secretary of education, gave a speech in Dallas. Taking great issue with Rizzo, Cheney talked about the need to teach our children about our history as well as about other peoples and cultures. Unquestionably, Cheney is correct.

Parents have been fleeing to private schools, and many are turning to home schooling to escape the substandard education and distorted values being imposed on our children. But it is imperative that the educational establishment be held accountable as well, because far too many children have nowhere else to learn. And as criminal as it is to relegate children to academic inferiority, we must also be aware of the collective effect this will have on our nation itself. Simply put, this nation will not remain great unless it returns to its roots of academic excellence. We can do it—and we must.

TURNING A BLIND EYE

With all this talk about choice, shouldn't we ensure that all children have a choice in education—that market forces be allowed to exert themselves in the fundamentally important area of education?

Of course we should. Yet tragically, liberals either turn a blind eye to such outrageous and long-standing evidence of educational decline—repeating their mantra, "More money! More money!"—or argue against the evidence, suggesting that the situation is actually improving significantly in our public schools.

I run into this all the time, on radio and TV. A few years ago, for example, Alan and I had on the program a guy by the name of Elliot Mincberg, legal director of the People for the American Way Foundation, to debate educational reform. Sure enough, Mincberg tried to defend the indefensible.

"Look at the evidence of the rise in SAT scores overall in the last five years," Mincberg told me, apparently willing to say just about anything in opposition to giving parents more freedom to choose schools that work for their children.

"We went up five points, Elliot," I responded at the time. "Five points. I'd hardly call that dramatic."

It didn't matter. Mincberg, like many liberals, had already made up his mind. He wasn't interested in letting a few facts get in the way. Yet actually, even that 5-point increase in SAT scores is suspect.

In 1994, after all, the Manhattan-based College Board—the company responsible for designing and distributing the Scholastic Aptitude Test—artificially rewrote the rules in such a way that average

SAT scores shot up by almost 100 points. In other words, a kid getting a 424 on the old test would suddenly get a score of 500 on the new test, a process the College Board called "recentering." The College Board also took antonyms off the test and gave kids thirty minutes more to complete it. Critics cried foul. They warned that the SATs were being "dumbed down," that scores were being "inflated," and that when everyone forgot about the recalibration, people would think their students were getting smarter and scoring higher even if they really weren't. But that didn't stop the educational elites from going ahead and doing whatever they wanted—and sure enough, the following year the country was treated to headlines like "HIGHEST SCORES IN YEARS ON NEW SAT."

TIME FOR A FREEDOM REVOLUTION

Something has got to change.

Remember back in the 1930s and 1940s when our parents were going to school and the biggest problems we faced in our schools were kids talking in class, chewing gum, and running in the halls? Today, in addition to woefully inadequate standards, curricula, and test scores, we face an epidemic of teen pregnancy, suicide, drug abuse, gangs, metal detectors, school shootings, and a deeply disturbing disrespect for authority and for life in general. More government rules and regulations aren't helping. More government money isn't helping. Neither are more government studies and more political speeches.

So what's the answer?

The answer is to permit competition to improve education. That means more accountability. It means more public school choice, more charter schools, private schools, parochial schools, home schools, and even same-sex schools. It means more vouchers, tuition tax credits, and educational savings accounts—and whatever else it takes to break the nearly total government monopoly on K–12 education in this country.

School choice works because freedom works. Just ask parents in Milwaukee. Just ask parents in Cleveland, Indianapolis, Washington, D.C., New York City, and elsewhere whose children are participating in small pilot voucher programs. They'll tell you how grateful they are for the chance to give their kids something better than they had before.

Indeed, a 1996 analysis by Professors Paul E. Peterson of Harvard University and Jay P. Greene of the University of Houston found that both reading and math scores of students participating in the school choice program for at least three to four years were demonstrably higher than those of a control group in public schools. In fact, the professors concluded that "if similar success could be achieved for all minority students nationwide, it could close the gap separating white and minority test scores by somewhere between one-third and more than one-half."

I've discussed vouchers with liberals again and again, and their responses are always the same. A few years back, for example, I debated Julianne Malveaux (you'll remember her from the last chapter) on *Hannity & Colmes,* and sure enough, her argument was perfectly predictable: don't let my people go.

Vouchers would work for both parents and students. The problem isn't the voucher program. The problem is that closed-minded liberals won't let the program expand so every parent has the freedom to choose.

"Come on," Malveaux shot back. "What you're saying here is they love it. If they love it, that's fine. But loving it is not a sufficient educational value."

But that was hardly the point, I reminded her. Parents—especially black and Hispanic parents—love school choice for a very specific reason. "Because it works."

Malveaux demanded that I prove it. Fine. Let's prove it.

First of all, kids who go to Catholic schools—even in urban areas—tend to do better academically than those who attend public schools. It's undeniable. A 1990 Rand Corporation study of New York City students found that only one in four public high schools students graduated, while 95 percent of Catholic students graduated. Moreover, only 16 percent of public school students took the SATs (however flawed), while a full 75 percent of students in Catholic schools did.

It's no wonder, then, that the Milwaukee school choice program has been a huge success and that it's gained a surprisingly diverse group of admirers along the way. Launched in 1990, it was a truly bipartisan effort, supported by then governor Tommy Thompson, a white conservative Republican, and State Representative Annette "Polly" Williams, a black liberal Democrat who ran Jesse Jackson's presidential campaigns in Wisconsin in 1984 and 1988. More than ten thousand low-income (and mostly minority) students participate in the Milwaukee program. During the 2001–2002 school year, they used vouchers worth about $5,700. Ninety-one participating private and parochial schools participate in the choice program, with great success.

Though opponents strenuously objected, Representative Williams stood firm. "Low-income families are not dumb," she said. "They're just poor. You give them money and you can't tell the difference. . . . Choice is the best thing that has come around for my people since I've been born. It allows poor people to have those choices that all those other people who are fearing it already have."

Will giving parents choice harm the public schools? Just the opposite, she says.

"We're constantly funding failure" in the public schools, says Williams. "We need to begin funding success and excellence."

Polly Williams is absolutely right, says one of the biggest supporters of the Milwaukee school choice program—Howard Fuller, the man who used to be the superintendent of the Milwaukee Public Schools. Fuller completely rejects the notion that public schools are threatened in any way by giving parents the freedom to make decisions on behalf of their children. In fact, he's repeatedly and bravely taken on his colleagues in the public school establishment when they've tried to criticize, undermine, or destroy the city's school choice experiment.

Also cutting against the grain in support of school choice is Milwaukee mayor John Norquist. But he's no George W. Bush "compassionate conservative" Republican. He's a Democrat, and darn proud of it. He, too, rejects the attacks made by fellow liberals against parents. There's nothing wrong, he points out, with creating real competition in education. Nor is there anything wrong with letting religious schools compete with public and private schools to win the trust and support of parents.

"There's something fundamentally wrong with a system where what the parents think isn't very important," says Mayor Norquist, dismissing left-wing attacks against religious schools. "For kids in our inner city, there's greater threats to their lives than religion."

Norquist is exactly right and deserves great credit for standing up to the liberal naysayers in his own party. When then vice president Al Gore attacked Milwaukee's school choice program during a speech to the antivoucher NEA, for example, the mayor and his team took exception to their party leader's remarks.

"School choice will not harm public schools; in fact it will push them to improve," said Norquist spokesman Jeff Fleming. "School choice is a reality in Milwaukee, and we invite the vice president to visit and see the results: improved educational opportunity for all Milwaukee students."

As a Democrat, was Norquist once skeptical of school choice?

Yes, he was, Fleming told the reporter. "But Representative Williams helped change his mind."

Good for her.

* * *

Other evidence in favor of school choice is mounting.

In February of 2002, researchers at Harvard and the University of Wisconsin released the findings of their three-year study of a voucher-like school choice program in New York City. Unlike Milwaukee, the vouchers in New York are paid for by a charitable foundation, not by taxpayers. But beginning in 1997, some thirteen hundred vouchers—called scholarships—each worth $1,400 have been used each year by low-income elementary school students who qualify for the federal school lunch program.

The results have been fascinating. In the first year of the program, twenty thousand families applied for just thirteen hundred slots, a powerful testament to the interest poor parents have in choosing a better school for their kids. A full 85 percent of the children who were accepted into the program were below-average students, countering the liberal argument that school choice programs only pick the "cream of the crop," those students who will easily achieve higher test scores down the road. On the contrary, teachers in the private schools that participate in the School Choice Scholarships Foundation program specifically want to work with disadvantaged, at-risk children, and they are clearly making a difference. Test scores for the "choice" participants were demonstrably and significantly higher than those of public school students of similar status in a control group, and four times more "choice" parents gave their child's school an A (42 percent) than did the public school parents (10 percent).

There's more. "A 1999 survey by Public Agenda, a nonpartisan research group, found that 68 percent of blacks favor vouchers," reported Michael Leo Owens of Emory University in an excellent *New York Times* op-ed piece explaining why support for school choice is strong and rising among African-Americans. "A similar poll by the Joint Center for Political and Economic Studies, a nonpartisan think tank, showed that the percentage of blacks supporting school vouchers rose to 60 percent in 1999 from 48 percent in 1996."

Owens went on to concede that his younger generation "knows that vouchers have severe limitations. We recognize that no voucher program can save a failing public system. Poorly funded vouchers don't offer much of a chance for poor children to enroll in expensive alternative schools. Vouchers can't ensure parental involvement in education. And vouchers can't end the resistance of many suburban schools to black enrollment." However, he concluded, vouchers "offer the only hope available to many poor students trapped in the nation's worst schools. For a limited number of children, they may make a crucial difference. That possibility is enough for black parents to take a chance.

Want more evidence? Come right here to New York, and tucked away in a little corner—largely unheralded by modern liberal elitists— you'll find a few brilliant little gems.

In the early 1970s, public schools in Harlem were horrific. They were so bad that administrators were ready to throw up their hands and give up. So when a handful of teachers and principals in District 4 asked if they could reorganize part of their school district into small, independently run alternative public schools to which neighborhood parents could choose to send their children, even liberal bureaucrats didn't have the heart to say no. After all, what harm could it do? The voucher movement hadn't really gathered steam yet, and no private, parochial, or otherwise religious schools would be allowed to participate. It wasn't exactly the brand of school choice I prefer, but it was a step forward—and it worked.

Read the wonderful book *Miracle in East Harlem: The Fight for Choice in Public Education* by Seymour Fliegel and James MacGuire. Dig through the newspaper clippings of these remarkable, innovative schools—schools where having just a little more freedom than traditional public schools has paid such big and valuable dividends in the lives of children and their parents—and you'll see what I'm talking about. Kids are learning in Harlem. They're being prepared for life. They're being given a chance to dream dreams and pursue them.

Oprah Winfrey came to Harlem in June of 2001 to deliver the commencement speech to the Young Women's Leadership School, part of the miracle in East Harlem. The school was started by Ann Tisch, a former NBC News reporter who got intrigued by the educational reforms going on in Milwaukee. So she quit her job, rolled up her sleeves, and dedicated herself to creating a school with a different way of doing things. Tisch's school is an all-girls school. That's right: no guys, just girls. All are minorities (60 percent are Hispanic, 40 percent are black). Most are poor. Most come from broken and disadvantaged families, and many are the children of single mothers. But because Tisch and her team have been given just a little more freedom than the usual public school teachers and principals, they've been able to design a school that works and thus attracts the trust of parents who choose to send their daughters there.

Liberals, of course, hated the idea of an all-girls school, which supposedly discriminated against boys. They hated the fresh breeze of creativity and innovation. So the New York Civil Liberties Union sued to shut the school down. Fortunately, they lost—I say fortunately because the school is already having tremendous results.

"Everyone in the school's first senior class will graduate," reported the New York *Daily News.* "All except one will go to four-year colleges; the exception is joining the Air Force. More than 80 percent of the girls at the grade 7–12 school read at or above grade level. Citywide, less than 50 percent do. On the English Regents [a statewide test], 100 percent of the girls passed, versus 42 percent citywide. On the Spanish and Math Regents, 100 percent passed; 97 percent passed the Biology Regents, and 94 percent passed the Global Studies Regents."

"At my old school, the kids didn't care, the teachers were burned out and parents weren't involved," said eighteen-year-old Monica

Diaz, once a D student, now a college-bound success story. "Before coming to this school, I had never even written an essay or knew what one was. This school definitely changed my life."

I could go on and on, but the point is simple and clear. Where it's being tried, school choice is working. It's giving parents more control, more involvement, and more peace of mind. It's giving teachers and principals more ownership and opportunity for improvement. And most importantly, it's helping students do better academically. Isn't that what we want in American education? Isn't that the whole point?

Yes, school choice programs are relatively new. Yes, relatively few students have been allowed to participate. But so far the news is very good.

EIGHT

I'M PRO-CHOICE

Liberals say they're pro-choice. But they're not.

They're pro-abortion.

Think about it. They insist that a woman's sovereignty over her own body (read: her convenience) trumps the right to life of an unborn innocent. Women, they say, should have the unfettered right to choose. But what about choice in other walks of life? Then it's a different story.

When it comes to women's freedom to choose better, safer schools for their children—many of whom are trapped in low-quality, dangerous public schools—they're anti-choice. The Left opposes tuition tax credits, vouchers, K–12 educational savings accounts, and most other forms of parental choice in education.

Similarly, when it comes to women terrorized by criminals, the Left doesn't support a woman's "freedom to choose" to buy a handgun and carry it in her purse or under her jacket should she need it to defend her life or the lives of her children. The Left doesn't trust the individual to make the right choices concerning her own personal security.

The Left doesn't believe in choice when it comes to hardworking folks choosing their own personal retirement accounts within the context of Social Security, with the potential of yielding two to three times the earnings of the Social Security system, which gives them less than a paltry 2 percent return on their money. The result: large numbers of seniors are living on poverty's edge in a situation that's only going to get worse as baby boomers retire and the ratio of producers to beneficiaries dramatically declines. But again, the Left doesn't trust individuals to make the right decisions concerning their own financial security.

So while the Left makes a lot of noise about the sanctity of choice, we see that choice itself is not the issue. The Left doesn't champion the individual's rights in a host of other areas and prefers to cede control over those decisions to government. No, this isn't about freedom, unless you mean it in the narrowest of contexts.

This is about a woman's freedom to terminate life within her womb. But even here, the driving force motivating the anti-lifers isn't freedom. If it were, the most engaged advocates of "choice" wouldn't be neutral on which choice the woman ultimately makes. They seem to have a strong preference for abortion. How else can you explain, for instance, their opposition to advising pregnant women of the potentially psychologically devastating impact of that procedure?

Check out the web sites of Planned Parenthood and some of the other most militant pro-abortionists and see if I'm exaggerating about their predisposition. See if "choice" is what they're really promoting. I think you will discover that freedom and choice are not their concern but that they use those terms to conceal their real agenda in a palatable wrapper.

ANTI-CHOICE EXTREMISTS?

Pro-abortion forces have employed the transparent strategy of demonizing pro-life advocates. Those of us who are pro-life are said to be "extremist anti-choice forces"—as if placing a woman's desire to terminate her pregnancy over an innocent unborn's very right to live isn't the extreme of the two positions in this debate. The examples are legion. As a Clinton TV ad put it during the 1992 Democratic primaries, "We need a president we can trust to protect our most fundamental rights. . . . this year the choice is clear. Bill Clinton strongly supports a woman's right to choose—he's spoken out against . . . the extremist anti-choice forces. As president, Bill Clinton will work to protect our precious freedoms. He supports the Freedom of Choice Act, and he'll work, as he always has, for equal rights and civil rights."

Al Gore has also attacked pro-lifers in the same terms. "I'm a Christian," Gore once told an audience in Philadelphia, but "we'll reject the anti-choice extremists." A Gore 2000 press release during the last campaign insisted that "Bush pandered to anti-choice extremists during the Republican primary.

And when left-wing feminist Gloria Steinem endorsed Gore in the 2000 campaign, she warned that "the Republican presidential nomination is in the hands of anti-choice extremists who don't represent the majority of even their own party."

Robin Duke, the president emeritus of the National Abortion Rights Action League and a member of the Planned Parenthood advisory board, also backed Gore during the 2000 campaign, telling fellow abortion rights proponents, "Let's cling to our friend Al Gore, who has supported us. We have enough trouble with anti-choice extremists in Congress."

As a conservative, I'm proudly pro-choice when it comes to matters of personal liberty, and passionately pro-life when it comes to matters of life and death.

Like the Founders of our country, I believe in certain absolute and "self-evident" moral truths. I believe in a God who created each one of us in His image, which makes each one of our lives sacred and precious and worthy of dignity. And I believe that life begins at conception—a fact that scientific advancements are making increasingly harder to deny. That's why we conservatives believe in the sanctity of life and protecting it. Furthermore, once life is protected, we should make sure all Americans have maximum personal freedom to make choices and pursue opportunities that improve their own lives and the lives of others.

In the previous chapter I mentioned how our Founding Fathers used the Declaration of Independence and the Constitution to build the foundation for what would eventually be the elimination of slavery. Some believe the Founders could have done more, and sooner, to end that awful institution. To them I say, why aren't you doing something today to help end the most unconscionable and immoral mistreatment of human life since slavery—abortion? Why are so many of you defending such a modern-day atrocity?

In 1857 the U.S. Supreme Court handed down the *Dred Scott v. Sandford* decision, ruling that slaves were property and that denying that property to a slave owner violated the Constitution. In 1973 the Court ruled in the case of *Roe v. Wade* that abortion is a privacy right and that denying that right to women violates the Constitution. The Constitution stands for neither slavery nor abortion. Therefore, in order to reach their conclusions, the justices in both cases had to treat human life as if it were something else. But just as the color of one's skin doesn't make someone a nonperson, neither does the inability of a baby to survive outside the mother's womb. These are fictions created by the justices to turn the Constitution upside down and deny certain human beings—whatever their physical appearance or stage in life—their God-given right to life. And don't tell me that in the case of slavery I'm confusing life with liberty. To me, life and liberty are inextricably intertwined. Oppressing human beings in the bondage of slavery does more than deny them their freedom. It destroys their dignity—the worth of their individual lives.

And there's another analogy between these twin blots on our nation's history. The advocates of both slavery and abortion have been characterized by a stunning zealotry. We know about the proponents of slavery, but look at the modern abortion movement. It has opposed everything from a twenty-four-hour waiting period and parental and spousal consent to pro-life counseling (both religious and medical) either outside or inside abortion clinics—again under the deceitful heading of "choice."

As a father of two young children whose beautiful, tiny, miraculous little fingers and toes I watched on that sonogram monitor in the earliest weeks of life, I find the contention that abortion is a choice, and that somehow our magnificent Constitution confers this right on a mother, absolutely appalling. When I think about that number—forty-two million unborn children killed by abortion over the past thirty years—it truly angers me. The fact that it is accepted by so many in society truly saddens me.

POLITICAL EXPEDIENCY

A good rule of thumb to help determine the relative righteousness of one side in a debate over the other is to check their respect for openness and truth. If one side is less than forthcoming about its positions or tries to disguise it in euphemistic language, you ought to be suspicious about the virtue of their cause. Truth has nothing to hide. Let me illustrate the point with a little quiz. The answers might surprise you.

Who said, "I am opposed to abortion and to government funding of abortions"?

a. Pat Robertson
b. Jerry Falwell
c. Bill Clinton

If you picked Robertson or Falwell, you wouldn't be wrong, because they've consistently held this position. But in this case, the correct answer is C—Bill Clinton. That's right, Clinton once purported to be a pro-life Southern Baptist. In 1986, then Arkansas governor Clinton wrote a letter to a constituent expressing his opposition to abortion and government funding of abortion. He even signed a parental notification law in 1989.

As a candidate for president, Clinton reversed himself. Once in office, he even repeatedly vetoed a ban on "partial birth abortion." During such an abortion, a baby is partially delivered, feet first. Before the baby's head comes out, the abortionist stabs the baby in the back of the skull with a pair of surgical scissors, inserts a vacuum cleaner, and sucks out the baby's brains. The skull collapses, the child dies, and the body is "delivered" dead on arrival. It is a terrible, gruesome act. A federal ban on partial birth abortion is supported by the American Medical Association and several leading Democrats, including former senator Daniel Patrick Moynihan (who has likened the procedure to "infanticide") and Senator Tom Daschle, who stunned colleagues in May of 1997 by voting with conservatives on this issue. Yet, bowing to the most extreme pro-abortion elements in his party, Clinton staunchly defended the procedure with the full force of federal law.

Let's try another question.

Who once voted for civil rights legislation defining an unborn baby from the moment of conception as "a person"?

> a. Jesse Helms
> b. Henry Hyde
> c. Al Gore

If you picked Helms or Hyde, you're not wrong. They are, after all, among the most strongly pro-life conservatives ever to have served in the U.S. Congress. Remarkably, however, in this case the correct answer is C—Al Gore.

In June of 1984, a Republican Congressman by the name of Mark Siljander introduced a bill to amend the Civil Rights Act. The bill stated that "for the purposes of this Act, the term 'person' shall include unborn children from the moment of conception." Although the House of Representatives, then controlled by the Democrats, defeated the Siljander amendment, Gore—then a congressman from Tennessee—voted in favor of the bill.

At the time, few if any were shocked by Gore's vote on the Siljander amendment because he was a reliable pro-life vote. In 1976, when he was first running for Congress, he told *The Nashville Banner,* "I don't believe a woman's freedom to live her own life, in all cases, outweighs the fetus's right to life."

During his House tenure, Gore actually voted pro-life 84 percent of the time.

In 1987 Gore wrote a letter to a constituent supporting Representative Henry Hyde's legislation banning federal funds for abortion. "During my eleven years in Congress," Representative Gore wrote, "I have consistently opposed federal funding of abortions. In my opinion, it is wrong to spend federal funds for what is arguably the taking of a human life. Let me assure you that I share your belief that innocent human life must be protected, and I am committed to furthering this goal."

In fact, Gore's early record was so pro-life that when he ran in the Democratic primaries for president in 1988, liberals attacked him. Representative Dick Gephardt, for example, denounced Gore as having a "near perfect anti-abortion record." Gore and his team realized that being tagged as pro-life was the kiss of political death in the Democratic Party—and that was unacceptable. But Gore's record was crystal clear. So what would he do? One Gore adviser explained Gore's plan to *U.S. News & World Report:* "Since there's a record [of pro-life votes] . . . what we have to do is deny, deny, deny," and that's precisely what Gore did. "I have not changed," Gore told Democrat voters, clearly a lie. "I have always been against anything that would take away a woman's right to have an abortion." Said the Gore adviser: "We've muddled the point, and with luck attention will turn elsewhere—or at least we'll be lucky enough so the thing doesn't blow into a full-fledged problem before Super Tuesday." Before long, Gore would go so far as to defend partial birth abortions.

Here's another question.

Who consistently voted for a constitutional amendment to ban abortion for a decade and proudly declared, "Life is the division of human cells, a process which begins with conception"?

> a. Tom DeLay
>
> b. Dick Armey
>
> c. Dick Gephardt

Yes, Republicans DeLay and Armey are strong pro-lifers. But the answer here is C—Dick Gephardt. Although we've seen how Gephardt attacked Al Gore during the 1988 Democratic primaries for flip-flopping on the abortion issue, Gephardt himself had done precisely the same thing just two years earlier.

When Gephardt, now the Democratic leader in the House of Representatives, began his career in Congress back in 1977, he was staunchly pro-life. During his first congressional campaign in 1976, Gephardt ran a newspaper ad headed "A PRO-LIFE PROMISE," in which he stressed his commitment to passing a pro-life constitutional amendment.

"In his first nine years as a Congressman," the National Right to Life Committee once noted, "Gephardt was a vocal spokesman for the pro-life cause. He co-sponsored an amendment to prohibit all abortions nationwide (except to save the life of the mother). [But] Gephardt reversed his position in 1986 as he positioned himself to run for president. He now states, 'As President of the United States, I would neither support nor initiate any effort to amend the constitution to make abortion illegal,' and, 'I do not believe current federal law regarding abortion needs to be changed.'"

How does Gephardt explain his flip-flop? "I'd rather change and be right than be rigid and wrong," he told reporters during the white heat of the 1988 campaign.

One final question.

Who said abortion is "black genocide" and

"a policy of killing infants"?

> a. Clarence Thomas
>
> b. Colin Powell
>
> c. Jesse Jackson

The answer is C—Jesse Jackson.

Back in the 1970s, early in his career, the Reverend Jackson was passionately pro-life. He spoke against abortion at black churches around the country. He spoke at a March for Life conference on January 22, 1977, marking the fourth anniversary of the *Roe v. Wade* decision. And he even spoke at a National Right to Life conference.

Jackson also wrote an article for the National Right to Life newsletter in which he argued that "in the abortion debate, one of the crucial questions is when does life begin. Anything growing is living. Therefore human life begins when the sperm and egg join . . . and the pulsation of life takes place. From that point, life may be described differently (as an egg, embryo, fetus, baby, child, teen-ager, adult), but the essence is the same."

Jackson went on to write that "those advocates of taking life prior to birth do not call it killing or murder, they call it abortion. They further never talk about aborting a baby because that would imply something human. Rather, they talk about aborting the fetus. Fetus sounds less than human and therefore can be justified."

"Some argue," Jackson continued, "suppose the woman does not want to have the baby. They say the very fact that she does not want the baby means that the psychological damage to the child is enough to abort the baby. I disagree. The solution to that problem is not to kill the innocent baby but to deal with her values and her attitude toward life—that which has allowed her not to want the baby."

Amen, Jesse! You were absolutely right.

But then politics intervened. Jackson's pro-life position rankled many fellow Democrats—especially devout liberals—and in time, particularly as he began considering a series of runs for president, Jackson hedged and then changed his position and became pro-abortion.

"Even our Creator did not make us puppets but gave us a free will to exercise a free choice," Jackson said during his 1984 presidential campaign. "Thus, as a matter of public policy I support the right of free choice relative to abortions."

Jackson's evolution from the pro-life to the pro-abortion camp— like Clinton's, Gore's, and Gephardt's—just happened to coincide with his presidential aspirations. And there's no question that today the Democratic Party is in the firm grip of the pro-abortion lobby. I'm not naive about politics, and I understand that at times politicians feel they have to adjust or change their positions to be successful. But it's completely reprehensible for them to do so with respect to a fundamental moral issue. Either these men never believed in their earlier stated moral position, or their lust for high office overpowered their moral convictions. In either case, their conduct is deceitful. And their attempt to besmirch those with whom they once stood as "anti-choice extremists" is cynical beyond description.

DEBATING THE DEVOUT

Protecting life is deeply important to me. It was important before my wife and I had kids but is even more so now because the stakes are so high. There is no more important issue.

Throughout my career, I've always made it a point to invite pro-abortion leaders onto my programs to discuss their views. I try to be firm and direct and ask pointed questions. I try not to be rude or offensive. It isn't my purpose simply to score debating points. My hope and prayer is that somebody out there listening by the radio or watching on television will consider both arguments—one that emphasizes life and morality, the other that emphasizes choice and convenience—and their minds and hearts will open to the pro-life position.

In September 1999, we had a particularly illuminating debate on this issue on *Hannity & Colmes*. Our scheduled guest was Patricia Ireland, president of the National Organization for Women (NOW). During show preparation, I came across an interesting article in a December 1993 issue of the *Philadelphia Inquirer* in which Kate Michelman—president of the National Abortion Rights Action League (NARAL)—was quoted as saying, "We think abortion is a bad thing. No woman wants to have an abortion."

Michelman had slipped off message. She had accidentally told the truth by conceding the moral point—that abortion is bad. This created quite an uproar in the pro-abortion movement, which forced NARAL to fire off a press release stating that Michelman "has never said—and would never say—that 'abortion is a bad thing.'" Michelman herself sent a letter to the *Inquirer* insisting that she'd been misquoted. But there was just one problem. The reporter had tape-recorded the interview. A review of the transcripts indicated that, sure enough, Michelman had said, "abortion is a bad thing." Michelman then withdrew her first letter to the editor, substituting another to "clarify" her remarks. The pro-abortion movement has been disavowing Michelman's moment of candor ever since. Are you beginning to see what I mean by the truth having nothing to hide (as well as the converse of that maxim)?

Armed with this research, I welcomed Ireland to the show.

"Welcome back to the program," I began. "Patricia, Kate Michelmen was quoted in the *Philadelphia Inquirer* in 1993 saying, 'We think abortion is a bad thing. No woman wants to have an abortion.' Do you agree with that statement?"

"Well, I don't think in every case it's a bad thing," she said. "I think often for a woman with a problem pregnancy in her life, it may be the best answer for her. And I think the big question is who gets to make that decision, the woman who knows herself, her circumstances, her responsibilities, her own religious beliefs, or some legislator off in Missouri or in Congress who really doesn't know that much about her."

It was an interesting response, for several reasons. First, by saying, "I don't think in every case it's a bad thing," Ireland was actually conceding that in some cases abortion is a bad thing, though I doubt she meant it to come out that way. Even in disagreeing with her pro-abortion colleague, she was skating on the thin ice of her own argument.

I then asked her about partial birth abortion. I reminded her of the gruesome procedure, which most pro-abortion advocates don't want described in public forums—again, because the truth damages their cause.

"When you hear that process described," I asked Ireland, "does that bother you? Does that get to you? How do you feel about that?"

Ireland admitted that such abortions "are always tragedies." But then she quickly asserted that she opposed a ban on such procedures and tried to turn the tables, attacking pro-lifers as "anti-abortion terrorists."

Again, her answer was instructive. If Ireland believes that abortion is not really the killing of an innocent child, then why would she concede that partial birth abortions are "always tragedies"? There is really only one answer. She knows full well that each of these procedures kills a baby that, in the overwhelming majority of cases, could survive outside the mother's womb. Later in that program, I pressed her further.

"Patricia, let me ask you this question because I asked you in the last segment [about] this procedure of partial birth abortion. I described these perfectly formed feet and legs and fingers and toes . . ."

"Yadda, yadda, yadda," she responded, like it was some kind of joke.

I told her how when my son was born, ten and a half months before that show, I'd prayed that he'd be born healthy. I couldn't understand how she could give me such a technical, clinical, cold answer.

She basically bumbled around. She talked about the health of the mother. I reminded her that the American Medical Association supported the ban on partial birth abortion and that former surgeon general C. Everett Koop had explained that, with all that modern medicine has to offer, partial birth abortion is never needed to save the life or health of the mother. There are other ways to care for the woman.

"You say, 'Yadda, yadda, yadda' when [we're talking about] a perfectly formed baby. Is that not callous, cold?"

"No," she replied, insisting to the end upon defending the indefensible. We reached an impasse, I truly believe, because she—like most on her side of the argument—was unwilling to deal with the issue honestly and fairly, even in her own mind.

A few years later, in March of 2001, Ireland and I revisited the issue on *Hannity & Colmes*. Again, I tried to get right to the heart of the issue.

"Are we better off with more abortion or less abortion in America?" I asked her. "Is abortion a good thing, a woman [wanting] to go through that?"

"Well, I think that's the wrong question. I think the question is—"

"No, no. I like my question."

"—do we want—"

"No, no, no, no, no. . . . I'm asking my question. Is abortion a good thing? Do we want more abortion? Would you like to see less abortion in America?"

"I would like to see us not go back to a time when illegal abortion was the leading cause of maternal death in this country."

Ireland insisted on ducking my question. But I refused to let go.

"Pat, I want to ask you a direct question, and I'm serious. Do you—"

"I know you are, and I'm giving you my direct answer."

"Would we better off with less abortion in America?"

"We are better off with legal abortion so that women aren't killed and maimed from back-alley abortions."

"You know why you're afraid to answer? The answer is obvious, and—"

"I'm not afraid to answer."

"The answer is yes," I said. "Women would be better off if they didn't have the experience of abortion."

"Then wouldn't we be better off if we had sex education that really educated students about sex?" she insisted. "Wouldn't we be really better off if we had access to birth control and information about birth control?"

"Just go to a pharmacy, Pat, there's a whole shelf—it says 'birth control'—go help yourself," I told her. Then I asked her one final time: "Why can't you admit that we'd be better off and it would be in women's best interest if they didn't have abortions? What is so hard? Why do you have to take this extreme position on abortion?"

You know what Patricia Ireland—the head of NOW—told me?

"It's my role in life."

In February 2001, I interviewed Kate Michelman of NARAL. It was during prospective attorney general John Ashcroft's Senate confirmation hearings. Michelman and her pro-abortion allies were doing everything they possibly could to derail Ashcroft's nomination.

"John Ashcroft's record is antithetical to everything Americans stand for in terms of rights and freedoms that they treasure and they expect their attorney general to protect and guard," Michelman insisted as the show began, ranting about his "unmitigated assault on women's rights of choice."

"His record is so extreme and so out of the mainstream," she declared.

Her attack against Senator Ashcroft reminded me of Senator Ted Kennedy's vitriolic and hysterical attack on Judge Robert Bork, a pro-life conservative, back in 1987. "Robert Bork's America is a land in which women would be forced into back-alley abortions, blacks would sit at segregated lunch counters, rogue police could break down citizen's doors in midnight raids," Kennedy declared, going on and on about the hellish society we would all live in if conservatives ran the government, sat on the Supreme Court, and governed by the actual U.S. Constitution, not a radical left-wing, hyperliberal interpretation of it.

In 1992, during another infamous confirmation hearing, Michelman herself warned that "Clarence Thomas is going to haunt this nation with his opinions" and "the specter of back-alley bloodletting."

Like Ireland, Michelman refused to address or even acknowledge the moral problem with abortion. Instead, she insisted on focusing on a woman's choice. And when asked about the horrific partial birth abortion procedure, Michelman claimed "there is no such thing. . . ."

I'm convinced that somewhere in the recesses of their souls, Michelman, Ireland, and the other pro-abortion leaders know that abortion is morally wrong, which is why they refuse to deal squarely with the issue.

A REASON FOR HOPE

Despite the enormity and militancy of the pro-abortion movement, I remain optimistic. In my heart I truly believe change is possible. One day *Roe v. Wade* will be seen to be as evil and abhorrent as *Dred Scott v. Sandford.*

It won't happen overnight. It won't happen easily. But it will happen.

I'm confident, in part, because I live by faith in a God of love and justice. I believe He will right the wrongs we commit, and if at all possible, He will do so mercifully.

I'm confident, too, because I truly believe in the value of debate and education and the power of persuasion. I utterly and completely reject the use of violence to stop abortion. Such actions are morally and legally wrong. What will get the job done is changing hearts and minds, one at a time if necessary, no matter how long it takes. Even though radical change is required, sometimes that magnitude of change must come about incrementally.

As we seek to change the law, we need to pray for a moral and spiritual awakening to end abortion in America. We as conservatives also need to redouble our efforts—noble as they already are—to reach every young, terrified, lonely pregnant woman and show them that we love them and care for them. We need to provide them with crisis pregnancy centers. We need to help them bring their babies to term, deliver them safely, and either help them raise them or find good, safe, loving married couples who want to adopt these children and give them a future. This is compassionate—and if self-proclaimed pro-choicers were truly pro-choice, they would try to make pregnant women aware of all their options and the potential consequences of each. After all, choice isn't meaningful if it isn't informed. Pro-abortionists, to earn their desired title as pro-choice, must first prove that they support informed choice, not a choice based in ignorance.

And when it comes to potential consequences I'm not merely talking in the abstract. The "choice" of abortion affects not only the life of the innocent unborn (by extinguishing it) but the life of the mother. One of the great joys and privileges of my life has been to interview a woman named Norma McCorvey. She was raised in a dysfunctional home. She abused drugs and alcohol. She became pregnant without being married, considered having an abortion, but couldn't because it wasn't legal. In 1970 she became the anonymous plaintiff in the landmark legal case that would change the legal status of abortion, and with it the course of American history. She was known only as "Jane Roe," and only recently has she made her identity known.

But there's more to Norma's story than meets the eye. In 1995, rather than attacking "Jane Roe," some members of the pro-life group Operation Rescue treated Norma with a little love and a little respect. They invited her to church, and for the first time in more than two decades, she agreed to go.

"I actually accepted the invitation," McCorvey told Alan and me on *Hannity & Colmes* one night. "I went to church on August the eighth of 1995. Pastor Morris Sheets's sermon that night was on John 3:16, 'For God so loved the world that He gave His only begotten Son, that whoever believes in Him shall not perish, but have everlasting life.' I was very touched by that. . . . When Pastor Sheets was doing his altar call, I went for it, you know? I just kind of let all my bridges and all my doors down. You know, I just kind of like opened up."

It is Norma McCorvey's story that gives me hope.

It gives me hope that we can make a difference through dialogue, compassion, and prayer. It shows me that lost, hurting women can find God and that He can transform them. It gives me confidence that peaceful pro-life activism can work—by changing one heart at a time. And every heart is worth it.

After all, if Jane Roe can change, isn't anything possible?

NINE

LONG LIVE THE PORCUPINE CARIBOU!

In the spring of 2002, Iraqi President Saddam Hussein declared he would stop exporting oil for thirty days or until Israel withdrew from the West Bank and Gaza. Iranian leaders called on fellow Islamic countries to stop shipping oil to the United States and all supporters of Israel to demonstrate the power of the OPEC cartel against the evils of the West.

"The United States has used wheat and food as a weapon," Ayatollah Ali Khamenei declared in a fiery speech to thousands in Tehran. "If Islamic and Arab countries do the same and only for one month suspend the export of oil to Israel and its supporters, the world would be shaken. The oil belongs to the people and can be used as a weapon against the West and those who support the savage regime of Israel."

Way up in the frigid and desolate Alaskan tundra, there is an answer to such problems: a massive coastal region of about nineteen million acres known as the Artic National Wildlife Refuge, or ANWR (pronounced *Ann*-wahr) for short. Few people would know anything about it—or care—but for one little fact: there's oil up there—lots of oil. Geologists believe the ANWR reserves could represent one of the largest onshore oil basins in U.S. history.

Tapping Alaskan oil would help America become far less dependent on foreign oil and less vulnerable to disruptions in the flow of oil imports from the Persian Gulf and other OPEC countries. After September 11 and new and persisting rumors of oil wars and embargoes against the United States by Islamic countries in the Middle East, tapping ANWR makes real sense.

There's just one problem: left-wing environmentalists hate the idea of drilling for oil in most places in the United States, on-shore or off. But they say they're particularly exercised about drilling in ANWR because of their concern for this barren acreage and a certain species of animal inhabiting it—the Porcupine caribou.

A Porcupine caribou? If you were in Congress, would you shape the economic and energy security of over 280 million Americans around the sexual migration patterns and birthing habits of a bunch of Porcupine caribou?

Named after Alaska's Porcupine River near where they live, the Porcupine caribou herd is strong and healthy today, numbering about 130,000. But because each year the herd gives birth to baby caribou in the ANWR region, environmentalists adamantly insist that drilling for oil in even small sections of ANWR would threaten the herd's ability to reproduce, fend off predators, and find adequate food supplies. So they have launched a withering campaign to block drilling in ANWR at all costs.

COURTING THE CARIBOU VOTE

During the 2000 presidential campaign, Al Gore, citing press reports on the controversy over drilling in ANWR, declared: "The Arctic National Wildlife Refuge encompasses nineteen million acres of land in Alaska and is home to some of America's most pristine wilderness and one of the most undisturbed ecosystems on earth" and warned that "the coastal plain, where drilling would occur, is where the one hundred twenty-nine thousand–head Porcupine caribou herd calves in the summer."

On *Hannity & Colmes*—just a few weeks after the initial terrorist attacks—I tried to convince former California governor Jerry Brown that we ought to drill for oil at ANWR. He wouldn't hear of it.

"Well, you've got to talk to the caribou on that one," Brown told me.

"Oh, the poor caribou," I said, shaking my head. "I should have known."

Then there was Brooks Yeager, vice president of the World Wildlife Fund's "global threats" program. "The Artic Refuge protects some of the world's most spectacular wilderness and wildlife, including the Porcupine caribou, who move to the refuge's coastal plain each spring in one of North America's last great mammal migrations, [and] the caribou rely on the coastal plain to give birth and raise their calves," he said, claiming that defeat of ANWR oil-drilling legislation was "an important goal-line stand for the environment."

According to a seven-state radio ad campaign engineered by the left-wing Sierra Club, caribou, polar bears, and the musk ox have so far survived "the ice age," "being hunted to near-extinction," and threatened by conservatives in the U.S. Senate "who caved to pressure from the big oil companies" that want to drill in ANWR.

A blizzard of issue ads and open letters demanded that Congress support psuedo-energy policies like "biomass fuels, solar power, and wind turbines" instead of drilling in ANWR's "critical wildlife area." After all, we've got to save the caribou! Among those lending their names to the campaign were former president Jimmy Carter, former vice president Walter Mondale, CNN founder Ted Turner, top advisers to President Clinton and Al Gore, and a plethora of actors like Brad Pitt, Jennifer Aniston, John Travolta, Mary Tyler Moore, Ed Asner, and Norman Lear.

All of this was part of the biggest environmentalist media and grassroots campaign in more than a decade—a blitzkrieg of TV ads, radio ads, print ads, direct mail, and media interviews all designed to block the pursuit of energy independence and court the caribou vote.

Oil drilling in ANWR is "bad energy policy" and "will do irrevocable harm" to the Porcupine caribou, among other supposed concerns, warned Senator John Kerry on NBC's *Meet the Press.*

"Special places like the Artic National Wildlife Refuge are part of our natural—and national—heritage," insisted Senator Hillary Rodham Clinton, also coming to the aid of the caribou. "The Artic Refuge is part of what makes our country so unique, so beautiful and so precious. It deserves protection, not exploitation."

But the real exploitation on this issue is coming from the Democrats. It wasn't enough for them to charge that Republicans had placed America's energy needs above the environment. As usual, they had to impute a sinister motive to the GOP. Drilling for oil is not about helping America achieve energy independence, they argue, but padding the pockets of their buddies in "Big Oil."

For example, Gore spokesman Douglas Hattaway said that caribou are severely threatened by conservatives like George W. Bush. Hattaway told reporters that "it's no surprise that Bush's energy policy is to open one of our great wilderness areas to drilling by his supporters in the oil industry. He has always put Big Oil before the environment and people's health. This is just another Bush proposal that promotes the interests of special interests rather than the American people."

That's why a plank in the Democratic Party's 2000 platform called for a ban on oil drilling in ANWR, even though Alaskan Democrats, who are closest to the situation, actually support drilling.

That's also why liberals in the Senate ganged up in the spring of 2002 to defeat any near-term prospect for ANWR drilling. The final vote was 54 to 46 against ANWR, and every major Democrat even remotely considering running for president in 2004—Hillary Clinton, Tom Daschle, Joe Lieberman, John Edwards, John Kerry, and Joe Biden—made sure to be in the caribou camp.

"I really think it comes down to this," said Senator Daschle. "We are just not going to allow Republicans to destroy the environment."

You've really got to hand it to the Left. They've got incredible message discipline. From environmental groups to top Democratic Party leaders, they are operating from the same radical playbook. They demonize most industries as polluters, and conservatives as antienvironment. And they turn a blind eye to the country's need to boost the economy, create new jobs, find new sources of energy, and become more self-sufficient—all the while blaming Republicans for the damage their actions cause to our economy and energy independence.

To illustrate the extent of their exploitation of the issue, let me share a highlight from an interview I conducted with Robert F. Kennedy, Jr., son of the late attorney general Bobby Kennedy and an environmental lawyer with the Natural Resource Defense Council. I confronted him about liberals who seem to be "more concerned about the spotted owl and the caribou in Alaska than they are about humanity and human beings."

"Yeah," Kennedy said, "and there's a radical right wing out there that wants to go live in paramilitary tents and, you know, shoot at black people."

Note the familiar tactic. Instead of either being humbled by the charge or vehemently denying it, Kennedy cynically dismissed it by hurling back a specious and irrelevant countercharge designed to divert. What do the indefensible positions of racist nutballs who are supposedly on the right wing have to do with mainstream positions of the Left? Conservatives and Republicans completely disavow such lunacy. But fringe elements, taken together, make up the Democratic Party. Their "mainstream" fully embraces radical, indefensible positions, from delaying the construction of a hospital in Southern California to save the Delhi Sands flower-loving fly, to halting the construction of a 320-unit apartment complex in the name of protecting the Wutu sewer rat. And I've yet to hear the Left seriously denounce the dangerous tactics of ecoterrorist organizations like the Earth Liberation Front (ELF) and Animal Liberation Front (ALF), which are responsible for substantial financial and personal damage throughout the United States.

FACTS, NOT FANATICISM

Few issues are more important to our economic strength and security than unfettered access to reasonably priced oil and gas, the lifeblood of any industrial society.

Remember when Arab nations slapped an oil embargo on the United States in 1973 to punish us for our support for Israel? Energy prices here skyrocketed and our economy plunged into the toilet. It took us years to recover from the ensuing recession. Remember, too, how Islamic extremists seized control of Iran in 1979, triggering a new wave of oil shortages, price spikes, gas lines, and the worst economy since the Great Depression with Jimmy Carter's infamous "misery index"? Then, of course, there was the recent energy crisis in California, spurring massive blackouts, price spikes, and serious hardships.

None of us wants to repeat the costly mistakes of the not-too-distant past. Yet if we follow the Left down this path that's precisely what will happen.

Now more than ever—particularly in the wake of 9/11—the American people deserve facts, not fanaticism, and the fact is that America is more dependent than ever on importing foreign oil. Back during the Arab oil embargo, the United States imported only about 36 percent of our oil needs. Thirty years later, that number has skyrocketed to almost 60 percent.

Worse, a higher and higher percentage of that oil is coming from the

Persian Gulf region. In 1973 less than 14 percent of our total foreign oil imports came from the Persian Gulf. By the year 2000, that number had climbed to more than 22 percent, making us increasingly more dependent on a hostile and volatile region to keep our economy humming.

The Clinton-Gore administration actually increased our dependence on foreign oil, and particularly on oil imported from the hotbed of Islamic radicalism. Between 1993 and 2000, U.S. oil imports from the Persian Gulf increased by more than 38 percent, from less than 1.8 million barrels a day to more than 2.4 million barrels a day. Worse still, when Clinton and Gore took office we imported no oil from Saddam Hussein's regime in Iraq, but by the time they left office we were importing more than 600,000 barrels a day from Iraq.

The U.S. Department of Energy predicts that if such trends continue unchecked, America's foreign oil imports will rise to 62 percent by 2020—half of which will come from the increasingly unstable (and hostile) Middle East.

THE CASE FOR ENERGY FREEDOM

Over the past few years I've talked to all kinds of experts on this subject, including current and former secretaries of energy and the interior, both Republicans and Democrats. I've also talked to radical environmentalists and the antigrowth crowd. Along the way, I've sifted through the rhetoric and facts and concluded that we have an incredible opportunity right in front of us, if we'll only seize the day.

If we choose to, America can achieve true energy freedom. But first we must overcome the Left's propaganda and obstructionism and proceed based upon the facts.

Right now, the United States has about twenty-one billion barrels of proven oil reserves, and estimates by the 1995 U.S. Geological Survey indicate that we have a "technically recoverable oil resource base onshore" of more than one hundred and ten billion barrels. Moreover, we have more than 1.2 trillion cubic feet of natural gas reserves, which when developed would last us for more than three decades.

At the heart of any such energy freedom strategy is the development of just a tiny sliver of ANWR. Of the nineteen million acres that make up the entire Artic Refuge, Congress has set aside a mere one and a half million acres for potential oil exploration and development—less than 8 percent of the total.

The Bush administration, however, isn't seeking to develop all one and a half million acres. The Bush plan calls for exploration on a mere two thousand acres. That means 99.99 percent of the land surface will be untouched—or just one one-hundredth of 1 percent!

Moreover, state-of-the-art developments in modern drilling technology now allow for a minimal amount of land and equipment to be used above ground. Petroleum engineers can put a hole in the ground in one place and then drill sideways as well as down, severely limiting man's "footprint" on environmentally sensitive areas. New technologies mean that energy development is no longer a zero-sum game. We no longer face a choice between our energy and economic needs and the environment. We can and should protect both.

The result of such high-tech development would be impressive, to say the least. The U.S. Geological Survey studies indicate that we could count on up to sixteen billion barrels of oil from ANWR. That's about as much as we would otherwise import from Saudi Arabia over the next thirty years, making it well worth the effort.

Meanwhile, it's important to keep in mind that ANWR is not exactly a bastion of tourism and trade, nor is it among America's most pristine and gorgeous wilderness areas. It's actually barren and practically uninhabitable. Senator Frank Murkowski, an Alaskan Republican, notes that ANWR "is a flat, treeless, almost featureless plain" where "temperatures can drop to minus forty degrees Fahrenheit" and where "there are fifty-six days of total darkness during the year, and almost nine months of harsh winter."

While humans can barely survive there, it's true that Porcupine caribou are among the few animals that can both survive and thrive. But the development of one one-hundreth of 1 percent of the land clearly won't destroy the caribou's habitat.

And this isn't just idle speculation. We have some empirical evidence that bears on the issue. When we developed oil fields on Alaska's nearby North Slope in Prudhoe Bay, for example, the caribou population flourished. In fact, "the Central Artic caribou herd that inhabits part of Prudhoe Baby has grown from 6,000 in 1978 to 19,700 today," notes Senator Murkowski, citing the most recent estimates by state and federal wildlife agencies. Columnist George Will has pointed out that "there is drilling for oil and gas in 29 wildlife refuges" that hasn't destroyed animals, birds, fish or the rest of the environment. Conservatives in Congress are even willing to give the secretary of the interior the power to stop oil development and exploration during the summer if the caribou are ever truly threatened. Conservatives passed such legislation back in 1995, but President Clinton vetoed the measure.

CUTTING THROUGH THE LEFT-WING SPIN

The evidence demonstrates overwhelmingly that the Left's argument for protecting the Porcupine caribou, the musk ox, and the polar bear in ANWR is a red herring. It's one more partisan political diversion designed to derail oil exploration and development anywhere—not just in Alaska but off the California and Florida coasts, in the Gulf of Mexico, in the Great Lakes, and on most public lands.

I once interviewed Deb Callahan of the League of Conservation Voters on *Hannity & Colmes* and she spelled out the radical environmentalists' case beautifully. After she insisted that "opening ANWR is a very poor idea," I challenged her to offer an alternative.

"Would you support drilling in the lower forty-eight states or not?

Would you support drilling off the coast of California or Florida or not? I mean, [in] which of these areas would you support drilling, if any?"

"That was a big area you just sort of laid out there," she stammered. "But first of all—"

"Well, pick one," I pressed. "I mean, tell me where you'd support drilling."

"Well, let me—let me talk about environmentalists supporting energy production and energy facilities. For instance, in California—"

"You can't name me one place you'd support drilling, can you?"

"Well, I—I—for instance—"

She wouldn't name one place where she'd support drilling for new sources of oil and natural gas. The best she would do was say that she wasn't for shutting down oil exploration, drilling, production, and shipping facilities in Prudhoe Bay.

"Do we think Prudhoe Bay should be shut down?" she asked rhetorically. "No."

Of course, that wasn't the question.

When Alan sat down for a one-on-one interview on *Hannity & Colmes* with Tom Daschle in February of 2002, Alan—to his credit—asked Daschle directly: Is the president right to tie the issue of oil drilling to national security?

"We can't go back, Alan, to the bad old days of simply finding places to drill," Daschle replied. "We're running out of places to drill in this country. But we can make much more efficient use of what we're using."

Despite the fact that those "bad old days" helped fuel America's industrial revolution and created the most prosperous economy on the face of the earth, no one is proposing lifting or suspending legitimate environmental requirements in the search for new sources of oil and gas, and Daschle knows it. No one is proposing using old technologies to explore for fossil fuels when new technologies exist. And no one is proposing changing the American landscape with oil rigs.

Agreeing with him completely, Alan then asked Daschle, "why this mania about drilling in this small area? What's behind that?"

"Well, I think what's behind it is just a mindset that many have had for generations that you go where the oil is regardless of the circumstances," Daschle answered. "What we have learned is that you can't always go where the oil is, especially in cases when there's so little oil there in the first place and where it doesn't provide more than about a six-month's supply of oil in the United States, and it isn't worth destroying permanently our most precious natural resources. . . . We're not going to go to ANWR."

Note that Daschle was completely unencumbered by the facts. As we've seen, drilling in ANWR would result in the destruction of no precious natural resources, much less permanently. But being hostage to their environmental constituencies, Democrats feel compelled to spew their destructive nonsense. And I do mean nonsense. These are the same people who painted Bush as a sadistic menace trying to poison our drinking water with arsenic merely because he spent a few months considering all the facts and deliberating carefully instead of making a knee-jerk decision on the arsenic standards—standards that were in place throughout the Clinton-Gore years and before.

And to think this man is not only the Senate majority leader and the highest ranking official in the Democratic Party, but he actually fancies himself presidential timber.

In a separate interview I had with Democratic senator John Kerry, he articulated his philosophical objection to pursuing oil drilling anywhere to solve our energy needs. He touted the benefits of solar power, wind power, hydroelectric power, and other alternative sources of energy. All that is fine. But just because Kerry or any other politician or activist imagines or demands these supposed energy alternatives doesn't make them economically viable now or in the future.

"[W]hat you have are two different visions," Senator Kerry told me. "The vision that has been expressed in the House legislation and the White House is one that depends on drilling our way out of our current problem."

"Well, that's part of their solution," I agreed, "and I know that Vice President—"

"I—" Kerry tried to interrupt.

"Wait a minute," I said. "I know Vice President Dick Cheney offered a series of solutions just last year. The vast majority talked about conservation. We have Gale Norton. She's been right here between us on this program and said that some estimates have the Arctic Wildlife Reserve where we'd only deal with .001 percent of the refuge, only two thousand acres, that it could be the second largest oil find in American history, and we could do it without harming the wildlife in any way, which is what we've been able to do at Prudhoe Bay. My only point is, you know, we have tried to perfect this alternative technology—solar, wind power—for decades, and we have not, obviously, been that successful. The Clinton-Gore administration had eight years to implement some of these new sources of energy. They weren't successful. If we want energy independence, I think part of that comprehensive plan has got to include lessening our depending on foreign oil and tapping into that resource."

"Well, what you said is partly correct," Kerry responded. "Yes, we have to lessen our dependence on foreign oil. The problem is, tapping into whatever might exist in the Arctic Wildlife Refuge does nothing to wean you from oil. It merely continues the dependency. It's like a narcotic. If you're on the narcotic, get more of it and don't worry about the alternative. We don't need to drill in the Arctic Wildlife Refuge, at least now, in order to provide for the energy needs of our country."

It is difficult to point to another issue in modern American history where a major political party's rhetoric is so divorced from reality. Let's think logically about this for a moment. Can you imagine how many solar panels and windmills would be required to replace our country's consumption of more traditional forms of energy? Even if it were feasible, where would we put them? In all those pristine places where the radical environmentalists claim to want to protect nature? Can you imagine their outcries then?

Can you imagine the kind of financial resources that would be required by homeowners, businesses, public facilities, public utilities, and the like, to convert our nation's energy infrastructure to deliver, receive, and make otherwise usable these new forms of energy?

And if these alternatives are truly viable and reasonable, why haven't any of the other major industrial nations—including Europe's socialist regimes and Japan—successfully instituted them?

Kerry and his fellow liberals are not only tilting at windmills, they're obstructing America's future economic growth and prosperity. Indeed, we would be doing them a substantial disservice just to take them seriously. Their ideas are so ill-advised that reasonableness requires us to assume something other than what they claim is motivating them. For if we accept their ideas at face value, we have no choice but to conclude that even in these most dangerous of times they would take us straight back to a Carter-vintage energy crisis.

THE ROAD AHEAD

Where, then, do we go from here?

In March of 2002, Alan and I interviewed Gale Norton, President Bush's interior secretary, on *Hannity & Colmes*. Secretary Norton commented that the administration was "working to have a bipartisan approach to solving problems for this country, but it is a little frustrating when we see things that get bogged down because of partisanship."

Liberals are "not only against the wildlife refuge for drilling," I noted. "They're against it in the Gulf of Mexico. They're against drilling off the coast of California and Florida. Left-wing groups are opposed to drilling in the Great Lakes, drilling in wilderness and parklands. They oppose nuclear power. They're against hydroelectric power plants. They don't want the construction of pipelines. I mean, I think the only thing left is a little battery-operated car."

She agreed, but said the Bush administration would continue looking for constructive ways to work with congressional Democrats for the sake of the country.

"We've been working hard to try and find those places where there is strong support for energy [development] going forward," Secretary Norton told me. "And, actually, the state of Alaska is somewhat unique with its approach to ANWR because they do strongly support the ANWR proposal in Alaska. They want to see the energy development in their backyards."

Americans know how important it is to expand domestic energy resources. Eight out of ten Americans, for example, believe the United States is likely to experience a serious energy crisis within the next few years, while 36 percent believe the United States is already in one, according to a Wirthlin poll taken in March of 2001. Nearly eight out of ten Americans say they want more oil produced here at home, and more than six out of ten have said they support development in ANWR when they understand the facts.

In fact, despite the Left's deceptions, more than 75 percent of Alaskans support oil development in ANWR.

Eskimos are also big supporters.

George N. Ahmaogak, Sr., is mayor of Alaska's North Slope Borough—part of ANWR—and he takes offense at liberal notions that he and his fellow Eskimos can't choose what's best for themselves, their families, and their land.

"We know that development of energy in ANWR is a responsible use of the land," the mayor says. "For thousands of years, we've had a reverence for the land, and part of our fundamental belief is that the land should be used responsibly.

"Conservation has always been part of our culture," the mayor adds. "Our people have been respectfully using the land long before Columbus discovered America. People who have never been to Alaska but are opposing ANWR oil development need to visit and speak to us."

Alaska's governor Tony Knowles—a Democrat—is a particularly big supporter of drilling in ANWR. He broke ranks with his party precisely because he knows the facts.

Alan and I invited Governor Knowles onto *Hannity & Colmes* to talk about ANWR. It was a good conversation. The governor is a very knowledgeable guy, and he's on the right side of this critically important issue. But Alan, of course, simply refused to take the word of an Alaskan Democrat that it is indeed possible to strike a healthy balance among energy security, jobs, economic growth, and protecting the environment. Instead, he went after President Bush.

"Should we be looking at the fact that George W. Bush got more than one point seven million dollars in campaign contributions from oil and gas companies, including BP and Exxon Mobil, two of the biggest companies that do business in Alaska?" Alan asked. "They always say 'Follow the money.' They're doing that with Clinton. Should that be part of the equation here?"

The governor responded with a zinger. "Well, I think you need to ask the senior citizen that was being pried from an elevator during one of the rolling blackouts in California as to whether we should . . . develop our oil and gas in America so we can provide energy for families and for jobs."

Union workers and their leadership also support drilling in ANWR.

"By tapping into petroleum resources in Alaska, we can create jobs and stabilize our economy by lessening our dependence on foreign oil," said Teamster president James P. Hoffa, explaining that developing ANWR could create more than 735,000 new jobs. "American jobs and environmental protection are not mutually exclusive. Alaskan oil fields currently use the most environmentally sensitive technology in the world. Only a small part of the Artic National Wildlife Refuge will be used, about two thousand acres—roughly one-fifth the size of Washington Dulles Airport."

The Teamsters—which represent more than 1.5 million workers in the United States and Canada—endorsed Al Gore in 2000. But in 2001, after President Bush, Energy Secretary Spence Abraham, and Interior Secretary Gale Norton courted them and invited them to join forces, the Teamsters backed the Bush energy plan.

And when the radical environmental groups used Martin Sheen—aka President Josiah Bartlett on NBC's *The West Wing*—to cut a commercial opposing oil development in Alaska, Jerry Hood, a top Teamster official, had some choice words. "I couldn't think of a more perfect champion for these pretend facts than a pretend president," he quipped. "The environmental lobby have repeated these half-truths for months, hoping that will make them true.

"I join President Bush in calling on the Senate to pass a comprehensive energy policy now," Hood added. "More than ever, we should listen to the commander in chief whose Oval Office is located in Washington, D.C.—not Hollywood."

The split between industrial union workers and white-collar environmentalists—both of which have been traditionally core Democrat constituencies—provides conservatives with an opportunity to force Democrats to choose between them. I believe George Bush won in heavily Democratic West Virginia in 2000 in large part because the coal miners, their union leaders, and their employers rejected Gore's history of radical environmentalism (with gun control being another pivotal issue). Bush deftly convinced many union voters that Gore's policies might jeopardize their jobs. Republicans can make similar inroads in the oil fields, the steel mills, the automobile factories, and many other important areas of American industry, by pointing to the Democrats' extreme positions.

President Bush campaigned on the promise of making this country more energy-independent and trying to achieve a reasonable balance between our environmental concerns and the nation's energy needs. And to fulfill that promise, he offered a serious and responsible energy plan—the first such plan in over a decade. When he unveiled his plan in May 2001, however, environmental activists went ballistic. In protest, Greenpeace dumped a truckload of coal in the driveway of Vice President Cheney's official residence. But neither Cheney nor Bush was deterred. Indeed, Bush proved that he was not going to be intimidated by those opposing ANWR drilling when he made it a centerpiece of his plan. This signaled a refreshing departure from the Clinton years.

Whereas the Clinton-Gore administration was largely in the pocket of environmental groups and therefore opposed the development of nuclear energy at all costs, the Bush plan included renewed nuclear energy development. In explaining the administration's position, Cheney even acknowledged its open-mindedness on the issue of global warming. In a speech at the Energy Efficiency Forum, he explained that an important motivating factor in the administration's decision to pursue nuclear energy was that it produces electricity without any polluting air emissions, which would be a way of addressing the global warming problem. But Cheney emphasized the hypocrisy of environmentalists, noting that they want to have it both ways. "We need to pursue the use of nuclear power," Cheney said. "But the people who yell the loudest on global warming are first to scream at nuclear power."

Further, the Bush administration has demonstrated an understanding that our energy and environmental problems are complex and not speculative.

On March 19, 2001, Energy Secretary Spencer Abraham delivered a speech in which he pointed out that "since 1980, the number of American refineries has been cut in half. There hasn't been a new refinery built in the United States in over twenty-five years." He added that environmental regulations prevent existing refineries from expanding and require them to produce more than fifteen types of gasoline. And he made a shocking revelation: "Refineries are so constrained that when President Clinton made the politically symbolic gesture of releasing thirty million barrels of oil from the Strategic Petroleum Reserve last fall, that oil had to be shipped overseas to be refined.

"Even if we find the supplies," Abraham said, "moving that gas to market will require an additional thirty-eight thousand miles of transmission pipeline and two hundred fifty-five thousand miles of distribution lines—at an estimated cost of a hundred and twenty to a hundred and fifty billion dollars."

Abraham's projections were also dire with respect to the production of electricity: "Over the next twenty years, the Department of Energy estimates that electricity demand in the United States will increase by forty-five percent. That rising growth rate will require the construction of over thirteen hundred new power plants—about sixty-five every year. Yet the last time we added that much power was 1985. During the 1990s, electricity consumption far outstripped projections, driven by the energy-hungry information economy. Some experts calculate that the demands of the Internet already consume some eight to thirteen percent of electricity. If demand grows at just the same pace as during the last decade, we'll need nearly nineteen hundred new plants by 2020—or more than ninety every year—just to keep pace."

Abraham also pointed out that "[t]here hasn't been a new nuclear power plant permit granted since 1979. Many of the one hundred and three existing nuclear plants are not even expected to file for a renewal of their licenses as they expire over the next fifteen years. Even hydroelectric power generation is expected to fall sharply. Relicensing a hydro facility can take a decade or more and cost millions. And now, even though consumers are faced with potential blackouts and chronic electricity shortages in the West, activists and some political leaders want to breach one or more of the four federal dams on the Snake River to help young salmon on their trek to the sea."

Abraham is right, and he deserves credit for communicating that these problems are difficult, multifaceted, and very important. And conservatives must continue delivering this message.

It is critical that we conservatives ultimately triumph on the energy issue because, as with so many others, it will determine what kind of country we leave the next generation. And the danger we face from failing to become energy-independent cannot be overstated. Decades of liberal no-growth policies have seriously endangered our economic and national security. And the problem is only getting worse.

TEN

THE TAXMAN COMETH, AND COMETH, AND COMETH

Few people on the Left are as likeable and genuine as Robert Reich. Fewer still are as passionate and knowledgeable about what they believe. Reich served as secretary of labor during most of the 1990s. He was one of President Clinton's top domestic policy advisers and has emerged as one of the most astute and influential liberal thinkers within his party.

On April 22, 2002—as I was working on this book, and just a week after tax returns were due to the Internal Revenue Service—I interviewed Reich on *Hannity & Colmes* on a subject near and dear to my heart and his: taxes.

"Are we overtaxed as a nation?" I asked him.

"I don't think we're overtaxed as a nation, Sean."

Amazing. Government spending is at an all-time high. And the tax burden on American families is at a record high, having skyrocketed during the Clinton-Gore years. The tax code is more complicated, convoluted, and corrupt than ever. Working families are paying four times more in taxes today than they did in the 1950s. Many are struggling just to make ends meet. They were hit hard by the recession that began in Clinton's final year and continued into Bush's first year, which was exacerbated by 9/11, the anthrax attacks and threats, and the fear and confusion they caused. We badly need significant tax cuts to get this economy roaring again, and not just for a few months but for the long haul.

Of course, Reich knew what I was going to say, and he didn't wait for my response. "When I was labor secretary," he said, "we downsized the Labor Department from . . . about eighteen thousand people to sixteen thousand people. I didn't fire anybody. It was through attrition. I got a lot of awards for good management. We made more do with less, and I think that anybody who is in the public sector has to be a good manager and not waste the taxpayers' money. . . ."

"But the average American is working [four] months a year to pay that tax bill," I argued. "Look, I bought a car for my wife over the weekend, and it cost me nearly five thousand dollars in taxes on the car. That's insane."

"I don't like taxes," he conceded. "The question is, are you getting your money's worth?"

"No!" I told him. "As a conservative, I want less government. I believe in the principles of freedom. I don't want a cradle to the grave society, I don't want government health care. . . ."

Reich then resorted to a typical liberal ploy. He recited several legitimate government functions and asked if I supported funding them, thereby implying that I, too, worship at the alter of Big Government.

"Sean, do you want the military?" he asked.

"That's what I want, and we have that. Thank God George Bush is in office."

"How about firefighters and police officers?"

"Yes. We have that on a local level."

"How about roads?" Reich asked, "Do you want good roads?"

Reich is a good debater. But his argument was nothing more than an attempt to obscure the point. The truth is that we don't need to pay government half or more of every dollar we earn at the margin to have a first-rate military, top-of-the-line police, fire, and ambulance services, and good roads. Yes, government has some functions it needs to perform, and perform well. Indeed, our Founding Fathers adopted a Constitution that is chock-full of enumerated governmental powers. But the Left has pushed the country way, way beyond that—and that's precisely the problem.

Through his questions, Reich highlighted the philosophical differences between liberals and conservatives on these issues. No matter how generous and compassionate liberals insist on being with other people's money, our government was never intended to be like a department store, where people choose what they want and charge it to someone else. The Constitution creates a limited government that respects the God-given rights of each individual, not a massive, centralized bureaucracy that oversees virtually all private sector activity, manages entitlement programs, confiscates property, and redistributes wealth. In other words, the Constitution does not support the establishment of a massive welfare state with few if any limits on its power.

But the Left rejects limited government, which is why they're forced to contort and ignore the plain language of the Constitution to advance their agenda. And more than anything else they detest tax cuts, which fuel private initiative and enterprise and thus impede their Big Government agenda and, frankly, their political power. They also oppose tax cuts because to do so is their weapon of choice in the ongoing class warfare they wage against Republicans.

CAUGHT IN THE ACT

Of course, most liberal politicians aren't as candid as Robert Reich. They usually won't admit that they're not too concerned about the heavy tax burden imposed on industrious Americans. When the camera is on, they talk a good line about the overtaxed little guy, and they claim to support tax relief in some form or another.

Sometimes, however, they slip up and disclose their true feelings. And when they do, it's priceless.

In October of 1997, for example, then Senate minority leader Tom Daschle was speaking with some journalists when he was asked if Democrats thought the American people were overtaxed, and whether he had any interest in working with Republicans to cut taxes.

"Do you envision tax cuts next year and going into the election campaign?" asked one reporter. "The Republicans are so fond of saying the American people are overtaxed. Do the Democrats think that? Or do you think the tax is just about right and maybe no more tax cutting is needed?"

"We have the lowest tax rate of any industrialized country in the world," Daschle replied. "That tax rate has, in large measure, been the subject of a great deal of debate about fairness for a long period of time. We have a great disparity between the richest and poorest in this country. Our view is that we've got to make the tax system more fair. But certainly I don't think that many people are overtaxed."

Of course, as soon as the comments started making the rounds in Washington, Daschle began to bob and weave. He claimed he was quoted out of context. But he wasn't. And Republicans immediately began criticizing him and drawing the nation's attention to his remarks.

"When NASA is done exploring Mars, they might want to send a probe to Planet Daschle," quipped Christina Martin, House Speaker Newt Gingrich's press secretary. "[It's] a loopy liberal land where nobody is overtaxed, the IRS is run by sweet old ladies, and audits are like winning lottery tickets."

"Tom Daschle either believes our high tax rates are just about right or even worse, too low," noted Republican National Committee

Chairman Jim Nicholson. "I can't think of anything else he could have said to show how out of touch he and his party are with the struggles facing Main Street Americans."

Two days later, Daschle was forced to "revise and extend" his remarks.

"Let me just say before I close out," Daschle told reporters, "people with a real fertile imagination are taking comments I made about taxes the other day totally, in my view, out of context. Let me be very clear. Americans are overtaxed."

Four sentences later, Daschle said it again.

"Obviously, Americans are overtaxed."

Seven sentences later, Daschle said it again.

"I believe Americans are overtaxed," he insisted, adding that he just wanted "to be sure everybody understands what my position was." I suppose this is why he consistently opposed President Bush's tax relief package four years later.

SEE DICK RAISE TAXES

Of course, Robert Reich and Tom Daschle aren't the only liberals who believe in their hearts that Americans are undertaxed. The man who wants to be the next Speaker of the House does, too.

During the summer of 2001—not long after President Bush's across-the-board pro-growth tax cuts were becoming a reality—House Minority Leader Dick Gephardt was on a campaign swing through Des Moines, Iowa. He was there to help fellow Democrats raise money, build their organizations for the midterm elections, and no doubt lay the groundwork for his own presidential campaign in 2004.

Everything seemed business as usual until the day after his visit, when the *Des Moines Register* published this headline: "TAX INCREASE POSSIBLE, GEPHARDT SAYS." The *Register* reported that Gephardt "hinted Saturday that tax increases would be on the horizon if Democrats gain control of the U.S. House in next year's elections."

Speaking proudly to a group of fellow Democrats about his support for the 1993 Clinton-Gore tax increase—the largest in history—Gephardt proclaimed: "Let me tell you something. I'm glad we did what was right in 1993, and I'll do it again because I believe in being fiscally responsible with the taxpayers' money." How about allowing people to be fiscally responsible in their own households without confiscating an ever-increasing portion of their earnings, robbing them of the funds with which to provide for their needs and wants?

You see, Democrats are unusually candid in the confines of their meetings with fellow Democrats. Often the best way to learn about their true intentions is by observing what they say to each other. And as you can see, their true intentions are to oppose tax relief and sponsor further tax increases.

Republicans rightly called Gephardt to task.

"The message is clear: Republicans giveth and Democrats taketh away," said Jim Gilmore, then tax-cutting governor of Virginia and chairman of the Republican National Committee.

"Mr. Gephardt's candor about raising taxes demonstrates that the Democrats are out of step with the American people," noted Representative Tom DeLay, the tax-cutting House majority whip from Texas. "The American people learned two things this spring: Mr. Gephardt and congressional Democrats opposed meaningful tax relief, and President Bush and congressional Republicans delivered. Dick Gephardt's campaign commitment to higher taxes is a vivid reminder of the Democrats' two-step solution to any problem. They expand the government and shrink your wallet."

"The ink isn't even dry on the tax-rebate checks, yet the leader of the Democrats in the House of Representatives is already plotting ways to raise taxes," warned Representative J. C. Watts, the House Republican Conference chairman from Oklahoma.

Gephardt and his advisers, of course, scrambled to take back what he'd said, deny he'd said it, and blame the media for allegedly misquoting him. Gephardt insisted that the story's "assumption that House Democrats would raise taxes could not be further from the truth," adding that "I never addressed the future of taxes in my remarks because I don't believe they need to be raised. I believe that the Bush administration must work to keep this budget in the black despite an overzealous tax cut that threatens our prosperity."

What struck me was what a "nondenial denial" Gephardt's various statements really were. During an interview on CNN's *Late Edition* the following Sunday, for example, Gephardt attacked the *Des Moines Register*, other news outlets, and Republicans for "a misquote and inaccurate reporting." But then he added this: "What I said was I would do it again if the circumstances were the same as they were in '93." I would respectfully suggest that it's hard to find any such qualifier in the transcript of Gephardt's remarks.

But what were those "circumstances" to which Gephardt was referring? Well, for one thing, Democrats controlled the House of Representatives. Aren't those the "circumstances" Gephardt has been campaigning so long and hard to change?

Alan and I couldn't help but duke it out on the air over the whole delicious controversy.

"Dick Gephardt," Alan began. "You're going to say that Dick Gephardt—"

"Got caught," I quickly agreed.

"—said he was going to raise taxes."

"Yeah, he did."

"He never said he was going to raise taxes," Alan protested. "That's not something he ever said."

Look, Alan, I said, you can spin it any way you want, but the fact is that Gephardt defended raising taxes and announced that he'd do it again. I even read Alan the quote. It made no difference.

"Do you believe that Dick Gephardt really wants to raise taxes if he had the opportunity?" Alan asked House Majority Leader Dick Armey a few moments later. "Do you really believe that's his agenda?"

Talk about a slow pitch right over home plate!

"Dick Gephardt fought for the '93 tax increases," Armey replied, knocking the ball out of the park, "even though they were on senior citizens, on working women, and on energy."

Perhaps Gephardt didn't know his remarks would be reported when he bragged about his role in raising taxes and his intention to raise them again should the Democrats regain control of Congress. When confronted publicly with his own words, he backtracked. He knew his real position would damage any chance he might have of winning the presidency in 2004. But the truth is that first and foremost the Democratic Party stands for increasing taxes whenever and wherever possible.

ONCE A MISTAKE, TWICE A TREND

This wasn't the first time Gephardt slipped up. Exactly two years before—in June of 1999—he gave a low-profile speech in Philadelphia in which he called for increased government spending, particularly on education. How would he pay for it?

"You've got to have a combination of taking it out of the defense budget and raising revenue," Gephardt told the audience. "We can argue about how to do that, closing loopholes or even raising taxes to do it. . . . I'd be proud to vote for tax increases for schools. You bet I would."

Not surprisingly, the moment the comments made news, Gephardt started backtracking. He sent aides out to spin away his comments. He wrote a letter to the editor of the *Washington Times* claiming he had no intention of raising taxes. He was even forced to go on NBC's *Meet the Press* to do some badly needed damage control.

"You've created a little stir with some comments in Philadelphia," Tim Russert noted, quoting Gephardt's "proud" support for more tax increases.

"Well, that's nonsense," Gephardt responded. "What I was saying, and what I believe, is that we can find room in the budget without changes in revenues in order to fund education, and that's what we ought to do." What a total falsehood. I guess he was just kidding about being proud to raise taxes for schools.

After Gephardt finished spinning, Russert pressed him on where this money would come from.

"Well, you did say you would take it out of the defense budget," Russert noted. "Where? What defense programs should be cut to pay for education?"

Gephardt didn't deny saying defense should be cut. In fact, he added that U.S. intelligence services should have their budgets slashed.

"I think we can find room throughout the entire budget," Gephardt said confidently. "We spend a lot of money, and I think in a repetitious manner, on intelligence. I think we could save money in that part of the budget. We have a Defense intelligence agency, and we have one in every service plus the Central Intelligence Agency. . . ."

Consider how shortsighted Gephardt was. If he had been successful in further cutting our intelligence capabilities—which are an integral part of our war on terrorism—imagine how more difficult it would be today to protect our homeland from more attacks.

The American people didn't buy Gephardt's "vision" of taxing, spending, and cutting defense in 1988, when he first sought the presidency, and they won't buy it in 2004 should he run again.

A LONG LINE OF LIBERAL TAX-RAISERS

On those infrequent occasions when liberals claim to support tax cuts, they are meager, disproportionately and unfairly skewed against the majority of producers, and designed as a political tactic to prevent meaningful tax relief offered by Republicans. But obviously their real preference is to raise taxes. You should understand that liberals begin with the belief that the money you and I produce is the government's money. The portion not taxed is what that beneficent government, in its abundant graciousness, allows you to keep. And those who harbor this worldview aren't much bothered by what this means for our freedoms. They seem wholly oblivious to the concept our framers intimately understood and incorporated into the Constitution: Political freedom is not achieved merely by giving people some voice (through voting) in the management of their government. Real freedom is only possible by imposing restraints on government. Liberals don't grasp the inverse relationship between the size and scope of government (in areas other than those in which it is authorized to function by the Constitution) and our individual liberties. So they rarely if ever hesitate to hoist their hands in favor of expanding the central government and raising taxes to fund the federal leviathan.

One of my favorite examples of an old-fashioned tax-raising liberal is Walter "Fritz" Mondale. The Minnesota Democrat not only served as Jimmy Carter's vice president but also had the misfortune of running in 1984 against one of the greatest American presidents, and the greatest tax-cutter, in our history—Ronald Wilson Reagan.

To this day, I can distinctly remember watching the Democratic Convention in the summer of '84 where Mondale said: "Let's tell the truth. It must be done, it must be done. Mr. Reagan will raise taxes, and so will I. He won't tell you. I just did."

Not surprisingly, the Left hailed Mondale's foresight and courage.

The editors of the *Washington Post* wrote: "It goes against all the political axioms to do what Walter Mondale did in San Francisco: to come out for a tax increase." But compared with Reagan's call for "tax simplification and reform," the *Post* wrote, "Mr. Mondale's ploy is better politics," because while "no one likes a tax increase," voters already had a sense that "a tax increase is coming, sooner or later. By promising that increase, and providing a vague sense of what it would be, Mr. Mondale has gone a long way toward shifting the focus of the campaign from a referendum on what is to a referendum on what is to be. This is to his advantage." In other words, it was inconceivable to the *Post* that Reagan could have been telling the truth, but in the unlikely event that he was, he was not dealing in reality. It's hard to escape the snobbery and elitism here.

The editors of the *New York Times* went even further, saying that defense spending should be slashed and taxes should be raised on everybody, not just wealthy individuals and business owners.

In one editorial, they wrote, "Mr. Mondale and other leading Democrats are ready to share the burden of asking the voters to face up to realities," arguing that a "combination of tax increases and cuts in defense and social spending" would be a chance to show real "leadership."

A few days later, the *Times* ran an op-ed piece by a Washington lawyer—described as "active in liberal and Democratic Party affairs since the New Deal"—entitled "HOW THE DEMOCRATS CAN WIN." The writer praised the Democratic Convention and a week of "electrifying liberal speeches"—including Mondale's speech, which "told the truth on the need to raise taxes." He added, "What more could anyone want?"

A few weeks later, the *Times* editors wrote, "Mr. Mondale is right to warn of a tax increase, wrong to imply it can come mostly from 'the rich.' But he and the budget deficit deserve a better reply than Mr. Reagan has yet given."

Not to be outdone, *Time* did a big story: "SCORING POINTS WITH CANDOR; MONDALE PUTS REAGAN ON THE DEFENSIVE BY PROMISING NEW TAXES." They even quoted Gephardt, who said that "there's something very politically attractive about being honest with the American people."

Despite the Left's celebration of Mondale, on November 6, 1984,

Ronald Reagan won the biggest landslide in the two-century-old history of American politics. He won forty-nine states (Mondale won only his home state of Minnesota). He won 59 percent of the popular vote (including an amazing 45 percent of the vote from union households, traditionally a Democratic stronghold). He won a record 525 electoral votes (FDR won 523 electoral votes in 1936). He also held the Senate for the GOP and picked up fourteen more Republican seats in the House. It was an absolute blowout. It was also a stunning testament to the power of a strong conservative leader standing up for his principles in the face of withering attacks by Big Government politicians and their media backers.

How did the losers react? Did they acknowledge the country's crystal clear ratification of Reaganite conservatism? Did they take it as a sign from the people that they'd better rethink their out-of-favor agenda? Of course not. Then Speaker of the House Thomas P. "Tip" O'Neill, a Massachusetts Democrat, spoke for most liberals when he said: "I don't think there was any mandate out there whatsoever."

Here the elitism graduates to arrogance, with the unmistakable message: liberals know better than the people what's best for them. I think it's fair to say that no matter what the outcome of any election, a liberal's job is never done. They live to increase taxes, increase spending, and cut national security. And they are rarely deterred, even by the will of the people, which as we've seen, they only pretend to respect.

THE TRUTH ABOUT TAXES

We all ought to be concerned by the incremental encroachments of our federal government and the freedoms they are eroding. Here's an axiomatic truth: The more expansive government becomes, the more difficult it is to dismantle. There is a certain inertia to government that militates against rollbacks. Part of the reason is that even many of those who might be generally opposed to Big Government become dependent on government benefits, creating a cycle of dependency. This can be difficult to break. Though not impossible, as recent experience, for example, has shown with welfare reform.

"The cost of federal, state and local government in America has exceeded the $3 trillion mark," wrote economist Steve Moore in a February 2002 study entitled "The Most Expensive Government in World History." "Not only does the United States spend more than the entire economy of France, but government spends more money in just a single year than it spent combined from 1781 to 1900, even after adjusting for inflation."

Moore—one of the brightest and most insightful policy analysts in Washington today—notes that while government consumed about 5 percent of America's national income during the days of FDR's New Deal, today it consumes between 20 and 25 percent. Worse, over the course of the next five years, the federal government alone is expected to spend "more money than was spent on World Wars I and II, the Civil War, and the Revolutionary War—even after adjusting for inflation."

What does that mean in practical terms? Moore puts it this way:

★ In 1900 total taxes per household were $1,900 (using constant 2000 dollars).

★ In 1950 total taxes per household were $11,000.

★ In 1999, total taxes per household reached $30,000.

Here's another way of looking at it. According to a report by the Washington, D.C.–based Tax Foundation:

★ In 1900, Tax Freedom Day—the day when Americans have earned enough money to pay off their total tax bill for the year—was January 20.

★ In 1950, Tax Freedom Day was March 29.

★ In 1993, the year Bill Clinton and Al Gore took office, Tax Freedom Day was April 20.

★ In 2000, Bill Clinton and Al Gore's last year in office, Tax Freedom Day was May 1.

During the Clinton-Gore years, the federal tax burden alone grew by a staggering 45 percent, from an average of $4,625 per person to about $6,690.

Moreover, we pay taxes on almost everything we do. There are federal income taxes, Social Security taxes, Medicare taxes, corporate taxes, federal airline taxes, gas taxes, cigarette taxes, alcohol taxes, and a dizzying array of excise taxes and fees. As if that weren't enough, there are state income taxes, local taxes, sales taxes, property taxes, hotel taxes, water taxes, electricity taxes, phone taxes, and on and on. Even when you're dead, your heirs have to pay the "death tax," a tax that from its inception has never been anything other than a socialistic measure primarily aimed not at producing revenues but at confiscating private property (a lynchpin of political and economic liberty) and redistributing wealth.

The cold truth is that the American taxpayer is being abused and plundered by his own government.

On top of all this, the federal income tax code, with all its byzantine rules and regulations, is more convoluted and complex than ever before. Between 1955 and 2000, for example, the total length of the federal tax code and its regulation grew by an astronomical 831 percent—from 744,000 words to some 6,929,000 words. Americans now spend (or, more accurately, *waste*) 5.8 billion hours filing out tax forms and we spend more than $194 billion a year complying with our out-of-control tax code.

It's no wonder, then, that a full 65 percent of Americans polled in October of 2000—just before the Bush vs. Gore election—said they were overtaxed.

Nor is it any wonder that even in the months following 9/11, according to pollsters, Americans still feared an IRS audit more than they feared anthrax.

As the late conservative icon Barry Goldwater once put it: "The income tax created more criminals than any other single act of government."

BUSH'S BOLDEST MOVE

President Bush has remained true to his campaign pledge in leading the fight for tax cuts. Without question, the $1.3 trillion tax cut plan passed in the summer of 2001 has been the boldest part of Bush's domestic agenda. And it has taken no small amount of courage and resolve. Both during the presidential campaign and after, the Left assailed Bush for seeking to reduce marginal tax rates and abolish the death tax. They accused him of seeking to bless the rich and soak the poor, courting big business instead of "the little folks," and lining the pockets of special interests at the expense of mom and pop.

"This may be the first budget in history that wasn't just dead on arrival, it was dead before arrival," bellowed Tom Daschle when the president's tax cut and spending proposals were first sent to Congress.

"You've got a Robin Hood in reverse—tax cuts that are crowding out other investments that are important to Minnesota," whined Paul Wellstone, one of the Senate's leading liberals.

"This whole budget and tax cut plan puts politics first and people last," charged Hillary Clinton. "We're in for a fight—I intend to be on the front lines on that fight."

Throughout the 1990s, our old friend Dick Gephardt railed against Republican attempts to let Americans keep more of what they earned, warning of "risky and irresponsible" tax cuts that would trigger "a rerun of the 1980s-style voodoo economics."

Not surprisingly, Gephardt launched a feverish (though ultimately unsuccessful) campaign to defeat President Bush's tax cut, calling the conservative approach "irresponsible," a "mismanagement of the economy," and "a risky gamble" that threatened to revisit the mistakes of the Reagan tax cuts in the 1980s.

"You'll remember back in the eighties, then Senate majority leader Howard Baker called [Reagan's tax cuts] a 'risky riverboat gamble,'" Gephardt told reporters. "Well, here we are again. After we fixed the problem, we had eight years of recovery. It's the best economy any of us had seen in our lifetime, and now we're tearing it down and breaking the confidence, both from rhetoric and from proposals, that had been created over a long period of time."

Day after day, week after week, Gephardt condemned the Bush tax cuts, arguing that marginal rate cuts would do little or nothing to revive an economy that was rapidly slowing in the spring of 2001.

"At a time when key indicators tell us that there is an economic slowdown," said Gephardt, "the president has sent a plan that ignores the needs of average Americans and provides a blueprint to fulfill a campaign promise to cut taxes first no matter what the cost." Can you believe these statements? Not even the most liberal of economists will argue for tax increases during a recession. There is a consensus among economists that during economic slowdowns tax cuts and other measures are advisable to stimulate the economy. Yet Gephardt characterized Bush's plan, designed to stimulate an ailing economy, as one that would be harmful to the average person experiencing the negative effects of the downturn. It was Gephardt and the Democrats, not the Republicans, who crafted their tax policy around partisan rather than economic considerations.

Gephardt likened the Bush tax cut plan of 2001 to the Reagan tax cut plan of 1981 and warned that Democrats would never stand by and let that happen again. "The one thing you're going to find unity in the Democratic Party about, I believe, is not repeating that mistake," declared Gephardt.

Gephardt's high dudgeon masks a serious measure of hypocrisy. For despite all his high-pitched rhetoric, he ultimately voted for the Reagan tax cut back in 1981. Indeed, he also backed Reagan's 1986 tax reform act. For this reason, during the Democratic presidential primaries in 1988, one of his rivals dubbed Gephardt "the godfather of the Reagan tax cuts."

Together, the two Reagan reforms brought the nation's top marginal tax rate (on the richest Americans) down from an outrageous 70 percent to just 28 percent.

And, by the way, Gephardt wasn't alone. When Tom Daschle was South Dakota's lone congressman back in 1981, he, too, wound up voting for the Reagan tax cut!

REAGAN WAS RIGHT, AND SO WAS JFK

Jimmy Carter left office with the American economy sinking fast— soaring unemployment, double-digit inflation, double-digit interest rates, a contracting economy, a loss of national self-confidence, and a sense that America's best days might be behind her. That was the bad news. The good news was that Ronald Reagan's economic leadership and dramatic tax cuts set into motion one of the greatest peacetime economic expansions in American history. For seven straight years, U.S. economic growth averaged 4 percent. Inflation plummeted. Interest rates were cut in half. Nearly twenty million new jobs were created, and the Dow Jones Industrial Average shot up an amazing 240 percent as new businesses flourished and middle-income Americans saw their pension plans create significant wealth.

Did the Reagan tax cuts cause the deficits of the 1980s? Not at all. In fact, government revenue nearly doubled during the Reagan years.

"Total tax revenues climbed by 99.4 percent during the 1980s," notes Dan Mitchell, one of the leading tax experts in Washington. "The results are even more impressive, however, when one looks at what happened to personal income tax revenues. Once the economy received an unambiguous tax cut in January 1983, personal income tax revenues climbed dramatically, increasing by more than 54 percent by 1989 (28 percent after adjusting for inflation)."

No, the deficits of the 1980s were caused by the insatiable spending demands of congressional Democrats, particularly the Democrat-controlled House.

As the budget information below demonstrates (and contrary to conventional wisdom), seven of the eight budgets President Reagan submitted to Congress proposed far less spending than Congress ultimately approved. In fact, had all of Reagan's budgets been adopted, federal spending would have been 25 percent less on a cumulative basis. But as congressional liberals used to say, Reagan's budget plans were always "dead on arrival."

FEDERAL BUDGET OUTLAYS PROPOSED (REAGAN) AND ACTUAL (CONGRESS), PERCENT DIFFERENCE, AND CUMULATIVE PERCENT DIFFERENCE (IN BILLIONS OF DOLLARS)

	Outlays			
Fiscal Year	**Proposed**	**Actual**	**% Difference**	**(Cumulative) % Difference**
1982	695.3	745.8	7.3	
1983	773.3	808.4	4.5	12.1
1984	862.5	851.8	−1.2	10.8

Fiscal Year	Proposed	Actual	% Difference	(Cumulative) % Difference
1985	940.3	946.4	0.7	11.6
1986	973.7	990.3	1.7	13.5
1987	994.0	1003.9	1.0	14.6
1988	1024.3	1064.1	3.9	19.1
1989	1094.2	1144.2	4.6	24.5
Totals	$7,357.6	$7,554.9		
Average			2.8	

Source: http.//reagan.webteamone.com/reagan_budgets.html

Did Reagan's tax cuts steal from the poor to give to the rich? Not at all. The rich did pay lower rates as a result of the marginal rate tax reductions. But because the economy flourished and more wealth was created, the richest Americans actually ended up paying a higher percentage of the total tax burden. In fact, economist Bruce Bartlett notes that in 1983 the total effective (that is, average) federal tax rate on the wealthiest 1 percent of Americans was 26.8 percent, but by 2000 it had climbed to 32.7 percent. At the same time, the effective tax rate on the poorest 20 percent of Americans dropped from 8.1 percent in 1983 to just 5.3 percent.

So the next time you hear some liberal complain about the 1980s, be ready with the facts to challenge them.

"The best sign that our economic program is working," Reagan once quipped, "is that they don't call it 'Reaganomics' anymore." (Of course, Bill Clinton resurrected the pejorative phrase *trickle-down Reaganomics* when he was misrepresenting the Reagan record during his first presidential campaign. But even Clinton's glibness cannot erase the historical record on "Reaganomics." President Bush's tax plan, like Reagan's before it, was the same approach John F. Kennedy urged in the 1960s.

Kennedy proposed reducing the top marginal tax rate from a suffocating 91 percent in 1963 to 70 percent in 1965. Tragically, Kennedy's life was cut short by an assassin's bullets. But guess who went on to pass the Kennedy tax cuts? Lyndon B. Johnson and the Democrat-controlled Congress.

"The Kennedy tax cuts helped to trigger a record economic expansion," notes Dan Mitchell. "Between 1961 and 1968, the inflation-adjusted economy expanded by more than 42 percent. On a yearly basis, economic growth averaged more than 5 percent." Moreover, Mitchell notes that "tax revenues climbed from $94 billion in 1961 to $153 billion in 1968, an increase of 62 percent (33 percent after adjusting for inflation)."

Kennedy was right about tax cuts. He understood that they create prosperity for all Americans by rewarding saving, investing, and working. Yet the current leadership of the Democratic Party, while routinely invoking Kennedy's name and memory, rejects his pro-growth economic legacy—which was among his greatest successes.

IF RUSSIA CAN DO IT . . .

I've interviewed Republican presidential contender Steve Forbes and House Majority Leader Dick Armey countless times, and the more I listen to these men, the more convinced I am that it's time to scrap this corrupt and indefensible federal income tax code.

Either a flat tax or a national sales tax would be preferable to the current mess. But personally, I lean toward the flat tax. We should start with something like a generous personal exemption of $15,000 for each adult and $5,000 for each child. That would mean that a family of four would pay no federal income tax on their first $40,000 of income—which would amount to a tax cut of between $1,000 and $2,000 for many Americans. Above the personal exemptions, we should tax income at a single fixed rate, say 15 or 17 percent, allowing deductions only for charitable contributions and home mortgage interest payments. Abolish the tax on capital gains. Abolish the marriage penalty. Abolish the alternative minimum tax. Abolish taxes on savings and investment. Abolish the death tax—permanently, not with some outrageous sunset provision that will cause the abolition to be lifted in ten years. Allow for immediate expensing of capital equipment for businesses. And we *should* create a tax form no bigger than a postcard or a single sheet of paper.

A flat tax would be simple to use. It would take about five minutes to complete. A flat tax would be fair. Everyone would be treated equally under the law.

Moreover, by removing the dead weight of 5.8 billion hours and $194 billion a year wasted in tax preparation and compliance, the flat tax would be pro-growth. Economists of all stripes agree it would bring interest rates down. They also agree it would unleash a serious economic boom. We would very likely see America's long-term and consistent economic growth rates averaging upwards of 4 to 5 percent a year. That, in turn, would cause government revenues to soar, providing much-needed additional funds to strengthen Medicare and save Social Security.

A flat tax would also prevent the torment of intimidating audits and would decriminalize honest mistakes resulting from the complexity of the current code.

Since January 2001, even formerly Communist Russia has embraced a 13 percent flat tax! It's lower than any other country in Europe. It's certainly lower than here. And it's working. As Russians pay far lower rates than they ever have before, they're working harder, creating more, and experiencing strong economic growth. In 2001 alone, some 400,000 new businesses were created—up 11 percent— and tax revenues soared a whopping 47 percent.

The fact is, tax rate cuts work every time they're tried, no matter what the country—or state, for that matter. But the question remains whether those of us who are trumpeting this truth will ultimately prevail in the war of ideas or be defeated by the boundless demagoguery of those who have a vested interest in distorting the truth. I believe we have reason to be optimistic. If we follow the lead of Ronald Reagan and George W. Bush, who overcame the class warfare tactics of the Left by taking our case directly to the American people, there's no reason we can't succeed.

ELEVEN

WINNING THE POLITICAL WARS

If there's one thing I've learned in my time in radio and television, it's this: It makes no difference how good your product or service is if you don't effectively market it.

In the world of ideas, conservatives have great products to sell. On the whole range of issues—from intelligence to immigration and national security to education and energy and taxation—conservatives have better ideas than liberals. They have superior prescriptions for governance, for solving society's problems, and for maximizing freedom.

The Republican Party is the vehicle through which conservative ideas have the best chance of thriving. Reciprocally, the Republican Party has its best chance of thriving by adhering to the precepts of conservatism. To the extent that Republican leaders have over time embraced a bold and principled brand of conservatism, they've been successful politically and in advancing their agenda. But when they have diluted their message for the sake of appeasing the center, they have suffered politically and their agenda has been compromised.

Liberal Democrats, by contrast, have largely lost the idealism they once had. Their ideas of Big Government have been in disfavor for some time, especially since the fall of the Soviet Empire. Whereas Republicans have generally benefited from remaining true to conservative ideals, Democratic presidential contenders have discovered that embracing full-blown liberalism has been the kiss of death for their political aspirations (e.g., McGovern and Mondale).

Bill Clinton both secured his party's nomination and won the general election by adopting the more centrist agenda of the Democratic Leadership Council. Often when he governed to the Left he alienated the electorate. By trying to ram the Hillary Care health-care debacle down the nation's throat, he handed the Republicans a congressional majority for the first time in forty years. And some of the things for which Clinton has received the greatest acclaim and for which he has taken credit were conservative policies enacted over his strenuous and repeated objections (balancing the budget and welfare reform among them).

So to a great extent the Democratic Party is no longer a party of ideas. Instead it has become a party of invective. Its divisiveness and demagoguery have little new to offer beyond expanding the welfare state. The Democrats talk a great game of compassion but can never explain what is compassionate about increasing government dependency and eroding our liberties.

That said, however, conservatives face a major problem. While conservatives have better ideas, liberals are generally better at politics—by a long shot. They play to win and they take no prisoners. In the process they often play dirty and dishonestly. Republicans face the challenge of fighting Democrats effectively without adopting their ruthless tactics. That's a tall, but necessary, order. The first step is for Republicans to shed their collective naïveté and realize they're in the fight of their lives. They can aspire to a new tone all they want to, but a rapprochement takes two, and the other side is offering nothing but the politics of personal destruction. Republicans can retain their decency, but they must fight—accepting the difficult challenge of fighting a clean fight against an opponent who plays dirty.

LIBERAL FEARMONGERING

Remember back in November of 1994 when voters swept Democrats out and Republicans into control of the U.S. House of Representatives and the Senate? Liberals were absolutely stunned—and desperate. They'd been so good at politics for so long—dominating the debate and control of Congress for decades—that it probably never occurred to many of them that they might one day lose power.

Faced with overwhelming rejection by voters who preferred the smaller-government agenda put forth in the Republicans' Contract with America, the Democrats unleashed a hysterical propaganda campaign.

House Minority Leader Dick Gephardt, not surprisingly, led the charge. Just one month after the Republican landslide, he branded Newt Gingrich and his fellow conservatives a "band of trickle-down terrorists." He said conservatives would use a "tried and tested GOP formula" of "division, exclusion, and fear" to implement their "Contract *on* America," apparently likening conservatives to a bloodthirsty Mafia family.

"When they swerve to the extreme, we'll champion the mainstream," Gephardt said in a speech broadcast live on CNN. "When they fly off to fiscal fantasy land, we'll guard America's real homes and jobs and families. When they stump for the wealthy, we'll stand for the workers, the people whose interests can't be protected by a Star Wars defense disaster. And when they try to impose the radical views of the few on all of America, we'll fight for the core responsibilities of work and responsibility and tolerance and diversity that always have been the creed of family life. And when they try to punish and pigeonhole those who are the most vulnerable, we'll work . . . to give them real opportunities, and when they try to rewrite the Constitution of the United States in a flash of ideological ink, we'll tell them 'Thanks, but no thanks,' our Founding Fathers got it right the first time."

Over the next few months, their vitriol got even worse. President Clinton said that conservatives wanted to "make war on the kids of this country." White House Chief of Staff Leon Panetta said that conservatives wanted to "literally take meals from kids" and "run over kids." Mario Cuomo likened conservatives to Nazi "storm troopers." Representative Jose E. Serrano, a New York Democrat, unloaded on conservatives and their "mean-spirited, reactionary, insensitive, indifferent, right-wing, extremist, anti-poor, anti-children, Constitution-bashing, bordering on racist 'Contract on America.'"

Simultaneously, the left-wing media dutifully chimed in.

One nationally syndicated columnist devoted an entire column to "WHY CONSERVATIVES DON'T DESERVE RESPECT," arguing that "no matter how smart or literate or successful they are," conservatives "do not deserve cultural affirmation." A local columnist in Denver couldn't simply disagree with Republican senator Ben Nighthorse Campbell on the issue of campaign finance reform. She also felt compelled to attack him personally by mocking his Native American heritage, describing him as a "pimp" in "a headdress." National Public Radio's Nina Totenberg made this outrageous statement about Senator Jesse Helms, the conservative's conservative from North Carolina: "I think he ought to be worried about what's going on in the good Lord's mind . . . because if there's retributive justice, he'll get AIDS from a transfusion or one of his grandchildren will get it."

As if that weren't enough, Hollywood got into the act. Barbra Streisand, for example, gave a speech at Harvard's Kennedy School of Government attacking Newt Gingrich, Jesse Helms, Rush Limbaugh, and the Christian Coalition. She ripped conservatives as the "far right," a "dangerous" group who were unwilling to tackle tough issues like racism, sexism, and global injustices like the Holocaust. A few years later, as the House of Representatives was impeaching Clinton for his high crimes and misdemeanors, Alec Baldwin said on *Late Night with Conan O'Brien:* "If we were in other countries, all of us together would go down to Washington and we would stone Henry Hyde to death! We would stone him to death! We would stone [him] to death and we would go to their homes and we'd kill their wives and their children. We would kill their families!"

As you might imagine, Representative Hyde—one of the most honorable and decent members of the United States Congress—wasn't amused. "Excuse me for not laughing," he told reporters. "[Baldwin] wants my family stoned to death by a mob. Imagine if a Republican said such a thing."

This incident was instructive for at least two reasons. One is that it caused absolutely no flap among the cultural elite. Only conservatives were appalled at Baldwin's ravings, proving once again that the liberals' self-proclaimed "tolerance" is a farce. Their tolerance extends to ideas and people of which they approve—no further, which means it's not tolerance at all. Among the tolerant Left, there is no respect, much less protection, for conservatives and their ideas.

The other lesson we can glean from this is that, despite their claims to have a corner on compassion, many liberals are capable of singular viciousness. One may protest that I'm being unfair for drawing broader conclusions from this; after all, it was only one actor spouting off. That would be true but for the facts that (1) Baldwin was not condemned by his ideological colleagues, (2) he is still respected in liberal circles, and (3) there are plenty more with tongues as sharp as his.

Another sharp tongue was unleashed on CBS's *Late Show with Craig Kilborn* in August 2000, when a violent graphic flashed briefly on the screen. The words *Snipers Wanted* were superimposed over footage of George W. Bush accepting the Republican nomination at his party's convention in Philadelphia. CBS, after being bombarded with complaints, reluctantly acknowledged that the graphic was "inappropriate and regrettable" and that CBS and the program's producer, Worldwide Pants, would investigate it. Bush, in his usually gracious way, accepted the apology and said he looked forward to seeing the results of CBS's investigation. You can rest assured that had Al Gore been the subject of the clip, heads would have rolled at CBS.

THE RACE CARD

One of the most reprehensible cards in the Left's deck is the race card. During the 1998 congressional elections, the Democratic Party ran an incredibly malicious anti-Republican television ad in Missouri.

"When you don't vote, you allow another cross to burn," said a male announcer. "When you don't vote, you let another assault wound a brother or sister. When you don't vote, you let the Republicans continue to cut school lunches and Head Start. When you don't vote, you allow the Republicans to give tax breaks to the wealthy while threatening Social Security and Medicare. Do vote, and you elect Democrats who want to strengthen Social Security and Medicare, make classes small by hiring a hundred thousand new teachers, and repair and rebuild public schools. When you vote, you elect Democrats committed to a Patient's Bill of rights that lets us, not the insurance companies, make choices about our health care. Voting will change things for the better. On November third, vote, vote smart, vote Democratic for Congress and U.S. Senate." A female announcer then concluded, "Paid for by Missouri Democratic Party, Donna Knight, Treasurer."

While the cynicism of this tactic speaks for itself, there was no apology, much less a retraction, from Democrats when confronted by Republicans. This Democratic Party, which prides itself on promoting civility among people and races, didn't even bother to distance itself from this discourse.

On *Hannity & Colmes,* I confronted Michael Brown—son of the late Clinton commerce secretary Ron Brown—about the despicable race-baiting tactics his party uses, such as that cross-burning TV ad.

"Michael, aren't you ashamed that your party ran an ad like that?" I asked him.

"No. Actually I guess I see why you're disappointed," Brown told me. "I mean, the facts hurt."

"You should be ashamed."

"I'm not ashamed at all," he shot back.

"So [if] you vote for a Republican, another cross is going to burn?" I pressed.

"That's the one sentence you pick out. They talked about specific issues."

"Are you ashamed of that sentence?" I pressed again.

Look, he said, "the Democratic Party has fought so hard for the American people, and the Republican Party has not. They never have, never will. . . . Sean, I may even agree with you that one of those lines may not be the best thing to do in an ad like that, but the facts are accurate."

What facts? This ad was clearly directed at potential African-American voters. It consisted of an admonition to vote Democratic, preceded by four racially charged, scaremongering statements grossly mischaracterizing the likely impact of Republican policies. According to the ad, voting Republican promotes cross burning, the commission of violent crimes against blacks, slashing of the school lunch program, Head Start, Social Security, and Medicare, and redistribution of tax revenues from the poor to the rich. Are those the "facts" to which Mr. Brown was referring? Utter shamelessness.

Another recent example of liberal race-baiting was a television ad from the 2000 election season, in which the National Association for the Advancement of Colored People tried to link George W. Bush to the sickening dragging death of a black man named James Byrd in Texas.

"I'm Renee Mullins, James Byrd's daughter," the ad began. "On June 7, 1998, in Texas, my father was killed. He was beaten, chained, and then dragged three miles to his death, all because he was black. So when Governor George W. Bush refused to support hate crimes legislation, it was like my father was killed all over again. Call George W. Bush and tell him to support hate crimes legislation. We won't be dragged away from our future."

My heart goes out to the Byrd family. I cannot imagine the pain and anguish they've been through. When the three men responsible for that evil act were arrested, convicted, and sentenced—two to die by lethal injection and the third to spend his life in prison—no one cheered louder than I.

That said, the ad was contemptible. It's one of the meanest ads I've ever seen in politics, and unfortunately I predict more of the same in 2002 and 2004 and beyond.

Conservatives didn't kill James Byrd. But thanks to conservative support for Texas's death penalty law—which, if liberals had their way, wouldn't exist—two of James Byrd's killers are to be executed.

It should be noted that among the other reasons conservatives oppose so-called hate crimes legislation is that they aspire to a color-blind society, not one constantly steeped in the degrading mire of color consciousness. They believe that by constantly placing race at the forefront of the national debate, we are reverting to the place from which Martin Luther King sought deliverance for blacks—that is, a society where men are judged by the color of their skin, not the content of their character.

But Democrats have so effectively demonized Republicans with the race card that they are often too intimidated to oppose race-conscious measures, like affirmative action laws or these hate crime bills, for fear of being falsely branded as bigots. That's probably why many Senate Republicans conspired with Democrats in 1999 to pass, under the anonymity of voice vote, the Hate Crimes Prevention Act.

Just the previous year, enough Senate Republicans opposed the bill (and in some cases vocally) to prevent its passage. But that was before the James Byrd murder, the fatal flogging of a gay college student in Wyoming, and a shooting spree in Illinois and Indiana by a man allegedly part of a white supremacist group.

Democrats are brilliant at parlaying such incidents to their political advantage. Everyone knows that hate crimes legislation would not have prevented James Byrd's murder by the savages that dragged him to death. But that didn't matter to Democrats, who shamelessly used these atrocities as a catalyst for their divisive legislation. They employed precisely the same tactic in their efforts to pass gun control legislation: Clinton used the Columbine massacre, knowing that the perpetrators broke more than sixty existing laws and that the legislation he was proposing would have had no deterrent effect on the killers. Ditto with campaign finance legislation: Democrats used the Enron scandal to rally support for this bill, despite the fact that Enron disproved the driving theory of reform; that is, that money leads to access and corruption. With Enron, it is clear that the Bush administration did not tailor its policy in favor of the corporate giant, even though it had contributed mightily to its presidential campaign coffers.

Democrats should be reminded from time to time that they don't have a stellar record of egalitarianism themselves. Indeed, if you look at history, you'll see that the Democrats have a shameful record of opening their big tent to racists and segregationists. Robert Byrd, the most senior member of the United States Senate—a man revered among his Democratic colleagues and the media as "the conscience of the Senate," who chairs the enormously powerful Appropriations Committee—was once a member of the Ku Klux Klan. Yes, Byrd quit. Yes, he says he regrets it. But then Byrd also went on to fight furiously against the 1964 Civil Rights Act. He even filibustered against the bill for nearly fourteen hours.

And Republicans have a better record on race than they are often given credit for. When former Klan leader David Duke tried to run for governor of Louisiana and then for president as a Republican, the GOP fought him tooth and nail. Former president Ronald Reagan, then president George Bush, his son George W. Bush, and other Republican leaders vigorously denounced Duke and actively worked against him. Reagan made radio ads supporting Duke's Republican opponent in 1989. Dubya personally traveled to Louisiana to denounce Duke and support his opponent. Conservatives took their stand against racism and the Klan, and they won.

And in point of fact, it was Republicans who provided the crucial winning margins necessary to pass the civil rights legislation of the mid-1960s, including the Civil Rights Act and the Voting Rights Act. Republicans were more supportive of these core civil rights bills than were the Democrats. "In the House," notes civil rights expert Linda Chavez, "80 percent of Republicans voted for the Civil Rights Act of 1964, compared with only 63 percent of Democrats. In the Senate, 82 percent of Republicans supported the legislation, compared with 69 percent of Democrats." Al Gore's father—then a Democratic senator from Tennessee—not only voted against the Civil Rights Act of 1964, he helped lead a filibuster of segregationst southerners against it. Also voting against it was Senator J. William Fulbright, a Democrat from Arkansas for whom Bill Clinton interned and who was one of Clinton's political mentors.

In addition to legislation aimed at enforcing equal rights, conservative Republicans have advocated policies that promote opportunity and prosperity for all Americans. It was the Reagan tax cuts and pro-growth economic program that led to an explosion of new wealth creation for black and Hispanic Americans.

"From 1982 to 1987, the number of black-owned firms increased by nearly 38 percent, about triple the overall business growth rate during that period," noted then Housing and Urban Development secretary

Jack Kemp at the ten-year anniversary of the signing of the tax cut bill he helped author. "Hispanic-owned businesses soared by 81 percent. The number of black families earning $50,000 a year doubled during the 1980s—a stunning accomplishment."

Black Enterprise magazine concurred. It took issue with some of the Reagan-Bush administration's policies, but it also agreed that the decade of the 1980s "was characterized by vigorous growth in the size and diversity of the nation's largest black-owned companies." Total sales more than tripled, from $2.3 billion to nearly $8 billion. "Average sales per company rose from $17 million to $45 million during the decade, [and] black-owned companies with sales exceeding $20 million became increasingly common beginning in 1984." By 1985, there were some 350,000 black-owned businesses in America, up dramatically from just 50,000 in 1968.

For the last several decades, conservatives have been fighting for educational freedom, choice, and opportunity in our inner cities—in places like Milwaukee, Cleveland, and elsewhere—so that all children, regardless of race, color, or ethnic background, have a chance to receive quality education. It is also conservatives who have championed enterprise zones, which are intended to significantly reduce the tax and regulatory burdens on businesses that locate or remain in economically poor areas, as an inducement for businesses to expand and employ more of the people who live there.

And consider this: it was Ronald Reagan who made Martin Luther King, Jr.'s birthday a national holiday. It was Reagan who extended the Voting Rights Act for an unprecedented twenty-five years. And it was Reagan who appointed Colin Powell the first African-American national security adviser. (Incidentally, it was also Reagan who appointed the first woman to the United States Supreme Court.)

More recently, among his first acts as president, George W. Bush appointed Condoleeza Rice the first African-American women to serve as national security adviser. And he appointed Powell as the first African-American secretary of state.

The party of Abraham Lincoln has a strong record of inclusion, and of supporting policies that are beneficial to minorities and all Americans. Republicans should proudly and confidently invoke this record as we continue to reach out to African-Americans and other minorities, as George W. Bush has done. There is *no* reason that an overwhelming majority of African-Americans and other minorities should continue to identify with the Democratic Party. The Democrats may be more shameless in trying to craft messages that minority-interest focus groups want to hear—but the principles and policies of the Republican Party are the only ones that will empower them to lay claim to the American dream.

THE CLASS CARD

Another favorite weapon of the Left is the class card, where they pit income groups against each other through the divisive politics of envy and greed. During the 1980s, liberals railed against President Reagan's "tax cuts for the rich." They did so even though, as I mentioned earlier, President Kennedy fought for cutting the top marginal tax rate on the rich from 91 percent down to 70 percent; many Democrats helped pass the Reagan tax cuts that brought the top marginal rate down from 70 percent to just 28 percent; and all the evidence showed that the rich ultimately pay a bigger share of the tax burden when their rates are cut and the economy booms—not to mention that under the Reagan tax cuts the economic plight of all income groups measurably improved.

During the 1990s, liberals hit the "repeat" button. They railed against Speaker Newt Gingrich's "tax cuts for the rich." They warned that tax cuts would lead to conservatives ending welfare benefits for the poor, endanger Medicare, and drain funds from Social Security. So instead, they passed the largest tax increase in American history.

Today is no different.

A political strategy memorandum prepared by James Carville and Paul Begala for congressional Democrats—entitled "A Battle Plan for the Democrats"—was published by the *New York Times* in the early months of the current Bush administration.

"Mr. Bush's agenda is neither compassionate nor conservative," wrote the two former Clinton strategists, now on the payroll of CNN. "It's radical and it's dangerous, and Democrats should say so. Mr. Bush is proposing a diminution of the government's ability to protect its citizens that is breathtaking in its scope.

"If Republicans want to run for re-election as the party that killed middle-class benefits in order to preserve tax breaks for the wealthy, Democrats can emerge with a healthy majority, and then we can defuse the time bomb of the Bush tax cut," Carville and Begala continued. "But we have to wage the battle in order to win it. . . . When forced to choose, the American people will demand that the savage inequalities of the Bush tax cut for the rich be tamed in order to fund important priorities for the middle class."

Economic class warfare is the card liberals play when they have nothing else to offer—which is most of the time.

Democrats seem to invoke it in almost every fiscal debate. Any time Republicans oppose another Democratic big-spending measure on grounds of fiscal responsibility (which, incidentally, is not often enough to suit me), Democrats charge that GOP opposition is necessary to protect or "pay for" their tax cuts. Remember the welfare reform debates of 1995 and 1996? Tom Daschle warned that the Republican plan "cuts welfare to pay for tax cuts for the rich."

Jesse Jackson charged that it would "plunge one million children into poverty."

Marion Wright Edelman of the left-wing Children's Defense Fund called the Republican plan a "moral blot" that would "make more than one million additional children poor, a majority of them from working families, increasing child poverty nationwide by 12 percent." She also claimed that it would "make children hungrier."

Senator Daniel Patrick Moynihan—citing an Urban Institute study—insisted that the proposal would cause 2.6 million Americans to be thrown into poverty, including 1.1 million children, and tried to explain that these were actually "quite conservative assumptions" and that "the actual impact could well be even worse than predicted."

President Clinton twice vetoed Republican welfare reform bills. But to their great credit, the conservatives never gave up. Eventually, President Clinton—who, of course, had promised repeatedly to "end welfare as we know it"—was the one who acknowledged the inevitable and signed the Republican bill when it was sent to him a third time.

So what happened? Were millions of Americans plunged into poverty? Were millions of children starved? Did the class warfare predictions come true? Of course not.

"Although liberals predicted that welfare reform would push an additional 2.6 million persons into poverty, there are 4.2 million fewer people living in poverty today than there were in 1996, according to the most common Census Bureau figures," note welfare experts Robert Rector and Patrick Fagan. "Some 2.3 million fewer children live in poverty today than in 1996. Decreases in poverty have been greatest among black children. In fact, today the poverty rate for black children is at the lowest point in U.S. history. There are 1.1 million fewer black children in poverty today than there were in the mid-1990s. . . . [and] hunger among children has been almost cut in half. According to the U.S. Department of Agriculture, there are nearly 2 million fewer hungry children today than at the time welfare reform was enacted."

The data also show that welfare caseloads are down nearly 50 percent. Employment of single moms between the ages of eighteen and twenty-four has doubled. The skyrocketing increase in out-of-wedlock births has come screeching to a halt. More and more low-income single moms are getting married and raising their children with a father in the home. There is still far more to do, given that a child is born to an unwed mother every twenty-five seconds in this country. But we're making progress—in large part because conservative ideas about work and individual social and fiscal responsibility have been put into practice.

THE AGE CARD

Heading into the 1996 elections, White House press secretary Mike McCurry used familiar scare tactics by warning that conservative Republicans want "to see the Medicare program just die and go away" and that "that's probably what they'd like to see happen to seniors, too, if you think about it." Representative Pat Williams, the Montana Democrat, alleged that Republicans "are gutting Medicare. Today, Medicare; tomorrow, Social Security, programs they have always opposed and oppose today." Representative Edward Markey, a Massachusetts Democrat, declared that the GOP—"Grand Old Party"— should now be thought of as "Get Old People." And Representative John Dingell, a Michigan Democrat, said of a Republican Medicare reform plan, "there is only one reason this bill is required—to finance tax cuts for the rich."

Gearing up for the 2000 elections, Vice President Al Gore charged, "I hear Republicans talking about fundamentally changing Social Security and Medicare, but I'll be damned if I'm going to see Social Security and Medicare destroyed or unraveled or unwound." And during the campaign for the 2002 elections, Dick Gephardt warned, "The Republican Party has always opposed Social Security and Medicare, and these latest scare tactics are part of a sixty-six-year drive to gut Social Security and let people fend for themselves at age sixty-five."

But facts are facts. No seniors have been harmed because of the Contract with America and conservative control of Congress for the past eight years. Medicare hasn't been destroyed because of the reforms President Clinton and conservative Republicans agreed to in the Balanced Budget Act of 1997. Moreover, no seniors will be wiped out by the expanded choices that would result if Congress passes the comprehensive Medicare reforms proposed by Senator John Breaux, a moderate Louisiana Democrat, and Senator Bill Frist, a Tennessee Republican and former heart surgeon.

President Bush is investing hundreds of billions of dollars toward strengthening Medicare over the next decade, above and beyond the already planned annual increases. He proposes fully protecting the Social Security benefits of current and imminent retirees while giving young people the choice to invest a small percentage of their payroll taxes into their own personal retirement account if they so choose. He has also empaneled a number of experts, led by former senator Moynihan, to advise him on Social Security reform.

The liberals, by contrast, propose no serious reforms for Social Security. In fact, their only solution is to continue subsidizing it out of general revenues instead of working to make it self-sustaining through partial privatization. Right now, American taxpayers face a nearly $20 trillion unfunded Social Security liability. Although today we have a large Social Security surplus, when baby boomers start retiring. Washington is going to start paying out more in benefits than it receives in payroll taxes. Around 2020, the Social Security deficit alone will be around $100 billion, and it will approach $300 billion a year by 2037. If we do nothing to improve the current system, we will eventually face three terrible options: (1) cut benefits to the bone, severely harming low-income seniors—and particularly women—whose benefits are already pathetically meager and who, unfortunately, have been conditioned to be dependent on these funds for their retirement; (2) radically increase payroll tax rates from 12.4 percent today to 18 percent or more (meaning that a family earning $30,000 a year and currently paying $3,720 a year in Social Security taxes could be forced to pay an additional $1,860 a year)—severely harming young families; and (3) a combination of severe benefit cuts and confiscatory tax increases.

Worse, even if Washington found another $20 trillion to pump into the existing system, it would still be a bad deal for Americans. Most of us working today receive less than a 2 percent rate of return on the money we put into Social Security. Much better rates of return are available from mutual funds and bonds or even bank certificates of deposits (CDs)—which offer a fixed rate of return and thus involve negligible risk to the consumer. Any privatized monies, upon death, could be passed on to a spouse, children, grandchildren, or a favorite charity.

Some twenty countries around the world give their workers the freedom to use personal retirement accounts to create real retirement security and personal wealth, and we should, too. In fact, a similar system is already at work right here in America, with remarkable results.

In the late 1970s, local officials in three counties in Texas—Galveston, Brazoria, and Matagorda, plus two cities and an appraisal district—wanted to improve the financial security of their employees. They began working with local banking officials and developed a retirement plan for government workers that would allow them to opt out of Social Security and instead invest their retirement fund privately. The funds were professionally and conservatively managed. Furthermore, as one of the architects of the plan—Judge Ray Holbrook—testified before the Social Security reform commission, the key feature of the plan was that it would use no stock market investments, only commercial banking products, annuities, and bonds that provide guaranteed fixed interest rates and no risk.

The program was instituted over strident liberal opposition, and twenty years later the results are in and they are impressive. The government workers are getting an average annual rate of return of between 7 and 8 percent on their money. They are accruing real wealth at a fairly rapid clip. They have disability insurance that pays up to 60 percent of a worker's salary (up to $5,000 a month) if something terrible happens to them. They also have life insurance that pays a worker's widow and family three times that worker's annual salary—up to $150,000.

"This matters to real people," says Judge Holbrook. "A county commissioner—a colleague of mine—passed away not long ago. His widow was quite young, about forty. From Social Security, she received a lump sum survivorship benefit of $255. Not per month. Not per year. That was it—$255. What did she receive from our Alternate Plan? She received a lump sum survivorship benefit of $150,000. Plus, she is entitled to a reserve account of $125,000, available at any time she wants to draw it down. So, from Social Security this widow received $255. From our plan she received more than a quarter of a million dollars."

This is the miracle of freedom. When you give people the freedom to make choices for themselves and don't force them into a one-size-fits-all system run by Washington, you'll be amazed at the good that can result.

"I know personal retirement accounts can work because I have one," says Judge Holbrook. "I know a commission can design a better system because I was part of one. I know it's possible to build public support for bold reform because I did it. I know it's possible to change the heart of a skeptic because I was one."

What a great example of American free enterprise and optimism Judge Holbrook and his Galveston project are. Let that be a lesson not only to liberals but also to fellow conservatives who sometimes fear we'll never be able to cut through the superheated rhetoric to get our message out. For even as I write this, there are some Republicans on Capitol Hill pressing for a vote that would put the GOP on record as being against honest, forward-looking Social Security reform that would protect seniors and give young people more freedom to save for their own futures. Unfortunately—but not surprisingly—they're being spooked by liberal fearmongering. But they shouldn't be. Galveston should serve as a model for Social Security reform. Just as conservative-sponsored welfare reform was the right thing to do and made life better for the neediest of Americans, so also conservative-sponsored Social Security reform would help Americans shore up their retirement security and give them more control over their financial destiny.

This is not to say that formidable political obstacles don't stand in the way of reform. Sadly, it's clear that the Left would rather have a political issue than to participate in protecting and saving the Social Security system. Even some Democrats have painfully acknowledged their party's ploy.

"I would urge my fellow Democrats to lower the rhetoric [and] stop the 'kill-the-messenger' strategy," says Robert Johnson, CEO of Black Entertainment Television and a member of President Bush's Social Security commission.

Fidel Vargas—a Democrat, an investment strategist, and also a member of President Bush's team of Social Security advisers—echoed Johnson's sentiment. "I am not here to gut Social Security," he said. "I am here to strengthen it."

These statements are encouraging for those who insist that reform is a hopeless cause. But Republicans need to push for reform with greater urgency *before* the system goes broke—so millions of retirees can have meaningful financial security.

VISION TO VICTORY: THREE MODELS

Knowing all the cards liberals will try to play is enormously helpful. But knowing how best to respond and to play the cards in our own hand is absolutely essential. For this we must look to three modern conservative leaders who offer an extraordinary model of how to move our ideas from vision to victory in the twenty-first century: Ronald Reagan, Newt Gingrich, and George W. Bush.

Each has been a strong leader. Each has been a man of ideas. Each faced withering attacks from the Left. One man's ideas triumphed, and he will go down in history as a great and beloved president. The second man's ideas triumphed, although history will show that he paid a severe, career-ending price. The third man is impressing the nation and the world as a phenomenal wartime president. History is still waiting to judge him.

Reagan, I believe, is our greatest modern American president and one of our most important presidents of all time. Ever since Reagan emerged onto the national stage during the Goldwater campaign of 1964, liberals have sought to destroy him, his ideas, and his character, for they understood right from the beginning the threat he posed to them and their agenda. They knew from the beginning of his political career that Reagan had been a Democrat, voted for FDR, initially supported the New Deal, worked in Hollywood, and not only served in a labor union but led one. They knew all too well that Ronald Reagan understood the liberal mindset—and ultimately had rejected it. He began speaking out. He began engaging in the political process. He began playing to win, and liberals knew it and did everything they could to stop him.

President Carter called Reagan's approach to foreign policy "extremely dangerous." He called Reagan himself "dangerous" and "radical." Carter's aides called Reagan "dumb," "trigger-happy," and a "Mad Bomber." Columnist Tom Wicker of the *New York Times* asked, "Do you really want Ronald Reagan . . . with his finger on the button?" Columnist Mary McGrory of the *Washington Post* described Reagan as a "shallow, nuclear cowboy." Walter Mondale described Reagan's conservative ideas as "dangerously destabilizing." Gary Hart worried that such ideas "could lead us to start World War III."

On and on it went. Liberals grasped for any fearmongering charge

and disparaging label available to defeat Mr. Conservative and his phi-
losophy and approach to government. But they could not have been
more wrong. They underestimated not only the Gipper, but the good
judgment of the American people—who weren't buying any of it.

Ronald Reagan had a vision of where he believed America must
go. He set out to defeat, not just contain, the Soviet Union and global
Communism. He set out to rebuild the American military and rein-
vigorate the country's sense of patriotism and self-confidence. He set
out to cut taxes, unleash the smothered spirit of entrepreneurship and
innovation, and revive the stalled American economy—or, as he put it,
to get the federal government out of Americans' wallets and off our
backs. But he didn't just have a set of goals. He also had a plan for
accomplishing them. He had a set of deeply held beliefs and fundamental principles to guide his steps. He had the ability and the desire
to speak clearly and directly to the American people. While liberals
uniformly underestimated and derided him as "the Great Communicator"—signifying all form and no substance—they failed to understand that his heartfelt message resonated with the overwhelming
majority of the American people.

Reagan also had a sense of optimism, mission, and destiny. He had
a loving, devoted, and instinctually insightful wife whom he relied
upon and trusted for honesty, candor, and wise counsel. What's more,
he had a great sense of humor, one that allowed him to laugh at himself and his opponents, and to never be deterred and derailed from his
mission.

Reagan was a leader and statesman who proved himself to be far
more than just talk. He got results—in a big way. Let's take a look at
his report card. He renewed the American can-do spirit and made
patriotism popular again; turned the economy around with deep,
across-the-board marginal tax rate cuts resulting in two decades of
unprecedented prosperity; rebuilt the U.S. military and intelligence
services and increased morale in both; defeated the Soviets and won

the Cold War; and drove the Communists out of Nicaragua and Grenada. He used his bully pulpit to inform and educate his fellow citizens about America's founding principles—limited government, individual liberty, and the rule of law. He spoke of God Almighty, morality, his opposition to abortion, and his support for voluntary school prayer. He was ceaselessly proud of his country, of all it had accomplished and would accomplish.

During his 1980 presidential campaign, Reagan was asked by a *New York Times* reporter why he thought his friend Barry Goldwater lost his 1964 presidential campaign. Understanding that the question was loaded, he responded, "I don't think Barry Goldwater was defeated because he was a conservative" but because his opponents "succeeded in creating an image of him as a dangerous radical."

Tragically, for all of Newt Gingrich's strengths—many of which we should learn from and employ—the man who led Stage Two of the Reagan Revolution by winning control of the U.S. House in 1994 never quite fully absorbed the Reagan lesson in a way that allowed him to survive liberal demonization—though his ideas clearly did. I say tragically because Gingrich is a friend, a colleague at Fox News, and one of the smartest men ever to serve in Washington and lead the conservative movement. He is without question a brilliant political strategist. Even back in the 1970s, he had a vision of winning back control of Congress for the Republican Party; he stuck with that vision, and he succeeded beyond the wildest expectations of even the most respected political experts. But along the way, he became the favorite target of the Left and the media. He was forced to retreat from the battlefield after the 1998 elections.

Representative Martin Frost, a Texas liberal who ran the Democratic Congressional Campaign Committee, once sent out a fundraising letter saying that Speaker Gingrich "promotes the policies of a terrorist." Columnist David Broder of the *Washington Post* called Gingrich and his Conservative Opportunity Society (a team of like-minded conservative congressmen) a bunch of "bomb throwers." In December of 1995, Representative Vic Fazio, a California Democrat, said that Gingrich was "acting like the Grinch who stole Christmas." The media started calling him "the Gingrinch who stole Christmas." Day after day after day, and no matter what he did, Gingrich couldn't seem to shake the image.

"They trumped us with 125,000 ads, coordinated with unions, paid for by the trial lawyers, [and] paid for by the Chinese Communists," he observed after leaving office.

Yet remarkably, his conservative ideas were so popular and so powerful that despite the concerted effort to vilify him, the message triumphed anyway. All ten items in the Contract with America were brought to a vote in the U.S. House in the first one hundred days, as promised. Nine passed the House. Six were signed by President Clinton. Taxes were cut for the first time in seventeen years. The budget was balanced for the first time since 1969. Welfare was reformed. Medicare was strengthened without raising taxes. Military spending was increased, though not nearly as much as conservatives had hoped, and missile defense research and development was at least kept on life support until a new conservative president could lead on the issue from the White House. All the while, he helped Republicans hold the House every year he was Speaker.

"My model [was] Ronald Reagan," says Gingrich, "who as California governor in 1970 proposed welfare reform at the National Governors Association. His peers voted him down, forty-nine to one. It took conservatives twenty-six years, but led by Gingrich, welfare reform was passed, and millions of Americans live better as a result.

That brings me to George W. Bush. During the 2000 campaign, Democrats and the liberal media treated him as stupid, shallow, unqualified, and unable to lead a great country. As with Reagan, they were wrong. I believe Dubya is one of the savviest and most likeable presidents in recent memory. He has a set of deeply held beliefs and goals and a great team around him to help him achieve them. Best of all, like Reagan, he instinctively understands the importance of the war of ideas.

That's precisely why Bush defined himself early on in his presidential campaign as a "compassionate conservative." Yes, it's redundant. But its purpose was to send a message to voters who had been exposed to eight years of liberal fearmongering and falsely characterizing Republicans. The message: true conservatives actually *are* every bit as compassionate as liberals believe themselves to be.

Despite the slimmest of margins in both the Senate and House, Bush succeeded in cutting taxes. He wanted to cut them more deeply. He wanted the tax cuts to be permanent. But he couldn't muster the votes to accomplish either. Yet he achieved what many thought was impossible, and it was no minor achievement. The entire liberal establishment—in and out of Congress—was dead set against him. And thanks to Bush's persistence, many believe his tax cut was just enough to help spur economic growth and end the recession early in 2002.

But events changed how the Bush presidency will be measured. On September 11, 2001, not only the American people but the people of the world found themselves looking to the new president for direction and leadership—and he provided them with both. President Bush was Churchillian in rallying our nation and allies to defeat the most dangerous threat to the free world since World War II. He led efforts at home to help those who suffered most horribly from the attacks on the World Trade Center and the Pentagon and the third attack, which failed. He led our military and the military of scores of other nations in the overthrow of the Taliban regime in Afghanistan. And he remains resolute in taking the war to the enemy no matter where that enemy hides and plots.

As we've seen, this war's end is not in sight. The enemy is like none other ever faced by our country. It breaks all the rules of war by refusing to identify itself as a combatant and deceptively blending in among civilian populations, it targets civilians, does not appear to fear death, and knows no borders. It seeks weapons of mass destruction in hopes of killing as many Americans as possible. Our nation's challenge is formidable. President Bush has demonstrated that he's up to the task, and thank God for that.

I'M NO KOOL-AID DRINKER

All that said, I'm an independent conservative first, a Republican second. When Republicans are right, I gladly support them. But when they're wrong—when they veer away from bedrock conservative principles—I will not pull my punches. I'm not going to defend bad ideas, even if they're proposed or pursued by my own party.

I'm no Republican Kool-Aid drinker. I never have been. I never will be.

Throughout the Clinton-Gore years, and particularly during the Monica Lewinsky scandal, I was always disturbed by liberals and Democratic Party loyalists who could come on my radio show or on *Hannity & Colmes* or other shows and defend President Clinton no matter what he said or did. It didn't seem to matter to these people that Clinton had lied to the country, lied under oath, harassed women, sought destruction of his political enemies, broken myriad laws, disgraced the office of the president of the United States, subjected America to ridicule and humiliation the world over. One after another, these liberals would just parrot the White House talking points and repeat whatever the high priest of the Democratic Party wanted them to say, no matter how indefensible. The quintessential Clinton Kool-Aid drinker is Vic Kamber. Vic is a Democratic strategist. He's a liberal loyalist. He stuck by the president to the bitter end. Over the years, Vic has been kind enough to appear on *Hannity & Colmes* many times.

But on one particular night—during the height of the Clinton-

Lewinsky scandal—Vic came on the show and just floored me. I pointed out that Monica had just cut a deal with Ken Starr and his team of prosecutors. She was scheduled to appear before the grand jury the next day to explain her side of the story. But Vic would hear none of it. He insisted Clinton had done nothing wrong. He insisted Clinton had broken no laws. He even insisted that Clinton and Lewinsky never engaged in sexual activity together, even though the evidence—including Lewinsky's own forthcoming testimony—was incontrovertible.

"If there is semen on the dress," Vic insisted (with a straight face), "it still may not be a sexual relationship as defined by the agreement with the judge." Of all the wagon-circling moments from Clinton Democrats, that one took the prize.

That, my friends, is a Kool-Aid drinker, and I'm not one of them. When I disagree with a leader of my party, I say so. When President Bush cut a miserable deal on education reform with Senator Ted Kennedy, effectively abandoning school vouchers and supporting a massive increase in federal money to and federal involvement in local education, I took issue with him. When President Bush abandoned his free trade principles by raising tariffs on steel imports, I took issue with him. When he signed that pork-laden farm bill raising federal spending by tens of billions of dollars instead of holding the line, I took issue with him.

Moreover, when he decisively established the Bush Doctrine on terrorism—you're either with us, or you're against us; you're either fighting terrorism, or you're supporting it—no one praised the president more than I. But in the spring of 2002, when he abandoned that principle in the Middle East crisis and sought to pressure Israel into holding its fire and negotiating with Yasser Arafat rather than encouraging Israel to fight and win its own war on terror, I took issue with the president.

The only way for conservatives to win the war of ideas in the twenty-first century is to hold fast to our fundamental principles—and, if compromise is necessary, make sure we advance our agenda rather than the agenda of the Left. We must confidently and repeatedly invoke our history, point to our record, and describe our vision for America. We must engage the Left, expose its positions, contrast its positions with our own, and make our case to the American people.

That's the formula for advancing the conservative agenda and, even more important, restoring America to its founding principles and thus promoting its tradition of freedom.

TWELVE

WINNING
THE MEDIA WARS

Have you ever stopped to think about just how much the Reagan Revolution accomplished in the face of withering attacks by a hostile, biased, almost slanderous liberal media?

It's amazing we got as far as we did. Conservatives fought valiantly and creatively in the 1980s to get our message out. But it wasn't easy. We had some great publications, great writers, and innovative media entrepreneurs leading the way. We had *National Review, Human Events,* the *American Spectator,* the *Wall Street Journal* editorial page, and the *Washington Times.* We had William F. Buckley, Jr., George Will, Bob Novak, Charles Krauthammer, and Cal Thomas. We had Paul Harvey, *The McLaughlin Group,* Jerry Falwell and the Moral Majority, and Pat Robertson and *The 700 Club.* Beyond this, we also had a smattering of other highly gifted and impressive conservative analysts and commentators across the country. But overall, Ronald Reagan and his team of conservative policy-makers in the White House, in the administration, and on Capitol Hill were more than matched by the liberal media.

He had the powerful bully pulpit of the White House, occasionally addressed the nation or Congress directly, and used his skills as the

Great Communicator to make the most of every opportunity to inform and persuade the American people about his vision for the country. But when you think about it, there were relatively few pipelines he could use to get his message out, because of the pervasive liberal slant of the dominant news organizations—CNN, CBS, ABC, and NBC—not to mention the bias of the reporters and editorial writers at most major newspapers and magazines.

There was no Rush Limbaugh, Matt Drudge, Sean Hannity, Ollie North, G. Gordon Liddy, Dr. Laura, or Dr. Dobson.

There was virtually no conservative presence on talk radio.

AM radio itself was a slowly dying medium, and most broadcast and cable television programs and networks were off-limits to conservatives.

Yet the Reagan Revolution triumphed. President Reagan signed into law the largest tax cuts in American history and ended double-digit inflation, high interest rates, and massive unemployment. At the same time, Reagan rebuilt the U.S. military, won the Cold War, and freed millions of people enslaved by Communism. And the American people adored him, despite the best efforts of the Left to tear him down. Reagan won two landslide elections, and his popularity helped secure the presidency for his vice president.

The power of Ronald Reagan's ideas, principles, and personality succeeded in overcoming what he frequently called Washington's "Iron Triangle"—Congress, the federal bureaucracy, and the media.

Imagine how much more he could have accomplished if he'd been able to get his message out to more Americans unadulterated by the Left's spin and bias.

THE COMING OF THE FOX

On October 7, 1996, American TV news changed forever.

You might not remember what happened that day. But believe me, Ted Turner and the executives at Time Warner remember. For that was the day the cable news wars began, with the launch of the Fox News Channel—and the day the liberal media's TV news monopoly was finally challenged. Finally the American people were being given a choice between "failed and biased" or "fair and balanced."

For decades conservatives have complained about the liberal media, and with good cause. The evidence of bias is overwhelming. Throughout this book I've cited examples of how conservative leaders and ideas are routinely maligned, sometimes in the most vicious of terms. That only begins to scratch the surface. Until Fox, for example, CNN was the most watched and influential cable news network in the country. It was founded by Ted Turner, a liberal loose cannon with a decidedly anti-Christian bent. Turner has called the Islamic extremist terrorists who attacked the World Trade Center "brave." He called Catholics on his own staff "Jesus freaks" for observing Ash Wednesday. He mocked the Pope for being Polish. He said Christianity is "for losers." He compared Rupert Murdoch—founder of the Fox News Channel and Turner's chief media competitor—to Adolf Hitler.

Did Turner's ideological views seep into CNN's coverage and analysis? Well, the network didn't earn its reputation as the "Clinton News Network" out of thin air.

CNN isn't alone. Brent Bozell's Media Research Center has done an outstanding job of chronicling the media's broad-based liberal slant. (See www.mediaresearch.org.) This bias is thoroughly documented elsewhere as well, including in Bernie Goldberg's amazing number one *New York Times* bestseller, *Bias: A CBS Insider Exposes How the Media Distort the News,* and in Ann Coulter's remarkable book *Slander: Liberal Lies about Conservatives.*

It's difficult to avoid the conclusion that this bias is leading directly to the demise of network news in this country. A recent article in *American Journalism Review* noted that the *CBS Evening News* with Dan Rather attracts just half the audience it did when Rather began anchoring in 1981. The *NBC Nightly News* with Tom Brokaw has seen its audience drop by 30 percent since Brokaw began anchoring in 1982. Peter Jennings on ABC's *World News Tonight* is doing even worse. His audience is down about 35 percent since he took over the anchor chair in 1983.

While the Big Three were losing viewers, Rupert Murdoch and Roger Ailes entered the scene. Both have decades of experience in the media business, Murdoch as a media baron and Ailes as a political and media strategist for Richard Nixon in 1968, a general adviser, strategist, and debate coach for Ronald Reagan in the 1980 and 1984 campaigns, and a senior media adviser for George H. W. Bush in 1988, before retiring from politics in 1991.

One day Murdoch reached a simple conclusion: rather than watch CNN, he decided to create his own news network.

From the beginning, Murdoch and Ailes realized that you don't have to create a "conservative" news network. You don't have to dictate, dominate, or control the content of news. Rather, the important thing is that news be reported *as news*—objectively, without letting undisclosed bias and editorializing seep into the cracks. Sure, Fox has opinion shows and opinion segments in news shows, but they are clearly identified as such—and, just as important, they allow both political viewpoints to be represented.

In effect, Murdoch and Ailes decided to do something radical: to go back to the fundamentals of journalism by telling both sides of the story. "Fair and balanced." "We report. You decide." They're not just marketing mottos. They're a different way of doing business. This traditional approach to news was reestablished in 1996, when these two men began building the Fox News Channel from the ground up.

WHY FOX SUCCEEDS

Few in the mainstream media really thought Fox would succeed. But the network's ratings proved that there was a wide, untapped audience out there, eager to hear a broader range of viewpoints and a more disciplined, hard-nosed approach to the news. Early on, the network surpassed MSNBC, the joint venture of General Electric's NBC News franchise and the deep pockets of Bill Gates's Microsoft Corporation. Later we rushed past CNN, making Fox the number one network in the cable news industry. The message couldn't have been clearer: people want news from anchormen and journalists, not liberal bias dressed up as news. They want good, smart analysis. And they aren't turned off by strong opinions—from both sides, which explains why I've had the good fortune of being able to do what I do with Alan Colmes every night on *Hannity & Colmes.*

But long before Fox brought these broader viewpoints to television, the real grassroots conservative movement had already begun—on the radio.

THE POWER OF RUSH AND RADIO

It's hard to imagine now, but by the late 1980s AM radio was nothing short of a dying medium. Most Americans listened to better music with greater clarity on FM radio, and the quality and creativity of news and talk programming on the AM dial was at rock bottom. Sure, there were a scattering of great stations and great personalities out there— among them people like Barry Farber and Bob Grant in New York, whom I listened to avidly. But they were the exceptions. The prognosis for the industry was decidedly grim. As an analysis by the Federal Communications Commission concluded, the radio industry was in "profound financial distress."

Then along came Rush Limbaugh, whose nationally syndicated radio show was launched in August of 1988.

At first Rush may have seemed an unlikely figure to revolutionize radio. After all, he'd already been fired from seven jobs. He was absolutely hated by the Left. But he had talent—a talent for delivering his conservative commentary not only with irreverent intelligence but with an infectious enthusiasm that made listeners want to keep tuning in. He loved radio, and listeners loved him. Not everyone agreed with him, of course. But conservatives (and an awful lot of liberals) found themselves mesmerized.

Against all conventional wisdom, Rush broadcast his three-hour daily radio program in the middle of the day, from noon to three o'clock eastern standard time—not during morning or afternoon drive-time, long assumed to be the most listened-to and lucrative time slot for talk radio. Most industry experts believed that the only thing more foolish than launching a national show on AM radio was to do so during pre-school and soap operas. Indeed, the very concept of talk radio syndication was dismissed by radio authorities as violating the immutable law that in order to succeed, talk shows had to be local, local, local. But Rush's success rewrote industry rules overnight. He soon had hundreds of stations signing up to be part of the Excellence in Broadcasting (EIB) network, and before long his show was heard on over six hundred stations by some twenty-two million listeners a week.

Now beside itself, the Left set out to destroy Rush—not conspiratorially but with a marked uniformity of purpose. They attacked him personally, publicly, and ferociously on CNN, in the *Washington Post,* the *New York Times, Newsweek,* the *New Yorker,* the *Nation,* the *New Republic, Time,* the *Los Angeles Times, U.S. News & World Report, USA Today,* on National Public Radio, at the National Organization for Women and the National Education Association. Al Gore attacked him. Al Franken attacked him. Even President Clinton joined in the hunt to demonize Rush. Remember Clinton's bizarre 1994 tirade on KMOX in St. Louis, in which he groused that Rush had three hours to speak his mind while he as president of the United States didn't have a way to get his own message out?

Yet the more the Left attacked Rush, the more interest and curiosity he attracted.

"Why do liberals fear me?" Rush asked in a fascinating cover story in *Policy Review* magazine in September 1994 (an article, by the way, in which he accurately predicted that "history will remember 1994 as a watershed year in American politics," a year in which liberalism would completely melt down). "I am not a distinguished member of Congress. I am not running for President, I do not control billions of dollars in taxpayer money. I can enact no policy, law, or regulation to affect a single American citizen's behavior. So why the high level of liberal emotion?"

His conclusion: "Liberals fear me because I threaten their control of the debate."

He was exactly right. The Left had never seen a conservative broadcaster so popular and so effective. For that matter, neither had any of us.

And the ripple effect was immediate. Rush's commercial and financial success—aside from his ascendant brand of commonsense conservatism—soon began spawning an entire industry of new talk radio stations and hosts, the vast majority of which were coming from a conservative or evangelical Christian worldview. In 1989, for example, there were only about three hundred radio stations in the United States with a news-talk format. But by 2001 that number had nearly quintupled, to more than fourteen hundred stations. Ratings soared throughout conservative talk radio. Ad revenues soared, too.

Rush is now the undisputed Babe Ruth of talk radio; his most recent nine-year deal with Premiere Radio Networks, a division of Clear Channel Communications, was worth an estimated $285 million—more than the combined salaries of the Big Three's anchormen. And statistics like those are a testament not just to Rush's formidable talent but to the size, commitment, and power of the American conservative community as it finally broke through the liberal media blacklist and found a voice.

RADIO AND ME

I'm a living testament to the talk radio tsunami Rush set into motion. Early in my career, Rush himself even gave me some breaks that really helped me get started.

But chronologically speaking, at least, my first debt of gratitude is owed to Ollie North.

In the late 1980s, as I've said, I became captivated and infuriated with the Iran-Contra hearings and by the efforts of liberal senators and congressmen to assassinate the reputations of Marine Lt. Col. Oliver North, Admiral John Poindexter, President Reagan, and his entire administration.

It was clear that the primary intention of these inquisitors was not to gather facts in the execution of their legitimate oversight function but to destroy the Reagan presidency and many of the outstanding patriots who served in it.

Like most people, my background and life's experiences inform my judgment about events and people. Like nothing before it, the Iran-Contra hearings struck a chord of discontent and urgency in me. It was as if they were calling me to action.

I was convinced that the liberals were wrong about North and Reagan. Some forget that terrorists threatened Americans then, too. You should read some of Reagan's antiterrorism speeches from that time—his words will amaze those of you who thought this menace began with September 11. Reagan recognized, even before George W. Bush, that at least two of the three nations designated by Bush collectively as the "axis of evil" were sponsors of terrorism.

In a speech to the American Bar Association in 1985 Reagan said, "In 1983 alone, the Central Intelligence Agency either confirmed or found strong evidence of Iranian involvement in fifty-seven terrorist attacks. . . . The extent and crudity of North Korean violence against the United States and our ally, South Korea, are a matter of record. Our aircraft have been shot down; our servicemen have been murdered in border incidents; and two years ago, four members of the South Korean cabinet were blown up in a bombing in Burma by North Korean terrorists. . . . Now, what is not readily understood is North Korea's wider links to the international terrorist network."

Reagan was also prescient about international terrorism's scope. George W. Bush was not the first president to recognize the war against terror as one of good against evil. "There is a temptation to see the terrorist act as simply the erratic work of a small group of fanatics," said Reagan in the same speech. "We make this mistake at great peril, for the attacks on America, her citizens, her allies, and other democratic nations in recent years do form a pattern of terrorism that has strategic implications and political goals. And only by moving our focus from the tactical to the strategic perspective, only by identifying the pattern of terror and those behind it, can we hope to put into force a strategy to deal with it."

Ollie North—decorated for courage and bravery in Vietnam with the Silver Star, the Bronze Star, two Purple Hearts and three Navy Commendation medals—was also keyed in to the gravity of the terrorist threat. He helped plan the Reagan administration's liberation of Grenada. He helped plan the raid against Libya, in response to repeated rounds of Libyan terrorism. He helped the Reagan-Bush administration wage a relentless campaign for freedom and democracy in Central America. And for his efforts, Ollie and his family were not heralded as American heroes. They were targeted—first by Libyan terrorists (physically), and then by liberal Democrats (politically and legally).

The outrage I felt watching the Left attack this man made me want to speak out and defend him. And it was only because of the existence of talk radio that I was able to start expressing my opinion to anyone beyond my friends and family. I'd grown up listening to Bob Grant, Barry Gray, John Gambling, and Barry Farber. That experience taught me early on that a passionate argument, well made, could make a difference—even if the person speaking was just a private citizen. And at a time when the liberal media was beating up on the Reagan administration daily, I quickly realized that tapping into the new phenomenon of conservative talk radio was one way I could help fight back—to defend Ollie and take on the liberals.

And what happened next amazed me: the things I had to say began attracting more feedback, spurring more people to call—until sometimes I was getting a bigger response than the hosts. Before long it dawned on me that I ought to be on the other side of the microphone, as a host rather than a caller. And that's how I began seriously pursuing a career in radio.

My first gig was with my own talk radio show at the University of Santa Barbara. But it didn't last long. I was too conservative, the higher-ups said, and they didn't like the comments one guest made on the show—so much for free speech on a college campus! The station was dominated by left-wing public affairs programs, including a gay-and-lesbian-perspective show, a Planned Parenthood show, and multiple shows that accused Reagan and Bush of being drug-runners and drug-pushers. The left-wing management had a zero-tolerance policy for conservative points of view. And I was promptly fired.

Once my voice was silenced, my destiny was set—do or die, I'd make my career in radio.

I put an ad in a radio trade publication and was eventually hired over the phone by WVNN in Huntsville, Alabama. I don't know if the guys who ran the station fully realized the risk they were taking with me. I was practically a kid. I had almost no idea what I was doing. And I'd never done two straight hours of radio, never mind five days a week. At the time I was just grateful for my first real break; looking back, I cringe to imagine what they thought of me.

For starters, the culture clash was pretty pronounced. I didn't know a single person who lived in Alabama, and I had no idea where this would all end up. I was downright frightened as I packed all my things in the back of a van and drove cross-country chasing my dream. When I got there, the first thing I discovered was that my New York accent—which I'd never even noticed—didn't go down easy in the South. But soon that concern faded. Being new to the business, I always thought I was on the verge of getting fired, so out of fear I worked like the devil just to make sure I kept my job. I tried to connect with callers. I read everything I could get my hands on, scouring newspapers and magazines (there was no Internet back then) in search of stories. All I knew was that I was making about $19,000 a year and loved what I was doing.

After about two years, I received an offer to come to Atlanta to work for WGST. A tremendous broadcaster there by the name of Neil Boortz—a feisty libertarian who has since become a good friend—had just left the station to go to rival WSB. But due to a noncompete clause in his contract, Boortz couldn't be on the air for a few months. That gave me the opportunity I needed. I knew that if I did well in Atlanta, it could lead to even greater opportunities. So I found a lawyer to negotiate a contract (it was my first), headed to Atlanta, and set out to win over Boortz's audience.

Somewhere along the way, I'd also begun appearing on television. I was horrible at it—it took me ages to feel comfortable in front of the camera—but I did it anyway, to gain more exposure for my views (and experience for myself). For a while I cohosted a TV debate show in Huntsville, Alabama, that was a kind of precursor to *Hannity & Colmes.* I cohosted with David Pearson, a fierce defender of the Left, and the show did very well from day one. Then, not long after I moved to Atlanta, I began getting requests to appear on national shows: *Donahue, Sally Jesse Raphael, Geraldo Rivera,* and Atlanta's own CNN, along with others out of Atlanta and New York.

On one of those trips to New York, after taping *Donahue,* I stopped in to see Rush himself. We'd met before over the years, but this visit to the seventeenth floor of Two Penn Plaza, the home of WABC—number one news-talk station in the entire country and flagship station of the EIB Network—was an absolute thrill for a kid who'd grown up in this very city dreaming of being on the New York radio airwaves. Little did I know how soon I'd have the chance.

On the same visit I also met Bob Grant, the King of Afternoon Drive in New York and one of the great pioneers of talk radio in America. Bob was a hard-hitting interviewer with in-your-face opinions, and one of the most entertaining hosts I'd ever heard. Early in my career I used to emulate Bob and was rough on callers, but I soon discovered his technique just didn't fit with my natural style. Grant was fired from WABC not long after I met him, for making controversial on-air statements, and for a while I was considered as a replacement for him, until Mike Gallagher got the job. Mike has since become a good friend, but I was still disappointed.

Not long after that, though, Roger Ailes gave me my big break on Fox with *Hannity & Colmes,* and I moved back to New York City. I also started doing radio on a fill-in basis on WABC, which soon led to an opportunity to host a weeknight show after *Hannity & Colmes,* from 11:00 P.M. to 2:00 A.M. To my delight, my show quickly doubled the ratings of its predecessor, and seemingly in no time WABC offered me the afternoon drive slot. *The Sean Hannity Show* quickly became the number one AM show in New York City in afternoon drive and the number one local talk show in New York. When a show like mine can achieve such a profile in the king of all "liberal-eastern-elite" cities, doesn't it say volumes about the real beliefs of average working New Yorkers?

As I've mentioned, on Monday, September 10, 2001, *The Sean Hannity Show* debuted in national syndication. In just the first seven months we've been picked up by two hundred stations and more than eight million listeners; we're now being heard in most of the key markets in the country, including WABC in New York, KABC in Los Angeles, WMAL in Washington, D.C., WSB in Atlanta, WDBO in Orlando, WLS in Chicago, WJR in Detroit, KSL in Salt Lake City, WBAP in Dallas, KNUS in Denver, KVI in Seattle, WLAC in Nashville, KFYI in Phoenix, and WRKO in Boston—just to name a few.

But for me the real pleasure in all this isn't about personal success or career milestones. It's about this outstanding media revolution that started back in the Reagan era and that has continued to grow with the help of phenomena like Rush Limbaugh's network and the rise of Fox News. It's about the fact that talk radio and fair and balanced TV are reaching the millions of people who are fed up with institutionalized bias in the mainstream media, and bringing them information that's unavailable elsewhere—along with great entertainment, of course.

There is talent all across the dial: Rush, Dr. Laura, Ollie North, Mike Reagan, Bob Dornan, Matt Drudge, Mike Savage, Howie Carr, Mitch Albom, Mike Gallagher, Laura Ingraham, Boortz, Michael Medved, Dennis Prager, Barry Farber, Ken Hamblin, Mark Davis, Bob Brinker, Clark Howard, the Dolans, Tom Martino, and Art Bell on the national level.

And great local guys like Curtis and Kuby, John Gambling, Steve Malzburg, Richard Bey, Larry Elder, Al Rantell, Bill Handel, Roger Hedgecock, Melanie Morgan, Lee Rodgers, Kirby Wilbur, Phil Valentine, John Carlson, Mark Fuhrman, Gary McNamara, Scott Slade, Jim Turner, Roe Conn, Gary Meir, Jay Marvin, Eileen Byrne, Jane Norris, Chris Core, Bill Cunningham, Scott Hennan, Martha Zoeller, Inga Barks, and many others all offer news, information, and opinion that you just won't find in the mainstream media.

DARE TO DO DIGITAL

In this dynamic technological society we live in, of course, TV and radio are no longer the sole sources of mass communication. The World Wide Web is another force that's shifting the landscape.

Who, for example, broke the Monica Lewinsky story to the world?

Was it the *New York Times?* Was it the *Washington Post?* Was it CBS News or CNN or NPR?

Of course not—not this, the story that almost led to the impeachment of a president. Not even *Newsweek* would publish the story, even though they had it first.

Suddenly, in the click of a mouse, a thirty-one-year-old Internet muckraker named Matt Drudge, working out of his apartment in Hollywood, broke the story. At that moment—and ever since—he has as much power as the highest profile and highest paid journalists on the planet.

"This is the most exciting moment in the history of news," declared Drudge. "Anyone from anywhere can cover anything. And send it out to everyone."

He was absolutely right.

It was Alan Colmes who actually first introduced me to Matt Drudge. Alan was one of the early subscribers to Matt's e-mail newsletter. In fact, *Hannity & Colmes* was one of the first to put Matt on national TV. We've had him on the show many times since, and without question he's one of the gutsiest media mavericks I've ever met.

I remember when we had Matt on *Hannity & Colmes* the night President Clinton gave his deposition to Ken Starr's team during the Lewinsky scandal. It made sense, after all, to have him on: he not only broke the story but continually provided new details and new insights into a drama that was at once sordid and sick yet undeniably mesmerizing.

"I've just talked to somebody who was pretty [close] to one of the principals who says Clinton was a mess," Matt told us. "He perjured himself all over the place. He countered documents and tapes that proved to the contrary."

"Matt, I had heard through the grapevine David Shuster and Jim Angle reporting earlier tonight that it was combative inside there," Alan piped in. "But as more and more details become available here, we're talking about significant legal issues, not the least of which is what I guess you're confirming here—that Ken Starr hit the president with many, many issues beyond Monica Lewinsky—"

"And let me stop you," Matt jumped in. "In the summer of 1974— a quick flashback—during Bill Clinton's race to become a U.S. representative from Arkansas, Clinton himself said—this was during Nixon—'If a president of the United States ever lied to the American people, he should resign.'"

"Wow, that's big," Alan agreed.

"I've never heard anyone else report that," I told him. "Where was that?"

It was on a stump speech, Drudge confirmed, adding: "This is [the] type of stuff you won't see down the dial."

Matt was right: the country is better off now that there are news outlets like his that won't shy away from important stories like the Clinton-Lewinsky scandal. But in the process of breaking the story, Drudge himself became one of the most despised and derided figures among the media because of his willingness to fly in the face of the liberal mainstream.

"Let's talk turkey," CNN political analyst Bill Schneider began his report one day. "Now, turkeys are foolish creatures, overstuffed, noisy, and self-important. On Thanksgiving Day, they get what they deserve. Come to think of it, they're a lot like politicians. Well, it's Thanksgiving Day, and politicians, too, should get what they deserve—especially those who have behaved foolishly. So bring on the political turkeys of the year, and let's carve them up."

So who was one of CNN's top turkeys? "Internet gossipmonger Matt Drudge," of course.

"Matt, there are people that despise you," I noted one night on *Hannity & Colmes* after the publication of his bestselling book, *Drudge Manifesto.* "There are people that won't put you on their show. There are people that think you are irresponsible. But yet you broke the cigar story, you broke the dress story, you broke Lewinsky's story, you're breaking stories every week. Why do they hate you so much?"

"I'm breaking water, you're getting me so excited," he replied in his typical provocative style. "I don't know why they hate me so much. You know, if the roles were switched and it was a Richard Nixon [scandal], and Drudge on his computer brought down an impeachment count on Richard Nixon, you don't think I'd be down at the Malibu Colony with Streisand doing the Chardonnay? Yes, I would."

"Yes, but Matt, they think what you do is irresponsible," I pointed out. "They look down and they think you're evil, that you are dangerous."

"Well, they think that because I have no editor," he explained. "I've got no boss. I will write whatever I want to write, and a million folks see it a day, and this is a new phenomenon. And you know, looking over the dial right before I went on the air, you've got a Ted Koppel sitting across from a Larry King. . . . You know, Ted Koppel scrapped the Lewinsky story . . . the night before the *Washington Post* [went with it]. Jackie Judd was ready to go with it. He said no. Why do these people still have jobs? They're supposed to be working for *us.*"

Good point. But at least we now have an alternative to the likes of Schneider, Koppel, and King.

When it comes to the media, I noted later in that show, everything's changing. "People seem to have sought out the alternative media, and they gravitate toward it because they want to bypass the established liberal bent."

"Exactly," Matt agreed. "And that is what this [Bush-Gore] election is exposing . . . there is a new breeze blowing, as Peggy Noonan probably would write, going toward individuals and rebels." He's right, and I say thank God that Matt Drudge is one of those rebels. Like Rush on the radio, Drudge is a pioneer on the Internet. Not every conservative needs to play the game his way. But we'd better play as hard and tough and tirelessly as he does.

Mark my words: conservatives will never win the war of ideas in the twenty-first century unless we continue to compete in, and ultimately dominate, the digital arena. And just as with radio, the groundswell has already begun on-line. National Review Online, Worldnetdaily.com, Townhall.com, Jewishworldreview.com, News max.com, Frontpagemagazine.com, Conservative News Service, Free Republic, and Lucianne.com—these and many other sites are already adding honesty and new ideas to the political conversation. We've got to win the Web, and the conservative-oriented news sites, webzines, and forums that are already out there are tools of enormous importance that will help us bypass the mainstream and speak directly to the American people.

As Walter Cronkite liked to say at the end of his news broadcast, "And that's the way it is."

[THIRTEEN]

WHAT REALLY MATTERS

When all is said and done, do the raging debates between liberals and conservatives really matter? Why? What's the difference whether liberals or conservatives set the direction of the country? Does anyone care whether Democrats or Republicans run Congress and the courts and occupy the White House? Why do I invest so much time and energy in exploring and debating these issues? Why do I get so passionate about them?

Well, I'll tell you: For me, the study of politics is not just part of my job. It matters to me very deeply—more than anything in the world except God and my family. (And of course politics even affects those parts of our lives.)

What is politics? Essentially it's the art or science of government. It's how we choose to run the country where we live our lives. How we govern ourselves affects so many things: how our children are educated; our freedom to worship as we please; our freedom to invest and use the money we earn. Indeed, this nation was founded primarily by people who wanted to escape Britain precisely because its government was smothering their free exercise of religion. So you better believe politics was important to them—important enough that they uprooted themselves and their families and risked their lives over tumultuous seas, just for the uncertain prospect of establishing a freer society.

So politics is not just some fascinating abstract subject that we pundits and commentators talk about for amusement—though it sure can be fun at times. It is not a spectator sport. Politics matters in very concrete ways.

Ultimately politics will determine who our leaders are because politics drives campaigns and campaigns decide elections. And—don't let the cynics steal your optimism—it matters who our leaders are. There are very real differences in the philosophies of the two parties. It matters what policies they advance because those policies will play a role in our quality of life, our prosperity, our relationships with other nations—and, most important, our freedoms. Just consider, for example, how liberal policies are damaging our children, our families, and our economy through inferior educational standards, environmental extremism, dependence on foreign oil, and the burden of overtaxation.

Don't let naysayers convince you that your individual participation in politics is meaningless. That's not the case. Even your individual vote matters, as we saw in spades during the 2000 presidential election, culminating in the battle for every single hanging chad in Florida.

But voting is not enough. If you understand the importance of politics in your life and that of your children, you'll be more likely to contribute to the process. The first step you must take is to keep yourself informed. With today's technology making the world's newspapers available at cyberspeed in our offices and homes, there is little excuse for us not to stay up-to-date on current events. Then we need to use the information we acquire to influence our friends and acquaintances. I'm not saying that everyone has to become a pundit, but we should all stay abreast of the issues and engage in the public debate—because the result of that debate may determine whether our children will enjoy the same freedoms we do.

I suppose it's obvious that our participation in the political process wouldn't much matter if everyone agreed with us about the concepts of limited government and freedom. But the reality is that an approximately equal number of people seem to have a different worldview. We've been referring to them through this book as liberals, or the Left. In general terms, they believe that most of the solutions for society's problems are to be found in government. Their focus tends to be on devising ways that the federal government can guarantee our economic security. They almost never factor into their policies the potential damage their ideas might have on freedom itself. They don't seem to consider the consequences of increasing government control, which inevitably involves a restriction of our freedoms.

And why should they? They're not alone. In addition to those who share their worldview—which tends to devalue political and economic liberties—there's another problem: political discourse in this country is dumbed down on the issue of freedom. Prior to the recent war on terror, how many from the baby boom generation and after have had to sacrifice anything—much less their lives—for the unprecedented freedoms we enjoy? We tend to be a spoiled lot, completely unappreciative of freedom itself, much less the hardships and other responsibilities involved in maintaining it. In short, we are a people ripe for the picking by those who wittingly or unwittingly want to rob us of our freedoms.

So we are engaged, as we will continue to be so long as this nation exists, in a peaceful struggle against those who value security over freedom and government over rugged individualism. Though peaceful, this struggle can sometimes grow vicious and mean-spirited. The war of ideas rages on, and the stage of politics is where it happens.

THE SHOOTING WAR

Had I written this book a generation ago, I doubtless would have approached it differently. I surely would have talked about the war of ideas because the war was going on then, too—as it has been since time immemorial. But twenty years ago the dynamic was different. Politics could be a dirty game then as well, but the bile seems to have reached new levels today—as the Clinton era has shown us.

It was one thing for Bill Clinton to engage in the types of immoral and criminal activities he did. (Though the president of the United States, he was just one person.) But it's another thing altogether for an entire political party to have embraced his misdeeds. It's sad to say, but the Democratic Party has done just that.

We conservatives had enough on our hands just combating the honest liberalism of the Democratic Party—not to mention moderates in our own Republican Party who didn't share our vision of limited government. But the Democratic Party is no longer just about implementing liberal ideas. It is also about demonizing conservatives and Republicans through distortion and disinformation.

It wasn't just that Democrats circled the wagons around their corrupt president in order to keep him and themselves in power. It was that they willingly adopted his approach to politics. They saw that it worked, and apparently they just couldn't resist its seductive appeal.

In years past, for example, Democrats and Republicans might have had a reasonable debate over whether to partially privatize Social Security. Today, though, all chance for a civil debate on the merits of the issue is lost, giving way to the politics of fear. Instead of merely trying to convince voters that their approach is superior, Democrats increasingly paint Republicans as heartless reverse–Robin Hood reprobates who steal from the poor and give to the rich, Republicans, they say, don't simply believe in less intrusive government and self-reliance; they want to take your children's lunch money and use it to buy themselves new Ferraris. We want to starve old people and bankrupt Social Security. We're not just less compassionate—Democrats have always accused us of that—we're downright sadistic people who enjoy hurting children and the elderly.

Democrats have perfected this politics of divisiveness and applied it across the board for purposes of shoring up their electoral prospects. But nowhere is this tactic employed more shamelessly and destructively than with the issue of race. As we've seen, the Democrats have actually stooped to equating a vote for Republicans with a vote for cross burnings and lynchings. That's the mindset we're up against.

One would hope that the Democratic Party would reject this approach to politics for moral reasons alone, in the interest of not pitting groups of people (race, gender, religion, class) against each other and thereby damaging the fabric of our society. But it doesn't seem like that's going to happen. Why? Because this kind of politics has a proven track record. It works. So when Bill Clinton was able to ride into the presidency largely on the lie that the temporary recession during the final year of George H. W. Bush's first term was "the worst economy in fifty years," why not continue with a winning formula? To Democrats, it doesn't matter how big the lie is—as long as it results in their guys getting more votes and acquiring and staying in power, they'll keep telling it. To them, the end justifies the means.

As low as Democrats stooped during the Clinton era and in the Florida election aftermath, even I didn't anticipate that they would go much lower. Their initial support for President Bush's war on terror was encouraging. At first, they even pretended to be softening their edge on domestic issues. But once a little time had passed after September 11, 2001, and people's sensitivities were slowly being numbed to the horror we all felt, the Democrats started back on the warpath. And by early 2002 they were back to their old tricks, placing raw politics above principle.

Apparently calculating that Bush would be more vulnerable to criticism with the passage of time, they latched on to the first opportunities that presented themselves to discredit our commander in chief in his conduct of the war effort. Three incidents are particularly noteworthy.

First, when President Bush's political strategist Karl Rove told a group of Republicans at a party luncheon in February 2002 that the GOP intended to tout Bush's record on defense and his conduct of the war in the upcoming campaigns, Democrats went ballistic. They accused Bush of "politicizing the war." The charge was as outrageous as it was preposterous. There is absolutely nothing improper about a party advertising the strengths of its leader in a political campaign. What better way to inform the public about the difference that his continued leadership will make? In truth, it was the Democrats who were using the disingenuous allegation to exploit the war for political purposes.

This pattern continued as the months unfolded, until two other similar events happened back-to-back in May. The Republican Party began to advertise a group of three pictures for sale, with the stated purpose of using the proceeds to help fund GOP congressional candidates. One of the pictures depicted President Bush seated in Air Force One on the telephone and looking out the window. The picture was very tasteful—not tacky, as some have suggested—and showed Bush looking quite presidential. You couldn't tell from the picture itself, apart from information in the accompanying caption, that it was connected with September 11. Among many other 9/11-related images they might have chosen—including the famous shot of Bush with the bullhorn addressing the rescue workers—it was as discreet a reference to Bush's wartime leadership as one could imagine. But the Democrats were beside themselves, accusing the Republicans of crossing a sacred line, of "politicizing the war."

No more than a week later the third major incident occurred. This one was particularly troublesome, showing the extent to which the Democratic Party would go in its desperation to discredit Bush and chip away at his phenomenal and persistent approval ratings. Someone leaked to reporters the fact that President Bush had been briefed in August—a month before September 11—that al Qaeda was planning to hijack American airplanes. There really wasn't much news here: there was no specific information in the briefing as to timing; there was no indication that these planes would be used as guided missiles on our military and civilian targets. The threat was not specific, and there was no way for Bush to have specifically responded to it.

That didn't stop the Democrats, who immediately took to the television and radio airwaves, as well as the print media, with their rallying cry, "What did Bush know and when did he know it?" They were quite deliberate in the phrasing of the question, using the vocabulary of Watergate to conjure up images of incomparable Republican corruption at the highest levels of government. Dick Gephardt, Tom Daschle, and Hillary Clinton, among the foremost leaders of the party, were in the thick of the action.

And let me tell you what's most disturbing about this. Gephardt, Daschle, Clinton, and other Democrats know, without question, that President Bush had by no means been told of the terrorists' plan to hijack our airplanes and guide them into our buildings. They know, beyond all doubt, that Bush would never have sat by and let 9/11 happen. Yet they couldn't resist the temptation to imply that he did. Here's what I saw in the Democrats' eyes in that moment: they are desperate, and they're showing it. They will continue to use these despicable tactics as long as they can get away with it—sacrificing the national interest all the while.

There is no question that we need to look into our intelligence services—whether or not you want to call it an investigation—to try to find out where the holes are and do everything that's necessary to fill them. We need to streamline communications between the FBI, CIA, INS, and other government agencies directly or indirectly involved in the chain of information. We face new threats every day, and we need to be willing to think outside the box, to reinvent the way we conduct our intelligence operations.

But that is not to say that we need a series of high-profile congressional investigations, whose hidden purpose may be to allow certain hot-dog politicians to posture before the cameras as they try to curry public favor. As corny as this may sound, our national security is one issue that should remain above politics. All of us, regardless of our political affiliation or leanings, have an interest in protecting ourselves and promoting the security of the United States. So we mustn't allow any commissions or hearings, however noble in their intent, to become political circuses.

Clearly, then, the debate between liberals and conservatives matters more than ever. Because right now—and for the foreseeable future— we are engaged in a shooting war. The actions and behavior of our leaders—and the attention with which we follow them—as we prosecute this war may literally mean the difference between life and death.

But there's another reason the war of ideas matters.

It matters because when the shooting is over, when our troops return home, when America successfully vanquishes our foes, we will be left with these questions: What will our children and grandchildren do with the freedom with which God blesses them? Will they understand how precious the gift of liberty really is? Will they cherish, nurture, and protect it? Will they pass the gift on to others desperately in need of it around the globe? Or will they ignore or misunderstand the magic of freedom and squander the many blessings of liberty?

LIVING THE AMERICAN DREAM

Years ago, I worked as a contractor in Rhode Island. I was just finishing a job at an office building late one Sunday night, and I got to talking with another guy who was working late that night. He was from Czechoslovakia. He'd grown up under communist oppression and persecution, but miraculously he'd gotten out and headed West, even at the height of the Cold War. Now he was living in the United States, working hard, trying to make ends meet, trying to build a new life for himself and his family. He was responsible for cleaning the entire office building every night, and his son was there helping him.

He struck me as a good guy—honest and sincere—and he had a fascinating story. He described his life under communism and his entire dramatic escape. He told me what it was like to come to America and start his life all over again. I must have sat there listening for two or three hours, captivated by his journey from tyranny to freedom.

And there was one image from that night that stayed with me more than any other. When he arrived in England, just before he and his family got the chance to come to the United States, all this fellow owned in the world was a bottle of champagne that someone had given him to celebrate his newfound freedom. That's all he had to his name: a bottle of champagne. Yet by the time I met him, though he'd been in the United States only two or three years, he already owned two houses. He owned several vans. He ran his own office-cleaning business. No sooner had he begun to breathe the air of freedom than he began pursuing his dreams, carving out a good life for himself in just a few short years.

It was only a chance encounter, but one that had a profound and lasting impact on me. I've often found myself marveling at the way this young Czech man appreciated America's freedoms. He drank them in with the thirst of one who had been deprived of liberties his entire life. So I've repeatedly wondered why so many Americans take their freedoms for granted and refuse to avail themselves of the limitless opportunities they provide.

Let's face it: there are too many Americans who have lived in freedom here for years but who act as though they aren't free—and who might as well not be. I'm not talking about all Americans, of course, or even most. But there are far too many people in this country who simply refuse to develop the gifts God has given them. Some are spoiled to the point that they don't even have real dreams. Some act as though they've been cheated—as if being given the *opportunity* to achieve is not enough. They act as though they expect material blessings to be bestowed upon them without any effort on their part. Some have bought into the lie that America is a racist, sexist, bigoted, homophobic country that keeps minorities down and does so intentionally.

How can that be?

How can so many people—like many who call my radio show— have grown up in this nation feeling bitter, angry, and resentful? They haven't grown up under Communism or some other despotic regime. They haven't had to run for their lives under cover of darkness. Yet often they, too, have little more to their name than a bottle of cheap champagne. They've had more opportunities to make something of themselves and create a real future for their families than most of the six billion people on this planet. But they talk as though America were a miserable, repressive country. They talk as though they've been ripped off, cheated, and scammed. They don't own a home or a car; they don't take their kids out fishing or hiking or camping on the weekends—and all they can do is sit back and wonder why.

What I tell such people usually isn't what they want to hear. But it's the truth. If you're not living your dreams in this country, if you're not living up to your highest potential, it's not America's fault. It's yours. You've got to start asking yourself not *What's America doing wrong to cheat me of my birthright?* but *What am I doing wrong that's holding me back from a life of spiritual, emotional, and financial success?*

I don't care how Pollyannaish it may sound—or how unconventional in today's climate—but America is a land of dreams, not nightmares. With the right attitude you can pursue and have a great chance of realizing your dreams. You don't have to be "somebody" to make something of your life, provided you're willing to roll up your sleeves and get to work. But remember: The American dream isn't necessarily a house with a garage and a pool and a dog and 2.2 children. It can be. But it doesn't have to be. It is whatever you want it to be. It's about having the freedom to pursue whatever goals you set for yourself.

How do I know? Why do I believe so passionately in the power of the American dream? It's simple: I'm living it. My parents didn't come over on the Mayflower. I wasn't raised in high society. I didn't grow up with a silver spoon in my mouth.

But so what? I had dreams—and still do. I'm far from satisfied yet; I'm just beginning. I've worked hard to achieve my dreams. I've seized opportunities as they've arisen. I've stirred up some opportunities when they've otherwise eluded me. I've sought to live a good and honest and honorable life. I've tried to be true to my faith in God and my faith in others. I've been blessed with a wonderful wife and two beautiful children, and I've tried—even with the considerable pressures of a three-hour radio show and a one-hour television show and other responsibilities—to be a blessing to them.

So when people call me up and tell me you can't make it in America—or that it takes welfare or a bunch of government handouts—I tell them they're crazy. *Of course* you can make it. If I'm doing it, you can. You don't have to make it big—that often takes breaks beyond one's total control. But you can make it and do quite well, if you're willing to invest the effort.

With all due respect to Al Gore, life itself is a "risky scheme." There are no guarantees, except one: You can't win if you don't play. You've got to be willing to jump from the high board. You've got to have the courage to take risks, to try new things, to seize new opportunities. And you've got to have the courage to make mistakes and learn from those mistakes, or trust me, you'll never achieve anything in life.

FREEDOM AND RESPONSIBILITY

That's the thing about freedom. It doesn't guarantee success. It guarantees your right to make your own choices. How you choose will go a long way toward determining your level of success. That means that with freedom comes responsibility. It means that freedom will do you little good if you are not willing to accept its sobering responsibilities. Life is about making wise decisions. It's about being disciplined, delaying gratification, and taking "the road less traveled." Otherwise you'll limit your chances for success.

Sure, you can stay up partying with your buddies all night. You can sleep in until noon. You can hang out at the mall or at the beach or sit around watching movies all the time. You can waste your money seeking pleasure through drugs and excessive use of alcohol. You can rack up credit card debt; you can be lazy with your schoolwork or on your job. You can squander your future if you want. It's a free country. But if this is the life you choose, you shouldn't blame other people when you fall flat on your face. Just polish your mirror and take a good look.

But let's say you show a little self-discipline—even if you haven't before. (One of the great things about this country is that it's rarely too late for another chance.) Let's say you go to bed at a reasonable hour at night and get up in the morning ready to tackle the day. Let's say you really work hard. You develop marketable skills. You help invent or produce or distribute some product or service that people want or need. You get out there and hustle. Rather than waste your money, you pay off your college loans and your credit cards and your car loans. You start socking some money away in a savings account or begin to invest it in a reasonable, responsible manner. You get into a twelve-step program, if you have to, to get out of a life of drinking or smoking or drugs or promiscuous sex. You get serious about your life and about your sense of worth and your sense of personal responsibility. What's going to happen? I guarantee you: You'll be on the road to success.

The point is, though, that the road to success is one paved by your own industry and determination, not by a caretaker government from Washington, D.C. So don't invest your hope for prosperity and happiness in government. Believe in yourself—and while you're at it, help to promote policies designed to keep government out of your way (and mine)—so that you'll possess the freedom to fulfill your dreams.

As Americans, we've inherited our traditions from men and women who made sacrifices to acquire and preserve freedoms—the freedoms we enjoy today. They laid the path for us. Let's not whine and complain about the hard work it will take to maximize our potential. Let's be grateful for the opportunities.

LESSONS FOR OUR CHILDREN

There's something about getting married, becoming a dad—and then witnessing something as horrible as 9/11—that's changed me. It's not just that it has kindled my desire to see America win the war on terrorism, to shut down the axis of evil before it's too late. More profoundly, it has also caused me (like countless others) to step back and reflect on what is important in life. It has given me an even greater resolve to teach my kids what really matters in life.

For Jill and me—as I suspect is true for many parents—it's more important than ever before that our kids not get swept up by all those debilitating lies that trap young people into feelings of loneliness, isolation, dependency, and bitterness. We want our kids to know that there *is* a God, that they *were* created in His image, that He loves them and *does* have a wonderful plan and purpose for their lives. We want them to discover for themselves the joy of a personal relationship with Jesus Christ. We want to see their souls come alive as they experience God's love and majesty.

The last thing we want is for our kids to gain the whole world— freedom and peace and prosperity—and lose their souls. We don't want them doomed to a world of psychiatrists and psychologists, a hypermedicated world of therapy and Freud and Ritalin. Some of the biggest challenges they will face are spiritual ones, and we want to help them truly understand the differences between right and wrong, good and evil. We want to help them keep in touch with their conscience—that silent voice within us that keeps us from veering off the tracks and into the abyss and helps to make us responsible human beings.

Kids need to understand their role and purpose in life. They need to understand what they can and cannot do and what they can and cannot control. They need to realize that their mission in life is to work hard and cheerfully at all they do, to live a righteous life, and that the basic necessities of life will be theirs by the grace of God. Their job is to dream some dreams, develop some skills, and then get off the couch and get into the game.

So we want our kids to know the Ten Commandments—to understand them, to internalize and live by them. We want them to see us trying to love God with all our heart and soul, our mind and strength, and trying to love our neighbors as we do ourselves. Moreover, we want them to understand that faith shouldn't be blind. It shouldn't be abstract. It involves going to church and praying and living on the straight and narrow—but that's just the beginning. To truly capture a child's soul and spark his imagination, faith must be real: it must be vivid, exciting, and powerful. Kids need role models. They need to see parents pray, and they need to see those prayers answered in a real and personal way.

God knows Jill and I aren't perfect. We're the first to admit it. But God isn't looking for perfection from parents. He's looking for willing and humble hearts. He's looking for parents ready, willing, and able to take seriously the solemn responsibility of raising children to navigate their way in a lost, confusing, and sometimes dangerous world. Now more than ever, that's the life we want to live for our kids.

After all, what will it profit our children to grow up in the greatest, freest, coolest country on earth, only to be spiritually lost and adrift in this world, without an anchor for their souls? We must help them know the truth, and the truth shall set them free indeed.

Upon this spiritual foundation, Jill and I want to help our kids

develop a deep and healthy appreciation of, and respect for, the sanctity of marriage and the power of strong, safe, healthy families,
unscarred by adultery and separation and divorce and searing emotional pain. Too many families are falling apart today. Too many parents are blowing up their marriages. Too many children are walking
wounded.

The whole notion of the traditional two-parent family, with a dad
and mom who are married and fully committed to each for the long
haul—regardless of what struggles come their way—is another of the
ideals that's under siege today. We live in an age characterized by the
maxim "If it feels good do it, regardless of the consequences." It's a
sex-drenched culture—from movies, music, and magazines to TV,
radio, and the Internet—that glorifies premarital sex, promiscuous sex,
extramarital sex, kinky sex, rough sex, and gay sex. You name it, you
can find it, and without looking that hard. No wonder our families are
melting down faster than an igloo in the Sahara. We've got to do better. While we fight to change the culture and win back the media,
we've got to protect our kids from such garbage and prepare them for
the challenges that lie ahead of them. As for Jill and me, we've got to
teach our kids how to deal with such temptations and how to have
such a deep love for and appreciation of God and marriage and family
that when those storms of temptation appear, they'll be empowered to
overcome them.

At the same time, Jill and I are passionate about the need to help
our kids develop a deep love for their country and for the ideals of
freedom and democracy and opportunity that America represents.
Our kids are young right now—just three and one years old—but it's
never too early to help them fall in love with America. You bet they're
going to learn the Pledge of Allegiance, and they're going to go to a
school that thinks the Pledge is a wonderful thing, not an act of racism
or sexism. You bet we're going to read them stories of the amazing
men and women who pledged "their lives, their fortunes and their

sacred honor" to this enduring experiment in freedom we call America. You bet they're going to learn all the great patriotic songs we grew up with, from "God Bless America" to Lee Greenwood's "I'm Proud to Be an American." Good music is good for the soul, and we don't ever want it to be said that we're not nourishing our kids' souls.

As our kids head into kindergarten and elementary school, middle school and high school, we're going to keep asking ourselves: Are we creating an environment where our kids really, truly, deeply understand how fortunate they are as Americans? Are they developing a sense of awe about what this country is all about? Do they have a sense of respect for the history and traditions of this country? Do they understand the mistakes we've made as a nation along the way, the lessons we've had to learn from those mistakes, and how we've sought to correct those mistakes and prevent them from recurring? Are they really developing a sense of how rare it is to grow up here in a world of peace and plenty and individual freedom?

We plan to take our kids on tours of the Mayflower, the Plymouth Plantation, and Ellis Island. We want our kids to see the Liberty Bell and the Capitol and the White House and understand the magic within them. We want them to understand why people come here from all over the world—people who have never tasted freedom; people who have never had the chance to pursue their own dreams; people who have never had the chance to truly succeed; people who nevertheless arrive here with little or nothing but the clothes on their backs and a fierce determination to work hard, play by the rules, and pursue their dreams without a dictator or despot telling them *no*. For when children understand why people will take such enormous risks to be free— even swimming through shark-infested waters to reach the American shoreline—they will begin to appreciate, and take seriously, the great gift of freedom.

Isn't that our mission as parents, to help our children not just to *be* free but to *live* free? If we do that—if we instill in our children and grandchildren not just knowledge but wisdom—then they will surely transcend the challenges that will come their way. And our lives will have been far richer for our love and service to them.

THE COMING STRUGGLE FOR OUR FUTURE

As I write these concluding thoughts, there are reports swirling through the media about new threats to civilization as we know it. The secretary of defense says it's a matter of when—not if—terrorists will strike the United States with weapons of mass destruction, be they chemical, biological, or nuclear. The director of the FBI says it's only a matter of time before "homicide bombers" arrive on our shores and seek to strike fear into the hearts of all Americans.

These are chilling thoughts. But this is the new world in which we live. It's a world of good versus evil. If it wasn't crystal clear before, it is now. The stakes are immeasurably higher. But we can rise to meet the challenge—we've seen volumes of evidence of that since September 11. Indeed, I'm frequently asked whether I think America will overcome the enormous problems she faces, especially the war against terrorism, and without hesitation I answer, Absolutely. The reason is simple: Americans have always faced daunting challenges, and we've not only survived, but we've become a better country and stronger people for it.

There are so many historical examples of America's resilience, and we're wise to acquaint ourselves with that history as we seek guidance and inspiration for what lies ahead. Perhaps the most compelling example is the Civil War. In the 1860s the very existence of our young republic was at stake. Nearly every family suffered the loss or maiming of a loved one in those few years. We were a nation of only thirty-one million people. Every soldier who died (an estimated six hundred thousand) or was wounded (an estimated four hundred thousand) was an American. *Twenty-five percent* of all enrolled soldiers suffered casualties. In other words, one out of four soldiers was either killed or wounded. Abraham Lincoln was assassinated. Reconstruction following the war was difficult and divisive. President Andrew Johnson, a Democrat from Tennessee, was impeached, and nearly convicted and removed from office, by the Republican-controlled Congress. Still, the Union not only survived, it was stronger. And the long march toward racial equality had begun.

In the next century, America's survival was again put to the test. On December 7, 1941, Japan attacked Pearl Harbor, destroying most of the Pacific fleet. The United States was suddenly at war with Tojo's Japan, Hitler's Germany, and Mussolini's Italy. Some wondered whether Americans had the mettle and resolve to defeat the Axis powers. I think British Prime Minister Winston Churchill answered them best when, the day after the attack on Pearl Harbor, he commented:

> Silly people—and there were many, not only in the enemy countries— might discount the force of the United States. Some said they were soft, others that they would never be united. They would fool around at a distance. They would never come to grips. They would never stand bloodletting. Their democracy and system of recurrent elections would paralyze their war effort. They would be just a vague blur on the horizon to friend and foe. Now we should see the weakness of this numerous but remote, wealthy, and talkative people. But I had studied the American Civil War, fought out to the last desperate inch. American blood flowed in my veins. I thought of a remark . . . made to me more than thirty years before—that the United States is like a gigantic boiler. Once the fire is lighted under it there is no limit to the power it can generate. Being saturated and satiated with emotion and sensation, I went to bed and slept the sleep of the saved and thankful.

Of course, Churchill was right. And again our country paid a high price. Nearly three hundred thousand American soldiers were killed in combat or died from combat wounds during World War II. Another one hundred fifteen thousand died from disease, starvation, or imprisonment. But we Americans not only recovered from Japan's devastating surprise attack, we led the Allies to a resounding victory over totalitarianism. We saved civilization and freed captive nations and people around the globe. And we ended one of the worst blemishes ever on the face of humanity—the Holocaust.

Before long, there was another enemy—Communist oppression—on the move. This war, the Cold War, was different: rather than directly attack the United States or confront us on the battlefield, the Soviet Union sought to create an empire by overthrowing governments (usually from within) and then instituting Communist regimes, which it would prop up with military and economic support. From Poland, Czechoslovakia, Hungary, and East Germany to the Korean peninsula, Southeast Asia, South and Central America, and Africa, the Soviet reach exceeded even that of Adolf Hitler.

For decades the United States engaged in costly efforts to contain the Soviet advance. Bloody wars were fought in South Korea and South Vietnam, killing nearly a hundred thousand American soldiers. Inside our own borders, the Left preached appeasement and conciliation. Some preached the demise of America. The nuclear freeze movement followed the antiwar movement, threatening our resolve and driving a wedge between our generations. Yet even with those factors going against us we ultimately won the Cold War. Today not only is the Soviet Union removed from the map, but the people of Russia have become an ally in the war against terrorism—a change of alliances unimaginable only a few short years ago.

As we've seen time and again, the American people have the strength and resolve to overcome the worst kinds of adversity. We are a just, kind, and God-fearing people. We don't seek to impose our will on others. We don't covet our neighbors' resources and territory. We're the first to bring humanitarian aid to those who are suffering in far-away places. And we're a loyal ally and friend to those who seek peace and goodwill.

It's a rare country that doesn't use its superior economic and military might for ill. Sometimes our enemies misinterpret this as a sign of weakness or timidity. But they do so at great risk. I believe that Osama bin Laden and his al Qaeda terrorists, like others who've come before them, have made just such a fatal miscalculation. Yes, these terrorists represent a different kind of challenge. They aren't organized into large standing armies. They're highly mobile, moving from country to country and region to region. They're not defending borders or regimes. And they're difficult to detect, even when they live among us.

As in the past, America will defeat this enemy. In fact, our brave servicemen and women have already toppled the Taliban government in Afghanistan and killed or captured thousands of al Qaeda terrorists. Our military has also deployed to other parts of the world in search of the enemy. But there will be temporary setbacks, some of which may be severe. As they already have, our leaders will continue to warn us of potential future attacks on our country, and sadly I have no doubt that they're right. It's important to remember that we've experienced setbacks in every major war—from the Revolution to the Cold War. Yet when this war's end comes, whenever that may be, we will again stand victorious over this latest ruthless enemy. Americans will tolerate no less.

BEATING THE LEFT

But after we defeat our latest foreign enemy, we will still face threats to our freedom, largely from left-wing extremists in our own country. While I don't in any way underestimate the difficulty of battling the Left, I'm also optimistic that we're making some progress in this struggle. Here are some recent reports from the front lines:

★ After eight years of cutting and slashing under the Clinton-Gore administration, our military and intelligence services will now receive the kind of respect and financial support they need in order to protect us.

★ President Bush has withdrawn the United States from the Anti-Ballistic Missile Treaty, created decades ago with the now-defunct Soviet Union, because it prevented us from building the defense systems we need to protect American soil from nuclear attack.

★ Despite a razor-thin majority in the House of Representatives and a one-vote Democratic majority in the Senate, in June 2001 President Bush signed his ten-year, $1.35 trillion tax cut plan into law. These are the most sweeping tax cuts since the 1981 Reagan tax cuts. And the Republicans aren't only looking at further tax cuts, they've vowed to make the Bush cuts permanent.

★ President Bush has withdrawn the United States from the Kyoto Protocols, which Clinton had signed without ever submitting them to the Senate, where he knew they would be rejected. The Kyoto Protocols, with their unrealistic and severe industrial emission standards, would have had a devastating impact on our economy.

★ While we lost the legislative battle over so-called campaign finance reform, and were deeply disappointed that President Bush refused to veto the bill despite his earlier strong objections to it, a wide array of individuals and organizations, represented by some of the top lawyers in the country, are now challenging the law in court. I'm confident that significant portions of the law—especially the prohibition against criticizing candidates thirty days before a primary election and sixty days before a general election—won't withstand the Supreme Court's scrutiny.

★ The United States Supreme Court has rejected an effort by the homosexual lobby to compel the Boy Scouts of America to employ openly gay troop leaders. In so doing, it upheld the precious right of freedom of association protected under the First Amendment, essentially holding that the Boy Scouts, as a private association, could make their own determination as to who should serve as leaders.

★ Attorney General John Ashcroft has formally recognized that the Second Amendment protects the right of *individuals,* not merely state militias, to keep and bear arms, thereby reversing the Clinton-Gore administration's official position. Moreover, where not long ago gun control was a popular target of Washington elitists, with all kinds of legislative gun-banning efforts gaining traction, this is no longer the case. Thanks largely to the educational and political efforts of Wayne LaPierre and his National Rifle Association, gun control can be a career-ending issue for more and more politicians.

★ Bush has eliminated the longtime role of the liberal American Bar Association (ABA) in screening the qualifications of potential judicial candidates. The ABA had used its unique position to skewer a number of conservative nominees, including Robert Bork and Clarence Thomas.

★ Since the Republican Congress passed the 1996 welfare reform bill, which had been vetoed on two previous occasions by Bill Clinton (before he ultimately signed it into law), the number of welfare recipients has dropped by half— which means that there are millions fewer people on the welfare rolls.

So we're making some headway. But much remains to be done. And frankly, we're going to have to do a better job at fighting the well-organized, recalcitrant Left.

We must understand that the Left's philosophical commitment to Big Government is stronger than ever—if only because their constituency includes so many whom they've made dependent on government largesse. The larger government becomes—not just in the now-shrinking welfare system but in areas from health care to environmental regulations—the more difficult it will be to dismantle.

These politicians, in order to preserve their power base, will continue to nurture this attitude of dependency and to divide society into factional groups. In response, we must claim the high ground and continue to preach racial color-blindness and egalitarianism—strongly and proactively. That's what conservatism is all about. That's the American ideal.

Finally, we must realize that our freedom depends on more than just our constitutional restraints on government, though we must fight to preserve them by electing officials who respect the concept of limited government and by appointing strict constructionists to the federal bench. No, as the framers warned, our freedom is dependent on the underlying morality of our people. They didn't mean that Americans must remain sinless to remain free. After all, the overwhelming majority of them were Christians who believed in man's fallen condition. No, they meant that as a society we must believe in, and strive to obey, absolute moral standards.

We must never lose sight of this moral dimension to our freedoms. And that is why, along with every other battle we wage, we must be willing to fight for our culture as well. In this age when moral relativism rules in our cultural institutions, it is important that those of us fighting for our culture never forget these admonitions of our framers. Though liberal politicians and thinkers continue to target our fixed standards, enabling the erosion of our culture, we must resist them at every turn.

One of the principal drawbacks of freedom is that it is inherently vulnerable to attack. By its very nature it permits, and perhaps even invites, assault from within and without. But freedom is worth fighting and dying for, and Americans have always risen to the challenge.

So we must. And so we will.

NOTES

1. Civilization in the Balance

"growing concentration of carbon dioxide . . .": Al Gore, *Earth in the Balance: Ecology and the Human Spirit* (Houghton Mifflin, 1992), p. 325.

Gore has even stooped to critiquing: Richard A. Oppel Jr., "Perhaps Looking Ahead, Gore Reflects With Regret," *New York Times*, June 30, 2002.

"I absolutely believe . . .": Alison Mitchell and Todd Purdum, "Lawmakers Seek Inquiry into Intelligence Failures," *New York Times,* October 22, 2001.

"We don't need a witch hunt . . .": Ibid.

"in 1996, a State Department dossier . . .": Judith Miller, Jeff Gerth, and Don Van Natta, Jr., "Planning for Terror But Failing to Act," *New York Times,* December 30, 2001.

"It wasn't the kind of thing . . .": Ibid.

Morris points out that . . . : Dick Morris, "Clinton's Priority: Political Correctness Over Fighting Terror," JewishWorldReview.com, January 3, 2002.

Clinton didn't even meet . . . : Dick Morris, "While Clinton Fiddled," *Wall Street Journal,* February 5, 2002.

Even after a bomb . . . : Ibid.

Clinton was apparently so afraid . . . : Morris in JewishWorldReview.com.

"Everything was more important . . .": Ibid.

"Frankly, I don't think . . .": Transcript, *Hannity & Colmes,* Fox News Channel, February 28, 2002.

"In February of 1996 . . .": Transcript, *Hannity & Colmes,* Fox News Channel, March 1, 2002.

Between 1996 and 2000 . . . : Mansoor Ijaz, "Clinton Let Bin Laden Slip Away and Metastasize," *Los Angeles Times,* December 5, 2001.

On April 5, 1997 . . . : S. Mitra Kalita, "Sources: U.S. Ignored Sudan's Overtures on Bin Laden," *Newsday,* December 2, 2001.

"the real danger for the West . . .": Mansoor Ijaz, "Prohibition on Financial Transactions with Countries Supporting Terrorism Act," Congressional testimony before the House Judiciary Committee's Subcommittee on Crime, June 10, 1997.

The silence of the Clinton . . . : Mansoor Ijaz in the *Los Angeles Times,* December 5, 2001.

"The militant Islamic terror . . .": Transcript, *Hannity & Colmes,* Fox News Channel, November 6, 2001.

"What is at stake today . . .": Benjamin Netanyahu, Congressional testimony, September 20, 2001.

2. The Left vs. the CIA

"a precious life given . . .": CIA director George Tenet, November 28, 2001.

His senior quote . . . : Blaine Harden and Kevin Sack, "One for His Country, and One Against It," *New York Times,* December 11, 2001.

He grew up feeding his mind on . . . : Shelby Steele, "Radical Sheik," *Wall Street Journal,* December 10, 2001.

"John loves America . . .": Sue Pleming, "Two American Sons: One Seen as Traitor, Other Hero," Reuters, February 13, 2002.

"Mike was a hero . . .": Ibid.

"Last month . . . at the grave . . .": President George W. Bush, State of the Union Address, January 29, 2002.

"Greater love has no man . . . : John 15:13.

"Well, we're doing really very well . . .": Transcript, *Hannity & Colmes,* Fox News Channel, February 19, 2002

"the number of Communist . . .": Kiron K. Skinner, Annelise Anderson, and Martin Anderson, editors, *Reagan in His Own Hand: The Writings of Ronald Reagan That Reveal His Revolutionary Vision for America* (Free Press, 2001), p. 121.

"makes one wonder . . .": Ibid, p. 124.

"made it sound as if the chief threat . . .": Ibid, p. 125.

"Is it time to get rid . . .": Ted Gup, "Clueless in Langley," *Mother Jones,* January/February 2002.

"Though the CIA is . . .": Robert Dreyfuss, "The CIA Crosses Over," *Mother Jones,* January/February 1995.

"an act of catastrophic terrorism . . .": Peter Pringle, "Bioterrorism: America's Newest War Game," *The Nation*, November 9, 1998.

"the national security cadre . . .": David Corn, "The Dark Smoke," *The Nation*, October 1, 2001.

In 1994 he wrote a book . . . : David Corn biography, www.thenation.com.

Vietnam Veterans Against the War . . . : Howard Fineman, "How Politics Changed on 9-11," *Newsweek*/MSNBC.com, January 2002.

"abandoned the responsibility . . .": Peter Kornbluth, "The Storm Over 'Dark Alliance,'" *Columbia Journalism Review*, January/February 1997.

The Agency's Inspector General . . . : Central Intelligence Agency, Office of Inspector General, "Report of Investigation Concerning Allegations of Connections between CIA and the Contras In Cocaine Trafficking to the United States," Overview, January 29, 1998.

Between 1996 and 1998 . . . : Transcript, *NewsHour with Jim Lehrer*, PBS, interview with Jeffrey Kaye, November 18, 1996.

Eventually, even the *Mercury News* . . . : See coverage by Todd S. Purdum, "Exposé on Crack Was Flawed, Paper Says," *New York Times*, May 13, 1997; Thomas Hackett, "The CIA-Crack Story; Anatomy of a Journalistic Train Wreck," Salon.com, May 1997; Peter Kornbluth, "The Storm Over 'Dark Alliance,'" *Columbia Journalism Review*, January/February 1997.

"I applaud Senator Kerry . . .": Rep. Maxine Waters, press release, July 17, 1998.

"The list of misdeeds . . .": Rep. Maxine Waters, press release, October 7, 1998.

"Central Intoxication Agency . . .": Peter Kornbluth, "The Storm Over 'Dark Alliance,'" *Columbia Journalism Review*, January/February 1997.

"Why is it that our vast intelligence . . .": Sen. John Kerry, *Congressional Record*, May 1, 1997, found on the web site of the Federation of American Scientists, www.fas.org.

"Without the Soviet threat . . .": Elaine Sciolino, "CIA Casting About for New Missions," *New York Times*, February 4, 1992, p. A1.

The Abolition of the Central Intelligence Agency Act . . . : Sen. Daniel Patrick Moynihan, S. 126, introduced January 4, 1995, 104th Congress.

"In the wake of disclosures . . .": J. P. Cassidy, "Torricelli Intel Reforms Said to Damage CIA," *The Hill*, October 10, 2001.

"In the mid-1990s . . .": Robert Baer, ABCNews.com, January 18, 2002.

agent scrub . . . : *The Hill*, October 10, 2001.

"I was very much opposed . . .": Ibid.

The CIA's London office . . . : Robert Baer, *See No Evil: The True Story of a Ground Soldier in the CIA's War on Terrorism* (Crown, 2002), pp. xvi–xvii.

"I never said I was afraid . . .": E-mails and conversations with Lt. Col. Oliver North.

3. Coast to Coast, Border to Border

"The Republican jihad . . .": Bob Herbert, "Inflicting Pain on Children," *New York Times*, February 25, 1995, p. A23.

"Human sacrifice is much in vogue . . .": Mary McGrory, "Human Sacrifice on the Hill," *Washington Post*, July 25, 1995, p. A2.

"I have no doubt that if . . .": Interview with Allen Ginsberg in article by Mathew Rothschild in *The Progressive*, August 1994, p. 34.

"What they want to do . . .": Transcript of press conference with President Clinton, February 24, 1995.

"the Republican leadership . . .": H. Josef Hebert, "Vice President Accuses GOP of Holy War against Environment," Associated Press, October 5, 1995.

"philosophical jihad . . .": Ann Devroy, "GOP and the White House Confront an Era of New Relations; Reasserting the Presidency Means Rethinking Almost Everything," *Washington Post*, November 14, 1994, p. A1.

"is one of the most dangerous . . .": Kenneth J. Cooper, "Democrat Offers Gingrich Apology for Harsh Words," *Washington Post*, May 6, 1995, p. A8.

"this country has lost control of its borders . . .": Mary Beth Franklin, "Reagan Says He Wants Immigration Bill," United Press International, October 19, 1983.

"symbol of American racism . . .": Dale Maharidge, "California Schemer: What You Need to Know about Pete Wilson," *Mother Jones*, November/December 1995.

"Conservatives are fond of fashioning . . .": Bill Berkowitz, "The Homeland Security Initiative," *The Nation*, February 21, 2002.

"David Duke with a word processor . . .": Eleanor Clift on *The McLaughlin Group*, November 17, 1991, quoted by the Media Research Center, November 25, 1991.

"draconian . . . anti-immigrant zealotry . . .": Anthony Lewis, "At the Heart of Liberty," *New York Times*, June 30, 2001.

"the immigration debate has reached a point . . .": Robert Pear, "Citizenship Proposal Faces Obstacle in the Constitution," *New York Times*, August 7, 1996.

"We really fall into a dangerous trap . . .": CNN, "Clinton Links Anti-Immigrant Sentiment to Church Burnings," www.Allpolitics.com, June 10, 1996.

"If a candidate wants to divide . . .": John Marelius, "Gore Blasts Ballot Initiatives at Latino Event," *San Diego Union Tribune*, July 18, 1999.

"The Republican leadership in Congress . . .": Rep. Dick Gephardt, "Democratic Hispanic Radio Response," http://democraticleader.house.gov, July 21, 2001.

"the anti-immigration forces . . .": Terry McAuliffe, www.democrats.org, July 18, 2001.

"the anti-immigrant proposals . . .": Rep. Luis Gutierrez, "Democratic Radio Response on Immigration," www.democrats.org, February 16, 2002.

"The majority Republican Party [is] basically anti-civil rights...": CNN, www.Allpolitics.com, December 14, 1997.

"a wave of scape-goating...": Paul Farhi and Kevin Merida, "House Rejects Tax Break; Viacom Sale to Minority Group Spurred Vote," *Washington Post*, February 22, 1995, p. A1.

8.7 million "unauthorized" immigrants...: "Evaluating Components of International Migration: The Residual Foreign Born," Working Paper Series No. 61, U.S. Census Bureau, December 2001.

3.4 million...: Robert Warren, "Annual Estimates of Unauthorized Immigration Population Residing in The U.S. and Components of Change: 1987 To 1997," Immigration and Naturalization Service, September 2000.

114,818 people from the Middle East...: "Intermediate Estimates of the Residual Foreign Born by Place of Birth and Sex, 2000," in "Evaluating Components of International Migration: The Residual Foreign Born," Working Paper Series No. 61, U.S. Census Bureau, December 2001.

an estimated two million foreign citizens...: Chris Adams, "Back on Front Burner: Push to Identify Foreigners Who Overstay Visas," *Wall Street Journal*, October 24, 2001; quoted on the National Center for Policy Analysis web site, www.ncpa.org/iss/imm/pd102401c.html

Mohammed Salameh...: Rep. Elton Gallegly (R-CA), *Congressional Record*, March 10, 1993, p. H1086.

Mir Aimal Kansi...: Ibid; see also statement by CIA Director George Tenet, press release, Central Intelligence Agency, November 10, 1997.

Gazi Ibrahim Abu Mezer...: Joseph P. Fried, "Jury Convicts Man in Scheme to Set a Bomb in the Subway," *New York Times*, July 24, 1998.

"no coverage of the border from midnight...": Michael R. Bromwich, "Northern Border Enforcement Issues," testimony before the House Judiciary Committee, April 14, 1999.

"In 1994," noted Sutherland...: Daniel Sutherland, "Abolish The INS: How Federal Bureaucracy Dooms Immigration Reform," Center for Equal Opportunity, January 1996.

"finding in reports released in...": Daniel W. Sutherland, "Immigration 2000: A Guide to the Issues," Center for Equal Opportunity, October 2000, p. 19.

"pushed the INS to speed up...": Stephen Barr, "Gore Turns to Making Reinvention Deliver," *Washington Post*, March 3, 1998, p. A15.

"more than eighty percent...": Rep. Elton Gallegly, "Terrorists at U.S. Airports? INS Doesn't Know and Doesn't Seem to Care," press release, January 28, 2002.

Consider a Harris Interactive poll...: Harris Interactive survey conducted for the Federation for American Immigration Reform, August 2001.

"By 85 percent to 11 percent...": Dick Morris, "When Terrorists Can Enter Legally, It's Time to Change the Law," JewishWorldReview.com, November 29, 2001.

And then, of course, there is the astonishing story: Adrian Sainz, "INS Approved Terrorists' Visas," Associated Press, March 12, 2002.

"INS is proud of its many successful...": U.S. Immigration and Naturalization Service web site, "Agency Awards" section, December 19, 2001.

Governor Don Sundquist actually signed the bill...: David Firestone, "In U.S. Illegally, Immigrants Get License to Drive," *New York Times*, August 4, 2001.

"The skyjackers had obtained...": "World Trade Center and Pentagon Terrorists' Identity and Immigration Status," Issue Brief, Federation for American Immigration Reform, October 2001; see also Issue Brief, "Driver's Licenses for Illegal Aliens," FAIR, June 2001.

"At Cal State campuses, for example...": Jill Leovy, "Tuition Law Praised, Attacked," *Los Angeles Times*, October 13, 2001.

labor unions called for blanket amnesty...: Steven Greenhouse, "Unions Urge Amnesty for Illegal Immigrants," *San Francisco Chronicle*, February 17, 2000.

"Our response is: Let's not call it an amnesty...": Gail Russell Chaddock, "Hispanic Voters Watch Immigration Battle," *Christian Science Monitor*, October 19, 2000, p. 3.

"I have no choice but to veto...": John Gizzi, "Clinton Demands Deal for Illegals," *Human Events*, November 10, 2000.

"To just give blanket amnesty...": Alan Fram, "GOP Defies Clinton on Immigration," Associated Press, October 26, 2000.

"In other words...": *Human Events*, November 10, 2000.

In the summer of 2001...: For coverage of controversy over Bush amnesty discussions, see Major Garrett, "Amnesty Could Help Win Hispanic Vote," CNN.com, July 16, 2001; see also column by Morton Kondracke, "Bush Could Score Coup with Amnesty for Illegal Aliens," *Roll Call*, July 16, 2001.

4. Daschle, Democrats, and Defense

"the gradual diminishment of...": Tom Hayden et al, "Port Huron Statement," Students for a Democratic Society (SDS), 1962.

On October 31, 1983, Senator Ted Kennedy...: See vote regarding Public Debt Limit Increase, Kennedy Nuclear Weapons Freeze Amendment, Vote Number 327, October 31, 1983, 98th Congress.

One nuclear freeze measure...: See "House Vote Descriptions" and "House Vote Ratings," 1983, American Conservative Union, www.conservative.org.

73 percent of all Senate Democrats . . . : See vote regarding Public Debt Limit Increase, Kennedy Nuclear Weapons Freeze Amendment, Vote Number 327, October 31, 1983, 98th Congress.

"I think the foremost responsibility . . .": Transcript, "The Second 1988 Presidential Debates," PBS, October 13, 1988, www.pbs.org. Note: Some liberal journalists believed Dukakis won the first debate, even though Dukakis lost the election less than a month later in a landslide for Bush. See "An Icy Duke Edges Out Bush in a Taut Debate," *Time,* October 3, 1988.

"for saving me from the draft . . .": Bill Clinton, letter to ROTC colonel, December 3, 1969, *Congressional Record,* July 30, 1993, p. H5550–H5551.

"loathing the military . . .": Ibid.

"The defense buildup . . .": Chapter 14, *Issues 2000,* The Heritage Foundation.

September 19, 1979 . . . : See "House Vote Descriptions" and "House Vote Ratings," 1979, American Conservative Union, www.conservative.org.

May 4, 1983 . . . : See "House Vote Descriptions" and "House Vote Ratings," 1983, American Conservative Union, www.conservative.org.

August 4, 1990 . . . : See vote regarding DOD Authorization Bill, SDI Funding Cut, Vote Number 226, August 4, 1990, 101st Congress.

October 15, 1990 . . . : See vote regarding FY 1991 DOD Appropriations Bill, Final Passage, Vote Number 273, October 15, 1990, 101st Congress.

January 12, 1991 . . . : See House vote regarding Use of Force Resolution, Pursuant to UN Security Council Resolution 678, Final Vote, Roll Call 9, January 12, 1991, 102nd Congress.

The Senate debate . . . : See Senate vote regarding Use of Force Resolution, Final Passage, Vote Number 2, January 12, 1991, 102nd Congress.

"I urge the Senate to reject . . .": Sen. Ted Kennedy, *Congressional Record,* January 12, 1991.

"I cannot look my seventeen-year old . . .": Sen. Tom Daschle, *Congressional Record,* January 10, 1991, p. S170.

April 25, 1991 . . . : See vote regarding Budget Resolution, Bradley Amendment, Vote Number 49, April 25, 1991, 102nd Congress.

the Clinton-Gore defense budget slashed . . . : See Senate Record Vote Analysis, Budget Resolution/Defense Cut, May 15, 1996, Republican Policy Committee.

Chart: Ibid.

May 15, 1996 . . . : See vote regarding Budget Resolution, Grassley Amendment, Vote Number 113, May 15, 1996.

June 25, 1998 . . . : See vote regarding Defense Authorization Bill, Harkin Amendment, Vote Number 175, June 25, 1998, 105th Congress.

June 13, 2000 . . . : See vote regarding Defense Appropriations, Wellstone Amendment, Vote Number 126, June 13, 2000, 106th Congress.

5. Threatcon Delta

"Unfortunately, we live in a dangerous world . . .": Transcript, *Hannity & Colmes*, Fox News Channel, December 29, 1999.

"Middle Eastern terrorist groups . . .": "Middle East Overview," *Patterns of Global Terrorism: 1999*, U.S. State Department, www.state.gov/www/global/terrorism/ 1999report/mideast.html.

"Clinton's antiterrorism policy is a joke . . .": Transcript, *Hannity & Colmes*, Fox News Channel, December 29, 1999.

"We can protect ourselves from . . .": Transcript, *Hannity & Colmes*, Fox News Channel, February 20, 2001.

During World War II . . . : Patricia Zengel, "Assassination and the Law of Armed Conflict," 134 *Military Law Review* 123, 137, 1991.

"I believe that what happened in 2000 . . .": Bill Cotterell, "Actor Compares 2000 Election to Sept. 11," *Tallahassee Democrat*, March 8, 2002.

"Bush is amateurish . . .": Lawrence Donegan, "Suddenly, It's Cool to Be Rude about Dubya Again," *The London Observer*, March 10, 2002.

"not convinced that voting . . .": Rep. Barbara Lee, "Why I Opposed the Resolution to Authorize Force," *San Francisco Chronicle*, September 23, 2001.

"we must do all we can . . .": Rep. Barbara Lee, press release, September 25, 2000.

"We need to know where we're going . . .": Marc Cooper, "Rep. Barbara Lee: Rowing against the Tide," *Los Angeles Times*, September 23, 2001.

"The enemy of America is not . . .": President Bush, address to the nation and a joint session of Congress, September 20, 2001.

"The trappings of a state of siege . . .": Rep. Dennis J. Kucinich, "A Prayer for America," speech to the Southern California Americans for Democratic Action, February 17, 2002.

"That's an outright lie . . .": Transcript, *Hannity & Colmes*, Fox News Channel, March 19, 2002.

"Persons close to this administration . . .": Juliet Eilperin, "Democrat Implies Sept. 11 Administration Plot," *Washington Post*, April 12, 2001, p. A16.

McKinney also made similar assertions . . . : Rep. Cynthia McKinney, *Congressional Record*, February 26, 2002.

"What did the president know . . .": See roundup of press stories on the subject, "Democrats Continue to Press for 9/11 Intelligence Investigation," *The Bulletin's Frontrunner*, May 21, 2002.

"Bush Knew": "White House Complains about Tabloid Headline on Bush Hijacking Briefing," Associated Press, May 17, 2002.

After a few days the story was debunked . . . : Bill Miller and Dan Eggen, "FBI Memo Author Did Not Envision Sept. 11; Phoenix Agent Who Marked Warning 'Routine' Finishes Congressional Testimony," *Washington Post,* May 23, 2002, p. A8.

"Those of us who come from . . .": Former President Bill Clinton, Speech at Georgetown University, November 7, 2001.

Then, in April 2002, during a speech in Austria . . . : Susanna Loof, "Clinton: Gaps Dividing Rich and Poor Must Be Diminished," Associated Press, April 13, 2002.

"Sleepers have been here for years . . .": Transcript, *Hannity & Colmes,* Fox News Channel, September 13, 2001.

"I think it'll take a period of years . . .": H. Josef Hebert, "Bush Officials Say High Alert May Be Needed for Years with Terrorists Possibly Lurking in U.S.," Associated Press, February 1, 2002.

"The Clinton-Gore administration shut down . . .": Jerry Seper, "Clinton White House Axes Terror-Fund Probe," *Washington Times,* April 2, 2002.

"The foreign terrorist threat . . .": Steven Emerson, Congressional testimony before the Senate Judiciary Committee's Subcommittee on Terrorism, Technology and Government Information, February 24, 1998.

Schiavo described a 1995 study . . . : Mary Schiavo with Sabra Chartrand, *Flying Blind, Flying Safe* (Avon Books, 1997).

"Every plane, every cabin . . .": "Clinton Imposes Stricter Airline Safety Measures," CNN.com, July 25, 1996.

"We will not rest in our efforts . . .": President Clinton, speech at George Washington University, *News Hour with Jim Lehrer,* PBS, August 6, 1996.

"Develop uniform performance standards . . .": "Vice President Gore Announces Aviation Security Recommendations," Office of the Vice President, press release, September 5, 1996.

"saw airport and airline operations . . .": "Gore Commission Report," in compliance with Executive Order 13015 of August 22, 1996, issued on February 12, 1997.

"According to industry experts . . .": Editorial, "The Luggage Loophole," *Boston Globe,* October 11, 2001, p. A14.

"Mary, I've got to tell you something . . .": Transcript, *Hannity & Colmes,* September 24, 2001.

There are eighteen thousand private airports . . .": Matthew L Wald and Elizabeth Becker, "Administration Considers Ways to Cut Terror Risk from Small Planes," *New York Times,* January 9, 2002, p. A12.

"For a few harrowing weeks last fall . . .": Massimo Calabresi and Romesh Ratnesar, "Can We Stop the Next Attack?" *Time*, March 11, 2002, pp. 25–35.

"Is it a strong possibility that one day . . .": Transcript, *Hannity & Colmes*, Fox News Channel, March 5, 2002.

"Our cause is just, and it continues . . .": President Bush, State of the Union Address, January 29, 2002.

"overly simplistic and counterproductive . . .": "Carter Rips Bush on 'Axis' Label," Associated Press, February 21, 2002.

"expansion without at least a clear direction . . .": "Daschle Says U.S. War Effort Lacks 'Clear Direction,'" Reuters, February 28, 2002.

I've interviewed Khidir Hamza . . . : Transcripts, *Hannity & Colmes*, Fox News Channel, January 18, 2002, and February 15, 2002.

It's an assessment James Woolsey . . . : Transcript, *Hannity & Colmes*, Fox News Channel, March 7, 2002.

"I don't think the success . . .": "Daschle Says U.S. War Effort Lacks 'Clear Direction,'" Reuters, February 28, 2002.

"blank checks to be written . . .": Ibid.

"bootstrapping this operation . . .": Alan Fram, "Democrats Criticize Bush Defense Plan," Associated Press, February 28, 2002.

6. The Pledge, the Declaration, and Patriotism

"We do have staff members . . .": Lee Sensenbrenner and Kathryn Kingsbury, "Pledge Banned in City Schools; School Board Also Nixes Anthem's Words," *Capital Times* (Madison, WI), October 9, 2001, p. A1.

"Indoctrination leads to . . .": Doug Erickson, "Can't Use Pledge of Allegiance to Comply with Law, Schools Told; Madison School Board Approves Using National Anthem But without the Words," *Wisconsin State Journal*, October 9, 2001, p. A1.

"I hope the good sense . . .": Stephanie Simon, "Intended to Unite, Displays of Patriotism Divide Some Schools," *Los Angeles Times*, October 12, 2001, p. A14.

"Mandating patriotism is . . .": Ibid; see also Don Feder's excellent article, "Left Unfurls Cynicism at Old Glory," *Boston Herald*, October 17, 2001, p. 31.

"makes our country as bad as . . .": Ibid.

"I think that religious patriotism . . .": Transcript, *Hannity & Colmes*, Fox News Channel, October 14, 2001.

"in your great zeal . . .": Doug Erickson, "Board Reverses Pledge Ban; Hundreds Speak at Meeting; Vote is 6-1," *Wisconsin State Journal*, October 16, 2001, p. A1.

"clear violation of the California . . .": Ryan McCarthy, "ACLU Orders School to Remove 'God Bless America' Sign," Scripps Howard News Service, October 5, 2001. See also Charles Lane, "Calif. School's Sign Runs Afoul of ACLU," *Washington Post,* October 12, 2001, p. A6.

"Well, there's a backdrop . . .": Transcript, *Hannity & Colmes,* Fox News Channel, October 15, 2001.

"DEMOCRATS KILL REQUIREMENT . . .": Steven K. Paulson, "Democrats Kill Requirement for Pledge of Allegiance," Associated Press, February 5, 2002.

"FLAG-DISPLAY MEASURE KILLED . . .": *Rocky Mountain News,* February 14, 2002, p. 16A.

public outrage eventually forced . . . : James B. Meadow, "Library Waves Old Glory, Ends Flag Flap," *Rocky Mountain News,* November 7, 2001, p. 14A, referencing an article in the *Boulder Daily Camera.* See also "Flag Goes Up at Boulder Library after Flap," Associated Press, November 6, 2001.

"brightly colored penises . . .": Ryan Morgan, "Flag Fight Draws Eyes to Ceramic Penis Art," *Denver Post,* November 9, 2001, p. B2.

"If you are here in this country . . .": "Tancredo Sponsors Bill Defending Old Glory," Associated Press, November 20, 2001.

"Senator Gordon . . . I'm glad . . . : Transcript, *Hannity & Colmes,* Fox News Channel, February 12, 2001.

"The politics of all this is just . . .": John Lehmann, Vincent Morris, and Tracy Connor, "New Olympic Flag Flap Unfurls; PA Wanted to Punish Banner Cop for Ripping IOC," *New York Post,* February 7, 2002, p. 6.

Matt Drudge was listening . . . Then the news wires . . . : See coverage by Matt Drudge, "IOC Won't Let WTC American Flag Fly at Olympics," www.DrudgeReport.com, February 5, 2002; Brady Snyder, "U.S. Delegation to Carry WTC Flag into Stadium," *The Deseret News* (Salt Lake City), February 6, 2002, p. A9; Shelly Emling, "WTC Flag Will Be Carried in Olympics Opening Ceremony," Cox News Service, February 6, 2002; Filip Bondy and Greg Gittrich, "Flag Gets Marching Orders; Honor Guard to Carry WTC Banner at Games," *New York Daily News,* February 7, 2002, p. 2; Jennifer Harper, "Flag from Ground Zero to Have Its Own Olympic Event," *Washington Times,* February 7, 2002; Joel C. Rosenberg, "Flash Traffic: WTC Flag Flies at Olympics," *World,* February 23, 2002; see also transcript, *Hannity & Colmes,* Fox News Channel, February 6, 2002.

"Greta Van Susteren . . .": Jim Mullen, "Hot Sheet," *Entertainment Weekly,* February 15, 2002, p. 12.

"If I asked you how to say . . .": Transcript, "Sean Hannity Show," ABC Radio Network; I played an excerpt of my radio interview with Jim Mullen on *Hannity &*

Colmes, see transcript, February 11, 2002; see also article by David Hinckley, "Hannity Has Fun with Barb-on-the-Brain," *Daily News* (New York), February 12, 2002, p. A1.

In the summer of 2001 . . . : Karin Miller, "ACLU Wants Speaker to Reconsider Request for Pledgeless Lawmaker to Leave Chamber," Associated Press, May 29, 2001; John Commins, "Pledge to Flag Stirs Capitol Flap," *Chattanooga Times/Free Press,* June 3, 2001 p. B6; Robert Stacy McCain, "Black Leaders Refuse to Pledge Allegiance to Flag," *Washington Times,* June 22, 2001, p. A1. See also transcripts of *Hannity & Colmes,* Fox News Channel, June 18, 2001, and June 26, 2001.

"it's ridiculous for black Americans . . .": See quotation and discussion in transcript, *Hannity & Colmes,* Fox News Channel, June 28, 2001.

"Do you know what they . . .": Transcript, *Hannity & Colmes,* Fox News Channel, March 22, 2002.

In 1977 Democratic Governor Michael Dukakis . . . : See Richard Cohen, "Nothing But Pudding; the Pledge of Allegiance Is a Frivolous Issue," *Washington Post,* August 30, 1988, p. A23; see also Editorial, "Abusing the Pledge of Allegiance," *New York Times,* August 26, 1988, p. A30.

But on June 11, 1990 . . . : See Flag Protection Amendment, Vote Number 128, June 26, 1990, 101st Congress.

Among those voting against . . . : Other potential Democratic presidential candidates voting against the flag protection amendment included Sen. Joe Biden, Sen. Christopher Dodd, Sen. Bob Kerrey, and Sen. John Kerry.

"The dispute centers only on . . .": Ranchanee Srisavasdi, "Student Group Cancels Performance after Words 'God' and 'Prayer' Banned," *Orange County Register,* March 9, 2002.

In the first few months of 2002 . . . : David Twiddy, "Bill Aims to Pay Lip Service to Liberty; the Declaration of Independence Would Be Required Recitation," *Tallahassee Democrat,* March 5, 2002, p. A1.

"September 11 has been used as a catalyst . . .": Alaine Griffen, "Patriotic Legislation Causes Split," *Hartford Courant,* March 12, 2002, p. A4.

"turn the state's educational system . . .": Daniel Ruth, "Turning Florida's Classrooms into the PTL Club," *Tampa Tribune,* February 20, 2002, p. 2.

"RELIGIOUS RIGHT ACTING LIKE . . .": See column by *St. Petersburg Times* writer Robyn Blumner, published in the *Lexington Herald Leader,* April 13, 2002, p. A11.

Yet another Florida Democrat wanted . . . : David Twiddy, "Bill Aims to Pay Lip Service to Liberty; the Declaration of Independence Would Be Required Recitation," *Tallahassee Democrat,* March 5, 2002.

Most recently, in June . . . : Randy Diamond, "GOP Push to Require Kids to Recite Declaration Fails By One Vote," *The Record* (Bergen County, NJ), June 29, 2001, p. A4.

"I would never allow my . . .": Eugene Kiely, "N.J. Senate Drops Declaration Bill," *Philadelphia Inquirer,* February 29, 2000, p. B1.

"This does not apply to me as a woman . . .": Randy Diamond, "GOP Push to Require Kids to Recite Declaration Fails By One Vote," *The Record* (Bergen County, NJ), June 29, 2001, p. A4.

"Well, what's right about it? . . .": Transcript, *Hannity & Colmes,* Fox News Channel, June 22, 1999.

"This smacks of the idea that . . .": Lisa Suhay, "On Pledging Allegiance to the Founders' Words," *New York Times,* December 19, 1999, p. NJ6.

In autobiographical notes penned in 1821 . . . : Paul Leicester Ford, *The Writings of Thomas Jefferson, vol. 1, Autobiography, with the Declaration of Independence* (1892), cited in Merrill D. Peterson, editor, *Thomas Jefferson, Writings* (Library of America, 1984), p. 18.

In October 1787, James Madison . . . : Robert A. Rutland et al, editors, *The Papers of James Madison, vol. 10, 27 May 1787–3 March 1788* (University of Chicago Press, 1977), pp. 206–19; *Jefferson Papers* (University of Chicago Press, 1977); Bernard Bailyn, editor, *The Debate on the Constitution, Part I: Sept. 1987 to February 1788* (Library of America, 1993), p. 202.

in the Fall of 1788, Philadelphia's *Independent Gazetteer* . . . : "An Examination of the Constitution of the United States," *Independent Gazetteer,* Philadelphia, 26–29 September 1788, cited in Colleen A. Sheehan and Gary L. McDowell, editors, *Friends of the Constitution (Writings of the "Other" Federalists 1787– 1788)* (Liberty Fund, 1998), pp. 469–70.

In March 1790 Thomas Paine . . . : Eric Foner, editor, *Thomas Paine—Collected Writings, Letter to Benjamin Rush (March 6, 1790),* (Library of America, 1995), p. 372.

7. Setting Parents Free

"The educational foundations . . .": "A Nation at Risk," National Commission on Excellence in Education, April 1983. I encourage you to read the entire report. You can find it at http://www.ed.gov/pubs/NatAtRisk/title.html

During the 1999–2000 school year . . . : These statistics come from the U.S. Department of education, cited in a report by Kirk A. Johnson and Krista Kafer, "Why More Money Will Not Solve America's Education Crisis," Heritage Foundation *Backgrounder,* Number 1448, June 11, 2001.

In a new report . . . : William J. Bennett et al, "A Nation Still at Risk," *Policy Review,* July–August 1998.

Last year, for example, 36 percent . . . : Kenneth Lovett and Carl Campanile, "City's Kids Flunk the Basic," *New York Post,* March 15, 2001, p. 18.

"Is it teaching? . . .": Ibid.

almost 330,000 kids . . . : "Record Number of Students Sent Back to Summer School," Associated Press, July 3, 2001.

actually held back a record number . . . : "Record Number Held Back in New York," Associated Press, September 2, 1999.

I remember a report back in the late 1980s . . . : Christopher Connell, "17 Percent of Prospective Teachers Flunk Certification Tests," Associated Press, August 27, 1987.

There was an almost unbelievable story . . . : Stefan C. Friedman and Carl Campanile, "Proof That Our Schools Have Hit a Bad Spell," *New York Post,* July 13, 2001, p. 6.

"I want to ask Joe Clark this . . .": Transcript, *Hannity & Colmes,* Fox News Channel, April 30, 1999.

"I certainly believe in the voucher system . . .": Transcript, *Hannity & Colmes,* Fox News Channel, August 30, 1999.

In fact, one out of every five members of . . . : For details on members of Congress who send their children to private schools, see survey by Nina Shokraii Rees and Jennifer Garrett, "How Members of Congress Practice School Choice," Heritage Foundation *Backgrounder,* Number 1377, June 14, 2000.

It was written by Ellen Sorokin . . . : Ellen Sorokin, "No Founding Fathers? That's Our New History; Overkill on Political Correctness Seen," *Washington Times,* January 28, 2002, p. A1.

"The names of these individuals . . .": Ellen Sorokin, "Founding Fathers Given New Life in New Jersey," *Washington Times,* February 2, 2002, p. A1.

The Ku Klux Klan was mentioned . . . : Connie Cass, "History Standards Criticized as Too Politically Correct," Associated Press, October 25, 1994; Editorial, "The Midnight Ride of the NEH," *Washington Times,* October 30, 1994, p. B2; Joyce Price, "Senate Lashes Historic Rehash," *Washington Times,* January 19, 1995, p. A12; Editorial, "Maligning the History Standards," *New York Times,* February 13, 1995, p. A18.

"Let's let the kids out of the prison of facts . . .": Charles Krauthammer, "History Hijacked," *Washington Post,* November 4, 1994, p. A25.

by a vote of 99 to 1 . . . : The one senator voting against the resolution denouncing the Clinton-Gore history standards was Sen. Bennett Johnson, the now retired Louisiana Democrat. See Joyce Price, "Senate Lashes Historic Rehash," *Washington Times,* January 19, 1995, p. A12.

"the recipient of such funds . . .": Ibid.

Thus in 1989 . . . : Lynne Cheney, "Once Again, Basic Skills Fall Prey to a Fad," *New York Times*, August 11, 1997.

The whole language method . . . : For more information, go to http://www.sntp.net/education/look-see.htm

"The success of America's domestic security . . .": Bob Chase, "One Nation, Unbowed: We Teach the Values That Make America Strong," *NEA Today*, November 1, 2001, p. 5.

Disarm Our Nuclear Forces . . . : See "Nuclear Freeze/Cessation" Resolution, National Education Association, 1982, 2002.

Disarm Our Conventional Military Forces . . . : See "Education on Peace and International Understanding" Resolution, National Education Association, 1982, 2001.

Reject English as an Official Language . . . : See "English as the Official Language" Resolution, National Education Association, 1987, 1993.

Encourage Mushy-Minded Multiculturalism . . . : See "Cultural Diversity in Instructional Materials and Activities" Resolution, National Education Association, 1969, 1995.

Encourage a Radical Sexual Agenda for Children . . . : See "Sex Education" Resolution, National Education Association, 1969, 2001.

On February 8, 2002, the NEA board . . . : Greg Toppo, "NEA Approves Resolution to Protect Gay, Lesbian, Bisexual Students and Staff," Associated Press, February 8, 2002.

In Novato, California, a group of parents . . . : Ellen Sorokin, "Gay-Themed Plays Prompt Suit; Parents Litigate for Right to Shield Public School Students," *Washington Times*, February 21, 2002, p. A5.

What They Didn't Tell You about Queer Sex . . . : Heidi B. Perlman, "Graphic Workshop for Gay Teens Run by Education Officials," Associated Press, May 16, 2000.

"Scott, you were there . . .": Transcript, *Hannity & Colmes*, Fox News Channel, May 25, 2000.

"went too far . . .": Mac Daniel, "2 Lose Jobs Over Workshop on Sex; Commissioner Calls Session Too Explicit," *Boston Globe*, May 20, 2000, p. B2;

"the actions of Massachusetts conservative groups . . .": Scott S. Greenberger, "Educator Fired for Sex Discussion Sues to Reclaim Job," *Boston Globe*, November 28, 2000. See also later discussions on *Hannity & Colmes* about the implications of this controversial case when then Massachusetts governor Paul Cellucci was nominated by President Bush to be U.S. ambassador to Canada. Transcripts include "Will Conservatives Try to Block Paul Cellucci's Ambassadorial Nomination," *Hannity & Colmes*, Fox News Channel, February 20,

2001; also "Investigating Massachusetts Governor Paul Cellucci," *Hannity & Colmes,* Fox News Channel, March 9, 2001.

The eggheads have dodgeball in their sights . . . : "Increasingly, Schools Move to Restrict Dodgeball," *New York Times,* May 6, 2001, p. A42.

"preserve the rights and dignity . . .": "Moves to Restrict Dodgeball on Increase in U.S. Schools," *Naples Daily News,* May 6, 2001.

"at its base, the game encourages . . .": Martin Miller, "Critics Aim to Bounce Dodge Ball Off the Schoolyard," *Los Angeles Times,* March 18, 2002.

The old neighborhood favorite cops and robbers . . . : Robert Sanchez, "Game Lands Boys in Trouble; School Punishes Kids for Pretend Shooting," *Rocky Mountain News,* May 14, 2002, p. 5A.

"Those people who said we don't need . . .": Valerie Strauss, "Sept. 11 Prompts Lesson Review; Educators Rethink Multiculturalism," *Washington Post,* October 1, 2001, p. B1.

"Look at the evidence . . .": Transcript, *Hannity & Colmes,* Fox News Channel, November 11, 1998.

In 1994, after all . . . : Michael Winerip, "SAT Increases Average Score, By Fiat," *New York Times,* June 11, 1994, p. A1; Dennis Kelly et al, "Revised Scoring for SAT Riles Some Academic Experts," *USA Today,* June 14, 1994, p. 6D; Tamara Henry, "Highest Scores in Years on New SAT," *USA Today,* August 24, 1995, p. 1D; Editorial, "A Curious Hike in the SAT," *Rocky Mountain News,* August 25, 1995, p. 45A.

"if similar success could be achieved . . .": Jay P. Greene and Paul E. Peterson, "The Effectiveness of School Choice in Milwaukee: A Secondary Analysis of Data from the Program's Evaluation," American Political Science Association Panel on the Political Analysis of Urban School Systems, August–September 1996, cited by Dorothy Hanks, "How Milwaukee's Choice Program Helps Poor Children Succeed in School," Heritage Foundation *F.Y.I.,* Number 120, September 23, 1996.

"Come on . . . what you're saying here is that . . .": Transcript, *Hannity & Colmes,* Fox News Channel, June 11, 1998.

A 1990 Rand Corporation study . . . : Dorothy Hanks, "How Milwaukee's Choice Program Helps Poor Children Succeed in School," Heritage Foundation *F.Y.I.,* Number 120, September 23, 1996.

"Low-income families are not dumb . . .": Representative Williams's support for school choice is legendary. For these quotes, see Donald Lambro, "Liberal Embraces Vouchers," *Washington Times,* April 2, 1990, p. A8.

Howard Fuller, the man who used to be the . . .": Fuller's support for school choice is well known throughout Milwaukee. As I write this, he's just spoken at a rally of hundreds of school choice supporters who were protesting against a plan by Wisconsin Democrats to slash the school choice program by $23 million. See Jesse Garza, "School Choice Supporters Urged to Go Beyond Rallying; It's Time to Vote Out Opponents, Fuller Tells Crowd," *Milwaukee Journal Sentinel,* April 12, 2002, p. 1B.

"There's something fundamentally wrong . . .": Mayor Norquist's support for school choice is also well documented. For this quote, see Joe Williams, "Norquist: MPS Needs to Satisfy Parents," *Milwaukee Journal Sentinel,* November 22, 1997, p. 3.

"School choice will not harm . . .": Joe Williams, "Gore Blasts Vouchers for Private Schools," *Milwaukee Journal Sentinel,* July 4, 1998, p. 1.

In February of 2002, researchers at Harvard . . . : Daniel P. Mayer et al., "School Choice in New York City After Three Years: An Evaluation of the School Choice Program Final Report," Mathematica Policy Research, Report No. 8404-045, February 19, 2002, cited by Kirk A. Johnson and Krista Kafer, "What the Harvard/Mathematica Study Says about Vouchers and Low-Income African-American Students," Heritage Foundation *Center for Data Analysis Report,* April 11, 2002.

"A 1999 survey by Public Agenda . . .": Michael Leo Owens, "Why Blacks Support Vouchers," *New York Times,* February 26, 2002, p. A25.

Read the wonderful book . . . : Seymour Fliegel and James MacGuire, *Miracle in East Harlem: The Fight For Choice in Public Education* (Times Books, 1994).

"Everyone in the school's first senior class . . .": Karen Hunter, "1st Graduating Class at All-Girls School a Huge Success," *Daily News* (New York), June 8, 2001 p. 30; see also Anjetta McQueen, "Harlem Academy Continues Despite Legal Challenges," Associated Press; see transcript of debate over single-sex schools, *Hannity & Colmes,* Fox News Channel, March 12, 1998.

8. I'm Pro-Choice

"We need a president we can trust . . .": "Clinton Rips Brown on Abortion Rights, Flat Tax Plan," *New York Times,* April 3, 1992.

"I'm a Christian" Gore once told . . . : A. Engler Anderson, "VP is A-OK: A1 Gore Charms Audience at Federation Banquet," Ethnic News Watch, *Jewish Exponent,* February 24, 1995, p. 6.

"Bush pandered to anti-choice extremists . . .": "Bush's Extreme Position against a Woman's Right to Choose Alienates Even Republican Women, Newspaper Reports," Gore 2000 campaign, press release, U.S. Newswire, March 12, 2000.

"the Republican presidential nomination is . . .": Gore 2000 campaign, press release January 27, 2000.

"Let's cling to our friend Al Gore . . .": Robin Duke, Letter to the Editor, *New York Times,* February 7, 2000, p. A18.

"I am opposed to abortion . . .": Felicity Barringer, "Clinton and Gore Shifted on Abortion," *New York Times,* July 20, 1992, p. A10.

He even signed a parental notification law . . . : Ibid.

repeatedly vetoed a ban on "partial birth abortion" . . . : James Bennet, "Clinton Again Vetoes Measure to Ban a Method of Abortion," *New York Times,* October 11, 1997, p. A9.

A federal ban on partial birth abortion is supported by . . . : See coverage by David Espo, "Modified Abortion Bill Wins Backing From AMA," Associated Press, May 20, 1997; Ronald Powers, "Moynihan, in Break with Clinton, Condemns Abortion Procedure," Associated Press, May 14, 1996; Darlene Superville, "Senate Passes Late-Abortion Limit," Associated Press, May 20, 1997; "Partial Birth Abortion Ban/Final Passage," Senate Vote Number 71, May 20, 1997, 105th Congress.

Who once voted for civil rights legislation . . . : Robin Toner, "Shifting Views Over Abortion Fog Gore Race," *New York Times,* February 25, 2000, p. A5.

"I don't believe a woman's freedom . . .": Ibid.

Gore actually voted pro-life 84 percent of the time . . . : "National Right to Life on Al Gore's Presidential Candidacy," National Right to Life, press release June 16, 1999.

"During my eleven years in Congress . . .": For full text of the Gore letter, see "Clinton's V.P. Pick Was Once Anti-Abortion," Ad Hoc Committee in Defense of Life, U.S. Newswire, July 10, 1992.

"near perfect anti-abortion record . . .": Michael Kramer, "The New (Low) Levels of the Game," *U.S. News & World Report,* March 7, 1988, p. 29.

"deny, deny, deny . . .": Ibid.

"Life is the division of human cells . . .": Bill Arthur, "Gephardt: Switch on Abortion Issue Stunned Supporters," Knight-Ridder newspapers, *Orange County Register,* January 3, 1988 p. K8; for more coverage of Gephardt's flip-flop on abortion, see Barry Massey, "Gephardt Dogged by Criticism of His Changed Positions," Associated Press, February 20, 1988; Harrison Rainie and Donald Baer, "The Gephardt File: Rebel without a Cause," *U.S. News & World Report,* February 8, 1988, p. 16.

"A PRO-LIFE PROMISE . . .": Maura Dolan and Robert A. Rosenblatt, "Doubts about His Character Possible; Charges of Flip-Flopping Pose Threat to Gephardt," *Los Angeles Times,* February 29, 1988, p. A1.

"In his first nine years as a Congressman . . .": Statement by National Right to Life, Business Wire, March 1, 1988.

"I'd rather change and be right, than . . .": Tom Wicker, "A Case for Flip-Flops," *New York Times,* March 1, 1988, p. A23.

"black genocide . . . a policy of killing infants . . .": Transcript of press conference by Dr. John Wilke, National Right to Life, Federal News Service, January 29, 1989; see also Associated Press story on Jackson and abortion, June 16, 1978.

"in the abortion debate, one of the crucial questions . . .": Colman McCarthy, "Jackson's Reversal on Abortion," *Washington Post,* May 21, 1988, p. A27.

"Even our Creator did not make us puppets . . .": James H. Rubin, "Democrats Agree on Most Civil Liberties Issues," Associated Press, March 31, 1984.

"We think abortion is a bad thing . . .": *Philadelphia Inquirer* article by reporter Jodi Enda, December 11, 1993, quoted in an article about the controversy by Howard Kurtz, "Poor Choice of Words from Abortion Rights Advocate?" *Washington Post,* February 7, 1994, p. C1.

"Welcome back to the program . . .": Transcript, *Hannity & Colmes,* Fox News Channel, September 22, 1999.

"Are we better off with more abortion . . .": Transcript, *Hannity & Colmes,* Fox News Channel, March 13, 2001.

"John Ashcroft's record is antithetical . . .": Transcript, *Hannity & Colmes,* Fox News Channel, February 2, 2001.

"Robert Bork's America is a land in which . . .": George F. Will, "The Democrats' Glass Chin," *Newsweek,* July 20, 1987, p. 66.

"Clarence Thomas is going to haunt this nation . . .": Transcript of press conference by Kate Michelman, National Abortion Rights Action League, Federal News Service, July 10, 1992.

"I actually accepted the invitation . . .": Transcript, *Hannity & Colmes,* Fox News Channel, February 1, 2001.

9. Long Live the Porcupine Caribou!

"The United States has used wheat . . .": Nazila Fathi, "Iranian Urges Muslims to Use Oil as a Weapon," *New York Times,* April 6, 2002 p. A9; see also "Iran's Supreme Leader Reissues Call for Oil Sanctions against Israeli Supporters," Associated Press, May 1, 2002.

"The Artic National Wildlife Refuge . . .": "Bush's Energy Policy Will Drill into Fragile Wildlife Refuge, Says Gore Campaign," Gore 2000 Campaign, press release, September 29, 2000.

"Well, you've got to talk to the caribou . . .": Transcript, *Hannity & Colmes*, Fox News Channel, October 30, 2001.

"The Artic Refuge protects some of the world's most . . .": Brooks Yeager, World Wildlife Fund, April 18, 2002.

"being hunted to near-extinction . . .": "Sierra Club Has a Unique Way of Saying Thanks on ANWR," *The Hotline*, April 25, 2002.

A blizzard of issue ads . . . : See series of advertisements and open letters, including "Americans Support Protection for America's Artic Refuge," Americans for Alaska, February 2002.

All of this was part of the biggest environmentalist media . . . : Melanie Fonder, "Enviros Launch Largest Campaign in 10 Years," *The Hill*, February 27, 2001.

"bad energy policy . . .": Transcript, *Meet The Press*, NBC, September 2, 2001.

"Special places like the Artic National . . .": Michael Kilian, "Battle over Alaska Begins," *Chicago Tribune*, March 1, 2001.

"it's no great surprise that Bush's energy policy . . .": "Bush's Energy Policy Will Drill into Fragile Wildlife Refuge, Says Gore Campaign," Gore 2000 campaign, press release, September 29, 2000.

That's why a plank in the . . . : Paul Query, "ANWR Plank Added to Democratic Platform with Only Minutes Left," Associated Press, August 14, 2000.

The final vote was 54 to 46 . . . : "Cloture Motion on Murkowski Amendment," Senate Roll Call Vote Number 71, April 18, 2002, 107th Congress.

"I really think it comes down to this . . .": Helen Dewar, "Senate Vote Blocks Drilling in Refuge," *Washington Post*, April 19, 2002, p. A1.

"Yeah . . . and there's a radical right wing . . .": Transcripts, *Hannity & Colmes*, Fox News Channel, January 24, 2001, and May 17, 2001.

36 percent . . . almost 60 percent . . . : See statements by Alaskan senator Frank Murkowski, including those on September 20, 2000, and September 29, 2000.

Worse, a higher and higher percentage of that oil . . . : See Table 5.4, "Petroleum Imports by Country of Origin, 1960–2000," Economic Information Administration, U.S. Department of Energy; see also "Annual Energy Review: 2000," EIA, U.S. Department of Energy.

Between 1993 and 2000, U.S. oil imports . . . : Ibid.

600,000 barrels a day from Iraq . . . : Ibid.

62 percent by 2020 . . . : Charli E. Coon and James Phillips, "Strengthening National Energy Security by Reducing Dependence on Foreign Oil," Heritage Foundation *Backgrounder*, Number 1540, April 24, 2002.

Right now, the U.S. has about twenty-one billion barrels . . . : Charli E. Coon, "Domestic Energy Production: Vital for Economic and National Security," Heritage Foundation *Executive Memorandum*, Number 787, October 30, 2001.

That means 99.99 percent of the land surface . . . : Charli E. Coon, "Tapping Oil Reserves in a Small Part of ANWR: Environmentally Sound, Energy Wise," Heritage Foundation *Executive Memorandum*, Number 763, August 1, 2001.

sixteen billion barrels of oil from ANWR . . . : Ibid.

"is a flat, treeless, almost featureless plain . . .": Sen. Frank Murkowski, "Drilling Won't Make It Less of a Refuge," *Washington Post*, December 10, 2000, p. B5.

"the Central Arctic caribou herd . . .": Ibid.

"there is drilling for oil and gas in 29 wildlife . . .": George F. Will, "Playing with Energy," *Washington Post*, April 21, 2002, p. B7.

Conservatives passed such legislation . . . : Sen. Frank Murkowski, "Drilling Won't Make It Less of a Refuge," *Washington Post*, December 10, 2000.

"Would you support drilling in the lower . . .": Transcript, *Hannity & Colmes*, Fox News Network, February 26, 2001.

"We can't go back, Alan, to the bad old days . . .": Transcript, *Hannity & Colmes*, Fox News Network, February 26, 2002.

"[W]hat you have are two different visions . . .": Transcript, *Hannity & Colmes*, January 22, 2002.

"working to have a bipartisan approach . . .": Transcript, *Hannity & Colmes*, Fox News Network, March 4, 2002.

Eight out of ten Americans . . . : Wirthlin poll, released via PR Newswire, March 20, 2001.

Nearly eight out of ten Americans say . . . : Charli Coon, "Drilling for Rational Answers on ANWR," *Washington Times*, April 1, 2002.

more than 75 percent of Alaskans . . . : Wirthlin poll cited above.

"We know that development of energy . . .": Mayor George N. Ahmaogak, Sr., "Eskimos Prove Balance Can Exist between Exploration and Environment," May 21, 2001.

"Should we be looking at the fact that . . .": Transcript, *Hannity & Colmes*, Fox News Network, February 26, 2001.

"By tapping into petroleum resources in Alaska . . .": James P. Hoffa, "Teamsters Support Opening Arctic National Wildlife Refuge; Tapping Alaskan Resources Eases Economic and Energy Needs Hoffa Says," International Brotherhood of Teamsters, press release, March 28, 2001.

the Teamsters backed the Bush energy plan . . . : Ron Hutcheson, "Bush and Teamsters Meet on Common Cause: Energy; the Union Sees New Jobs in His Plan to Open an Alaska Refuge," *Philadelphia Inquirer*, January 18, 2002, p. A10.

"I couldn't think of a more perfect champion . . .": Jerry Hood, "Teamsters Applaud Martin Sheen's Acting in ANWR Ad; Pretend President Champions

Pretend Facts," International Brotherhood of Teamsters, press release, November 5, 2001.

gun control being another pivotal issue . . . : Liz Marlantes, "Democrats Tone Down Gun-Control Stance," *Christian Science Monitor,* May 10, 2002, p. 2.

Gore's policies might jeopardize their jobs . . . : John Nichols, "Teamsters Not Turtles," *In These Times,* June 25, 2001, p. 17.

In protest, Greenpeace dumped a truckload . . . : Liz Halloran, "Environmentalists Mine Bush Energy Plan for Publicity," *Hartford Courant,* May 18, 2001, p. A1.

In a speech at the Energy Efficiency Forum . . . : Suzanne Struglinski, "Nuclear Power: Cheney Cites Nuke Power as Possible Global Warming Answer," Greenwire, June 14, 2001.

"since 1980 the number of American refineries . . .": U.S. Secretary of Energy Spencer Abraham, "A National Report Card on America's Energy Crisis," speech to the U.S. Chamber of Commerce at the National Energy Summit, March 19, 2001; for the text, go to www.energy.gov/HQDocs/speeches/2001/marss/energy_speech.html.

10. The Taxman Cometh, and Cometh, and Cometh

"Are we overtaxed as a nation? . . .": Transcript, *Hannity & Colmes,* Fox News Channel, April 22, 2002.

"Do you envision tax cuts next year . . .": Transcript of Daschle press briefing, FDCH Political Transcripts, October 20, 1997; see also "Daschle Throws Cold Water on Additional Tax Cuts," *White House Bulletin,* October 20, 1997, and "Daschle Adds Fast Track to List of Bills Dems May Block," in "Congress Daily," *National Journal,* October 20, 1997.

"When NASA is done exploring Mars . . .": Christina Martin, "Response to Daschle Remarks on Taxes," Office of House Speaker Newt Gingrich, press release, October 20, 1997.

"Tom Daschle either believes our high tax rates . . .": Jim Nicholson, Republican National Committee, press release, October 21, 1997; see also "Daschle Backtracks on Tax Statement, Claims Quote Taken 'Out Of Context,'" Republican National Committee, press release, October 24, 1997.

"Let me just say before I close out . . .": Transcript of Daschle press briefing, FDCH Political Transcripts, October 22, 1997.

"TAX INCREASE POSSIBLE . . .": *Des Moines Register,* July 22, 2002, quoted by Donald Lambro, "Gephardt Hints at Increase In Taxes," *Washington Times,* July 24, 2001, p. A1; see also *The Bulletin's Frontrunner* news roundup report, July 23, 2001.

"The message is clear . . .": Ibid.

"Mr. Gephardt's candor about raising taxes . . .": Rep. Tom DeLay, "Majority Whip Urges Democrats to Campaign on Gephardt Tax Hike In 2002," press release, July 23, 2001.

"The ink isn't even dry on the . . .": Donald Lambro, "Gephardt Hints at Increase in Taxes," *Washington Times,* July 24, 2001.

"assumption that House Democrats . . .": Ibid; Gephardt also claimed the story was misreported on CNN's *Inside Politics,* July 24, 2001.

"a misquote and inaccurate reporting . . .": CNN's *Late Edition,* July 29, 2001, quoted in *The Bulletin's Frontrunner,* July 30, 2001.

"Alan and I couldn't help but duke it out on the air . . .": Transcript, *Hannity & Colmes,* Fox News Channel, July 23, 2001.

"You've got to have a combination of . . .": See Representative Gephardt's speech first quoted in a column by Larry Eichel, "Gephardt's Bold, Traditional Vision," *Philadelphia Inquirer,* June 2, 1999, p. A19; see also articles by Donald Lambro, "Gleeful GOP Assails Gephardt for Urging Defense Cuts, Tax Rise," *Washington Times,* June 3, 1999, p. A3; "If I Were Speaker . . ." *National Journal,* June 4, 1999; Jake Tapper, "Search for a Boogeyman," Salon.com, June 11, 1999.

He wrote a letter to the editor . . . : Rep. Dick Gephardt, Letter to the Editor, "Tax Position Clarification," *Washington Times,* June 8, 1999, p. A18.

"You've created a little stir . . .": Transcript, *Meet the Press,* NBC, June 13, 1999.

"Let's tell the truth . . .": Transcript of Walter Mondale's speech, Associated Press, July 19, 1984.

"It goes against all the political axioms . . .": Editorial, "Mr. Reagan's Tax Problem," *Washington Post,* July 29, 1984, p. C6.

"Mr. Mondale and other leading Democrats . . .": Editorial, "How Much for Your Vote?" *New York Times,* July 26, 1984, p. A22.

"HOW THE DEMOCRATS CAN WIN . . .": Joseph L. Rauh, Jr., "How the Democrats Can Win," *New York Times,* July 29, 1984, section 4, p. 23.

"Mr. Mondale is right to warn of a tax increase . . .": Editorial, "New Year's Tax Increase," *New York Times,* August 3, 1984, p. A22.

"SCORING POINTS WITH CANDOR . . .": Kurt Anderson, "Scoring Points with Candor; Mondale Puts Reagan on the Defensive by Promising New Taxes," *Time,* August 20, 1984, p. 20.

biggest landslide . . . : Howell Raines, "Reagan Taking 49 States and 59% of Vote, Vows to Stress Arms Talks and Economy," *New York Times,* November 8, 1984, p. A1

"I don't think there was any mandate . . .": Ibid.

"The cost of federal, state and local government . . .": Stephen Moore, "The Most Expensive Government in World History," Institute for Policy Innovation, *IPI Policy Report,* Number 161, February 12, 2002; see also accompanying press release, www.ipi.org.

Tax Freedom Day . . . : J. Scott Moody and David Hoffman, "America Celebrates Tax Freedom Day," Tax Foundation, *Special Report,* Number 112, April 2002.

federal tax burden alone grew by . . .": Steve Forbes, *A New Birth of Freedom* (Regnery, 1999), p. 66.

from 744,000 words to some 6,929,000: Scott Moody, "The Cost of Tax Compliance," Tax Foundation Report, www.taxfoundation.org, February 2002.

a full 65 percent of Americans . . . : Terry Jones, "Is 'Massive' Bush Tax Cut Too Big?" *Investor's Business Daily,* August 16, 2001, p. A1.

"feared an IRS audit than anthrax . . .": Cited by Rep. John Linder, "King George's Tax Code; It Is Time for a 1040 Revolution," *Washington Times,* April 17, 2002.

"This may be the first budget in history . . .": Martin Crutsinger, "Dems to Fight Bush's Spending Plan," Associated Press, April 10, 2001.

"You've got a Robin Hood in reverse . . .": See roundup of anti-Bush tax and budget quotes, in "The Hotline," *National Journal,* April 10, 2001.

"This whole budget and tax plan . . .": Ibid.

"risky and irresponsible . . .": Transcript of press conference with Representative Gephardt and Senator Daschle, Federal News Service, July 20, 1999.

"irresponsible . . . mismanagement . . . risky gamble . . .": Transcript of press conference with Representative Gephardt and Senator Daschle, Federal News Service, March 15, 2001.

"You'll remember back in the eighties . . .": Ibid.

"At a time when key indicators . . .": House Minority Leader Richard Gephardt, quoted by Bloomberg News, April 9, 2001.

"The one thing you're going to find . . .": David Espo, "Dems Ready to Compromise with Bush," Associated Press, January 24, 2001.

"the godfather of the Reagan tax cuts . . .": Charles Stafford, "Gephardt Gets a Going-Over from Rival Democrats," *St. Petersburg Times,* February 14, 1988, p. 6A.

Daschle . . . wound up voting for the Reagan tax cut . . . : Associated Press, August 5, 1981.

For seven straight years . . . : Lawrence Kudlow, "Lest We Forget: Ronald Reagan Changed the World for the Better," *Investor's Business Daily,* February 15, 2002; see also Grover Norquist, "Reagan's Legacy 20 Years Later: The Kemp-Roth

Tax Cut Anniversary," U.S. Newswire, August 13, 2001; Dinesh D'Souza, "How Reagan Elected Clinton," *Forbes* cover story, November 3, 1997.

"Total tax revenues climbed by 99.4 percent . . .": Daniel J. Mitchell, "Lowering Marginal Tax Rates: The Key to Pro-Growth Tax Relief," Heritage Foundation *Backgrounder*, Number 1443, May 22, 2001.

"In fact, economist Bruce Bartlett notes that . . .": Bruce Bartlett, "Not So Stimulating," *National Review*, November 16, 2001.

"The best sign that our economic program . . .": Dinesh D'Souza, "How Reagan Elected Clinton," *Forbes* cover story, November 3, 1997.

"The Kennedy tax cuts . . .": Daniel J. Mitchell, "Lowering Marginal Tax Rates: The Key to Pro-Growth Tax Relief," Heritage Foundation *Backgrounder*, Number 1443, May 22, 2001.

I lean toward the flat tax . . . : For more on the flat tax and answering liberal criticism of tax reform, see Steve Forbes, *A New Birth of Freedom* (Regnery, 1999); see also Jack Kemp and Ken Blackwell, editors, *The IRS v. The People* (Heritage Foundation, 1999).

Since January 2001, even formerly Communist . . .": Sabrina Tavernise, "Russia Imposes Flat Tax on Income, and Its Coffers Swell," *New York Times*, March 23, 2002, p. A3.

11. Winning the Political Wars

"band of trickle-down terrorists . . .": Transcript of Gephardt speech, *Live Report*, CNN, December 13, 1994.

"When they swerve to the extreme . . .": Ibid.

"make war on the kids of this country . . .": Jeff Jacoby, "How the Right Is Demonized," *Boston Globe*, December 21, 1995, p. A19; also see Jacoby's column "More Hate Speech from the Left," *Boston Globe*, December 30, 1997, p. A15.

"literally take meals from kids . . .": Ibid.

"likened conservatives to Adolf Hitler . . .": Ibid.

"storm troopers . . .": Ibid.

"mean-spirited, reactionary . . .": John McCaslin, "Inside the Beltway," *Washington Times*, February 27, 1995, p. A7.

"no matter how smart or literate . . .": Richard Reeves, "Why Conservatives Don't Deserve Respect," *Baltimore Sun*, May 19, 1995, p. 19A.

"pimp . . . in a headdress . . .": Diane Carman, "Payoffs: A Plague in Politics," *Denver Post*, October 28, 1999, p. B1; see also excellent column by Cal Thomas,

"What to Do about Outrageous Speech," *Times-Picayune* (New Orleans), December 29, 1999, p. 7B.

"I think he ought to be worried . . .": Transcript, *Inside Washington,* Federal News Service, July 8, 1995.

Barbra Streisand, for example, gave a speech . . . : Excerpts published in the *Washington Post,* February 12, 1995.

"If we were in other countries . . .": "Earth to Alec: You're Not Funny," *New York Post,* December 17, 1998, p. 12.

"Excuse me for not laughing . . .": Ibid.

Snipers Wanted . . . : Lynn Elber, "Violent Anti-Bush Graphic Was 'Regrettable,' CBS Says," Associated Press, August 9, 2000.

"When you don't vote . . .": Transcript of Democratic Party television ad, replayed on *Hannity & Colmes,* Fox News Network, May 10, 2002.

"Michael, aren't you ashamed . . .": Transcript, *Hannity & Colmes,* Fox News Network, May 10, 2002.

"I'm Renee Mullins . . .": Transcript of Democratic Party television ad, replayed on *Hannity & Colmes,* Fox News Network, May 10, 2002.

two of James Byrd's killers are to be executed . . . : C. Bryson Hull, "Brewer Sentenced to Death for Dragging Death," Associated Press, September 24, 1999; see also Patty Reinert, "3rd Defendant Gets Life Sentence in Jasper Man's Dragging Death," *Houston Chronicle,* November 19, 1999, p. A1.

Robert Byrd . . . once a member of the Ku Klux Klan . . . : Transcript, *Inside Politics,* CNN, December 20, 1993; Martin Tolchin, "Byrd Facing a Re-Election Threat by a 'Sleeper' in West Virginia," *New York Times,* April 13, 1982, p. A18; Ken Ringle, "Who's Afraid of the Ku Klux Klan?" *Washington Post,* November 26, 1982, p. A17; John Aloysius, "Byrd's Mastery of Senate Life Keeps Stimulus Bill on Track," *Boston Globe,* March 28, 1993, p. 16.

When former Klan leader David Duke . . . : Peter Applebome, "Klan's Ghost Haunts Louisiana Vote," *New York Times,* February 16, 1989, p. A22; "National GOP Leaders Formally Denounce Duke," Associated Press, February 24, 1989; Bush adviser David Demarest, Letter to the Editor, "Bush Backed Klansman's Rival in GOP Race," *New York Times,* March 6, 1989, p. A16; Cal Thomas, "Democrats Should Disown Race-Baiters," *St. Louis Post-Dispatch,* August 2, 1990, p. 3C; "GOP Governors Denounce Duke," Associated Press, October 22, 1991; Roberto Suro, "Bush Denounces Duke as a Racist and Charlatan," *New York Times,* November 7, 1991, p. B18; John King, "State GOP Leaders Denounce Duke," Associated Press, December 9, 1991.

"In the House . . . 80 percent of Republicans . . .": Linda Chavez, "What Frightens Democrats?" Creators Syndicate, posted on www.TownHall.com, August 4, 2000.

"From 1982 to 1987 . . .": Jack Kemp, "A Tenth Anniversary Celebration of the Kemp-Roth Tax Cuts: The Importance of America's Victory Over Washington," *Heritage Lectures,* Heritage Foundation, August 13, 1991.

Black Enterprise magazine concurred . . . : Editors' Report, "A Tale of Two Decades: 20 Years of Black Business Leadership," *Black Enterprise,* June 1992, p. 207.

A political strategy memorandum . . . : James Carville and Paul Begala, "A Battle Plan for the Democrats," *New York Times,* May 27, 2001, section 4, p. 9.

"Mr. Bush's agenda is neither . . .": Ibid.

"cuts welfare to pay for tax cuts . . .": Sen. Tom Daschle, press release, June 21, 1996.

"plunge one million children into poverty . . .": Carolyn Skorneck, "Senate Nears Passage of Welfare Overhaul Over Critics Cries," Associated Press, August 1, 1996.

"moral blot . . . make more than one million . . .": Marion Wright Edelman, Children's Defense Fund, press release, July 31, 1996.

2.6 million Americans to be thrown into poverty . . . : Sen. Daniel Patrick Moynihan, press release, August 1, 1996.

"Although liberals predicted that . . .": Robert Rector and Patrick F. Fagan, "The Good News about Welfare Reform," Heritage Foundation *Backgrounder,* Number 1468, September 5, 2001.

The data also show . . . : Ibid.

"see the Medicare program just die and go away . . .": Jeff Jacoby, "How the Right Is Demonized," *Boston Globe,* December 21, 1995; also see Jacoby's column "More Hate Speech from the Left," *Boston Globe,* December 30, 1997.

"are gutting Medicare . . .": Adam Clymer, "Reshaping Medicare: The Overview," *New York Times,* October 20, 1995, p. A1.

"Get Old People . . .": Ibid.

"there is only one reason this bill is required . . .": Ibid.

"I hear Republicans talking about . . .": Donald Lambro in the *Washington Times,* March 21, 1999, cited by "The Hotline," *National Journal,* March 22, 1999.

"The Republican Party has always opposed Social Security . . .": Larry Lipman and Lisa Helem, "Critics Blast Social Security Panel's Call for Private Accounts," Cox News Service, July 24, 2001; see also op-ed piece by Peter Ferrara, "Social Security Scare-Mongering; Gephardt, Daschle Rail against Social Security Reform," *Washington Times,* August 29, 2001, p. A17.

Around 2020, the Social Security deficit alone . . . : For more about Social Security's unfunded liabilities and the resulting policy implications, see Daniel J.

Mitchell, "Social Security Trust Fund Report Shows Program's Finances Getting Worse," Heritage Foundation *Backgrounder,* Number 1273, April 16, 1999; see also Wade Dokken (a lifelong Democrat and CEO of American Skandia), *New Century, New Deal: How to Turn Your Wages into Wealth through Social Security Choice* (Regnery, 2000).

In the late 1970s, local officials . . . : Judge Ray Holbrook, "An American Model for Social Security Reform," United Seniors Association testimony before the President's Social Security reform commission, www.unitedseniors.org, September 6, 2001.

"This matters to real people . . .": Ibid.

"I would urge my fellow Democrats . . .": Sara Fritz, "Social Security Panel Under Siege," *St. Petersburg Times,* July 25, 2001, p. 1A.

"I am not here to gut Social Security . . .": Ibid.

"extremely dangerous . . .": Terence Smith, "Carter Sharpens Attacks on Reagan's Arms Stand," *New York Times,* October 30, 1980, p. B14.

"dangerous . . . radical . . .": Barry Schweid, "Carter Hints Reagan 'Dangerous,'" Associated Press, October 28, 1980.

"dumb . . . trigger-happy . . . Mad Bomber": Meg Greenfield, "Taking Reagan Seriously," *Washington Post,* July 23, 1980, p. A21.

"Do you really want Ronald Reagan . . .": Tom Wicker, "After the Convention," *New York Times,* August 15, 1980, p. A23.

"shallow, nuclear cowboy": Mary McGrory, "Shallow: Reagan Proved He's a Smoothie, but Don't Scratch Too Deep," *Washington Post,* June 10, 1982, p. A3.

"dangerously destabilizing": Strobe Talbott, "The Case against Star Wars Weapons," *Time,* May 7, 1984, p. 81.

"could lead us to start World War III": Scott Sonner, "Hart Blasts Reagan on MX," United Press International, July 23, 1983.

"I don't think Barry Goldwater was . . .": Howell Raines, "Reagan Seeks to Stress Arms Issue without Seeming 'Trigger Happy,'" *New York Times,* June 2, 1980, p. B10.

"promotes the policies of a terrorist": Kenneth J. Cooper, "Democrat Offers Gingrich Apology for Harsh Words," *Washington Post,* May 6, 1995, p. A8.

"bomb throwers": David S. Broder, "Rebels without a Pause," *WP Magazine, Washington Post,* December 31, 1995, p. W8.

"acting like the Grinch . . .": Representative Vic Fazio, press release, December 11, 1995.

"the Gingrinch who stole Christmas": Tom Brazaitis, "Gingrich May Hold Key to Clinton's Survival," *Cleveland Plain Dealer,* December 18, 1994, p. 2C.

"They trumped us with 125,000 ads . . .": Newt Gingrich, "Political Lessons for 2000," *The American Enterprise,* April 2000, p. 26.

"My model [was] Ronald Reagan . . .": Ibid.

"If there is semen on the dress . . .": Transcript, *Hannity & Colmes,* Fox News Channel, August 5, 1998.

12. Winning the Media Wars

Turner has called the Islamic extremist terrorists . . . : Matt Kempner, "Turner Rues Words 'Reported Out of Context'; Terrorists Were 'Brave,' He Said," *Atlanta Journal and Constitution,* February 13, 2002, p. 3A.

"Jesus freaks": "Resignation at CNN," *New York Times,* March 15, 2001, p. C6.

He mocked the Pope for being Polish . . . Christianity is "for losers" . . . compared Rupert Murdoch . . . : Matt Kempner, "Turner Rues Words 'Reported Out of Context'; Terrorists Were 'Brave,' He Said," *Atlanta Journal and Constitution,* February 13, 2002, p. 3A.

A recent article in *American Journalism Review* noted . . . : Paul Farhi, "Nightly News Blues," *American Journalism Review,* June 2001.

"profound financial distress": Joe Flint, "NAB Confab Celebrates Radio Revival," *Daily Variety,* October 10, 1994, p. 3.

"Why do liberals fear me?" . . . : Rush Limbaugh, "Voice of America: Why Liberals Fear Me," *Policy Review,* Fall 1994, p. 4.

Three hundred radio stations . . . more than fourteen hundred stations . . . : Don Kaplan, "A Salary the Size of Mt. Rushmore, or Was Viacom Boss Just Kidding?" *New York Post,* July 19, 2001, p. 82.

an estimated $285 million . . . : Dan Weil, "Source: Limbaugh's New Radio Contract Worth $285 Million," *Palm Beach Post,* July 20, 2001, p. 1D.

"In 1983 alone, the Central Intelligence Agency . . .": President Ronald Reagan, "The New Network of Terrorist States," speech to the American Bar Association, July 8, 1995 (published in the *Department of State Bulletin,* August 1985, p. 7).

"This is the most exciting moment . . .": Matt Drudge, *Drudge Manifesto* (New American Library, 2000).

"I've just talked to somebody . . .": Transcript, *Hannity & Colmes,* Fox News Channel, August 17, 1998.

"Let's talk turkey . . .": Transcript, *Inside Politics,* CNN, November 27, 1997.

"Matt, there are people that despise you . . .": Transcript, *Hannity & Colmes,* Fox News Channel, October 13, 2000.

13. What Really Matters

one out of four soldiers was either killed or wounded . . . : See http://
www.geobop.com/World/NA/Topics/History/Civil_War/reference/compare/.

"Silly people—and there were many . . .": Winston S. Churchill, *The Grand Alliance*
(Houghton Mifflin Company, 1950).

nearly three hundred thousand . . . : see http://www.geobop.com/World/NA/
Topics/History/Civil_War/reference/compare/

killing nearly a hundred thousand American soldiers . . . : Ibid.

INDEX